To our children

Joanna, Samantha, Christopher and Amanda

Crime Prevention and the Built Environment

Richard H. Schneider and Ted Kitchen

LONDON AND NEW YORK

HV7431
.S354
2007

.71006681

First published 2007
by Routledge
2 Park Square, Milton Park, Abingdon, Oxon OX14 4RN

Simultaneously published in the USA and Canada
by Routledge
270 Madison Ave, New York, NY 10016

Routledge is an imprint of the Taylor & Francis Group, an informa business

© 2007 Richard H. Schneider and Ted Kitchen

Typeset in Akzidenz Grotesk by
Keystroke, 28 High Street, Tettenhall, Wolverhampton
Printed and bound in Great Britain by
The Cromwell Press, Trowbridge, Wiltshire

British Library Cataloguing in Publication Data
A catalogue record for this book is available from the British Library

Library of Congress Cataloging in Publication Data
Schneider, Richard H. (Richard Harold), 1947–
    Crime prevention in the built environment / Richard H. Schneider and Ted Kitchen.
       p. cm.
    Includes bibliographical references and index.
    ISBN 0-415-37324-7 (hbk : alk. paper) – ISBN 0-415-37325-5 (pbk : alk. paper)
1. Crime prevention. 2. City planning. 3. Crime prevention and architectural design.
I. Kitchen, Ted. II. Title.
    HV7431.S354 2007
    364.4'9–dc22
    2006026303

ISBN10: 0–415–37324–7 (hbk)   ISBN13: 978–0–415–37324–1 (hbk)
ISBN10: 0–415–37325–5 (pbk)   ISBN13: 978–0–415–37325–8 (pbk)
ISBN10: 0–203–09881–1 (ebk)   ISBN13: 978–0–203–09881–3 (ebk)

Crime Prevention and the Built Environment

Both planning and crime affect the quality of life and the sustainability of cities, nations and lives. Worldwide interest is at an all-time high in the role that planning processes and the design of the physical environment can play in reducing the opportunity for crime, the fear of crime and the risk of terrorism. In seeking to advance the field of crime prevention planning, this book builds upon established theory and incorporates original research on the evolving relationships between planning systems, police and citizens. Surveying classical place-based crime prevention as well as concepts such as space syntax and new urbanism, it provides an international perspective on these issues and takes a look at the ways in which terrorism and technology affect place-based crime prevention. It also seeks to investigate the connection between crime prevention and development planning at a policy level, looking at the bureaucratic and administrative hurdles to cooperative action.

For professionals, students and researchers working in planning, design and criminology, the need to respond effectively to these problems represents a huge challenge. By linking theory, evidence and practical application, this book seeks to bridge gaps within and across these areas. The second book produced by this transatlantic writing partnership, *Crime Prevention and the Built Environment* provides a comprehensive analysis of some of the most important issues affecting quality of life in urban areas across the world.

Richard H. Schneider is Professor of Urban and Regional Planning at the University of Florida College of Design, Construction and Planning. His research has included work on the design and implementation of technology for crime analysis, the evaluation of crime prevention strategies and the comparison of crime prevention programmes at an international level.

Ted Kitchen is Emeritus Professor of Planning and Urban Regeneration at Sheffield Hallam University. Since his work as a professional planner, his academic research has centred on planning and urban regeneration practice, focusing in particular on the relationship between planning and crime prevention.

Contents

Figures

Tables

Boxes

Preface

Having already written a general textbook in the field of planning for crime prevention, *Planning for Crime Prevention: A Transatlantic Perspective* (Routledge, 2002), we were conscious of two things in particular. The first was that, while that book was written mainly for the planning community, the interest in its subject matter turned out to be much more extensive than that. So this time we wanted in particular to engage with a broad spectrum of built environment professionals and police officers with an interest in this field, because we are conscious that they all have an important part to play in moving the field forward. The second point was the rather more personal one that we felt that our first book had tried to encompass the field, but as a consequence of this desire to achieve breadth it had not been able to look in as much depth as we would have liked at some particular topics which we felt were of emerging importance. So, we wanted in this book to take the opportunity to treat some of the issues that we think are important to the future development of the field in a greater degree of depth.

These two considerations have played an important part in shaping this book, as has our desire to see the field as being essentially about the inter-action of theory and practice. So, Part One of this book tries to introduce both the classical theories in the field and some of the more recent challenges to them in a relatively succinct manner, while Part Two debates five particular elements of practice development in the context both of these theoretical discussions and of the real-world issues that are shaping what happens on the ground. As before, our working method was to allocate the responsibility for taking the lead on individual chapters to one of us, and then to exchange drafts and comment on them as critical friends until we were satisfied collectively with what we had produced. So, Richard Schneider took the lead with Chapters 2, 3, 7 and 8, and Ted Kitchen took the lead with the remaining chapters and acted as overall editor. The process of electronic exchange is, of course, of fundamental importance to the successful functioning of a trans-atlantic writing partnership, but in this particular case it was supplemented by the fact that Richard Schneider spent the period September–December

2005 on sabbatical at Sheffield Hallam University, during which time first drafts of around half of the book were produced. We hope this combination of electronic communication and propinquity has enabled us to produce a book that readers will enjoy reading as much as we have enjoyed writing.

We are both very conscious that our backgrounds, perceptions and writing styles are different, and that this could be a real barrier in a cooperation of this nature. But if people worried too much about issues of this nature, transatlantic writing collaborations like this one simply would not happen. And in any event, we see differences of this nature as sources of strength rather than as problems, and we have tried to ensure that our writing process has capitalised on this potential. It is, of course, for others to judge how successful this endeavour has been.

Acknowledgements

Richard Schneider is grateful to the University of Florida and to its College of Design, Construction and Planning for supporting a semester-long sabbatical in Britain in autumn 2005, during which time he was able to research and write parts of this book. While in Britain he served as a visiting professor at Sheffield Hallam University's Faculty of Development and Society, and he is appreciative of the munificent provision of office space, facilities and staff support which allowed him to pursue the research and to participate in the life of the university. In this and other regards he is especially indebted to co-author Ted Kitchen and to his wife, Ann Kitchen, for opening doors at the university as well as to their own home at crucial junctures. The value of their friendship, good advice, and warm and generous spirit cannot be overstated as contributions to this work. Special thanks are due to Dr Richard Walton and to the Reverend Ann Walton, who were gracious landlords and hosts throughout the time spent in Britain. Finally, but certainly not least, Richard is indebted to his partner and friend, Zulma Chardon, for her loving companionship, encouragement, good humour, and patience in supporting Richard as the work was completed in both the United States and Britain.

Ted Kitchen would like to thank his colleagues in the Urban and Regional Studies Group in the Faculty of Development and Society at Sheffield Hallam University (SHU) for all their support during the life of this project, even if at times they may not have realised they were giving it. For his last year at SHU before retirement, Ted had two book contracts to deliver (one of which was this present book), and the work planning process in the group created for him the time and space to undertake this task, with inevitable knock-on effects on colleagues. In particular, it was important, with Richard Schneider in the university between September and December 2005, for Ted to have the time and space to work effectively with him, and again this need was taken into account in the process of adjusting work commitments among group members. He would also like to thank the Dean of the Faculty at the time, Professor Kevin Bonnett, and his colleagues for agreeing enthusiastically to the idea that Richard Schneider should come to SHU on sabbatical, and then for doing the necessary things to make this happen. There is no doubt that work on this book benefited enormously from this sabbatical arrangement. Finally, Ted would like to thank his wife, Ann, for all her love and support during the life of this project, when she lived with both a husband and two books. He hopes the latter were more awkward than the former, but somehow doubts it.

Richard and Ted would both like to thank Ann Wilson for her work on the book from start to completion. In Ted's case she turned his handwritten scripts into conventional text quickly and efficiently, like the experienced reader of his handwriting that she had become after dealing with his other recent book in the same way. In Richard's case she converted American English into English English with grace and good humour (and a little help from the appropriate spell-checker). But more than this, she helped us standardise the presentation of our figures, our notes and the bibliography, and thus contributed a huge amount to the transatlantic effort, for which we are very grateful. We would also like to thank police architectural liaison officers Stephen Town (Bradford) and Peter Knowles (Bedfordshire) for showing us round parts of their areas, for hosting us for a day each, for responding to our many questions, and for offering us comments on drafts of parts of this book. We both hope that Ann, Stephen and Peter feel that all of their efforts on our behalf are properly reflected in the end product. We would like to thank Dr Ilir Bejleri for his helpful comments on a draft of Chapter 8, and Peter Harrison for the several improvements he suggested at the editorial stage.

Most of the photographs, diagrams and other figures in this book have been created by us, but where we have sourced them from elsewhere we have acknowledged these sources in our text and where necessary obtained the relevant permissions to republish. We are grateful for the cooperative approach to the creation of illustrations for this book that we have experienced from all sides.

Note: Figures 7.3 and 7.4 and Tables 7.1, 7.2 and 7.3 are kindly reprinted by permission of Dr Brian Taylor of UCLA and the Mineta Transportation Institute. This report was sponsored by the Mineta Transporation Institute at San Jose State University, which is funded by the US Department of Transportation and the California Department of Transportation. Additional funding was provided by the UCLA International Institute.

Abbreviations

ACPO	Association of Chief Police Officers
AIP	American Institute of Planners
ALO	architectural liaison officer
ANPR	automatic number place recognition
AT/FP	Anti-Terrorism and Force Protection
BOMA	Building Owners and Managers Association
BRAC	Base Realignment and Closure
BSI	British Standards Institution
CCTV	closed-circuit television
CDRP	crime and disorder reduction partnership
COP	crime opportunity profile
COPS	community-oriented policing; Crime Opportunity Profiling of Streets
CPTED	crime prevention through environmental design
CRAVED	concealable, removable, available, valuable, enjoyable and disposable
CSO	community support officer
DHS	Department of Homeland Security (United States)
EDRA	Environmental Design Research Association
GIS	geographic information system(s)
GPS	global positioning system(s)
HUD	Department of Housing and Urban Development (United States)
IRA	Irish Republican Army
JIATFE	Joint Interagency Task Force East
MAPS	Mapping and Analysis for Public Safety
NAF	Naval Air Facility
NCTC	National Counterterrorism Center (United States)
NTD	neo-traditional development
ODPM	Office of the Deputy Prime Minister (United Kingdom)
POP	problem-oriented policing
PPS1	Planning Policy Statement 1 (United Kingdom)

RFID   radio frequency identification
SBD   Secured by Design
TND   traditional neighbourhood design
TOD   transit-oriented development
TRIA   Terrorist Risk Insurance Act 2002 (United States)
UCR   Uniform Crime Reports
UL   Underwriters Laboratory

1

Introduction

Introduction

We commence this book with a short discussion of the relationship between crime and the design of the built environment, since aspects of those relationships are our primary focus. We then discuss, again relatively briefly, the phenomenon of fear of crime, which is not our primary focus here but which in many people's minds is inextricably linked with the issue of crime prevention. After this, we set out our approach to this book, and follow that with an outline of its structure, before closing with some brief concluding remarks.

Crime prevention and the built environment

There is no doubt that the form and layout of the built environment have a huge impact on the opportunity to commit crime, and therefore at least potentially on thinking about crime prevention (Tilley, 2005, chapter 1). A high proportion of crime takes place in particular locations, and the characteristics of those locations in terms both of their general settings and their specific attributes influence very considerably the crimes that do (and don't) take place there. This broad understanding has probably been around for nearly as long as crime has existed as a recognised phenomenon, although the process of writing about it systematically is somewhat more recent than that. What is rather more challenging than this broad proposition, however, is the idea that we might manipulate the physical environment at both the micro and the macro scales in order to reduce or even eliminate the opportunities for crimes to be committed. This is challenging, because, for such activities to be effective, we need to know what the relationship is likely to be between particular interventions and crime outcomes; and while there is much that can be said about this, there is also much that we do not know with any degree of certainty (Sherman *et al.*, 1997). Additionally, while we can say with confidence that the characteristics of the built environment influence the opportunity to commit crime, rarely will this be the only explanation of why a crime did (or did not) occur. So, a second major challenge is around understanding the significance of the process of manipulating the form of the built environment in order to reduce or eliminate the opportunity to commit crime alongside all the other activities that societies might sanction to this end. And there is almost certainly a third major challenge here as well, which is around the concept of public acceptability, both collectively and individually. Human beings are by no means all the same, and so what some would regard as sensible preventive measures (for example), others might see as unacceptable inhibitions or as unappealing fortifications.

These three challenges are by no means the only ones that exist in this field, but they are at the heart of what we are trying to do in this book. We want to contribute to the growing understanding of the ways in which the built environment can be manipulated in order to reduce the opportunity for crimes to be committed. We recognise that initiatives of this nature almost never occur in isolation (even if that is how they might be seen in the minds of some of their protagonists), but are almost always part of a complex, multifaceted and ever-shifting process of modifying the environments in which people live in order to improve the quality of that experience. And we recognise in particular that initiatives of this type need to be undertaken *with* people rather than done *to* them, seeking consent, providing knowledge and understanding, and responding constructively to individual and collective preferences. There is a long way to go before it could be said that we are on top of this agenda; after all, if that were the case, wouldn't we already be manipulating the built environment successfully across the world, and be a long way down the road towards eliminating crime? We believe that, starting from where we are now, this will be a long journey, but we hope that this book can make a contribution to this process.

In particular, we are interested in the relationship between the work of architects, planners, civil engineers and other designers of the built environment and the experiences of crime that their layouts produce, because it is surely better (and, in the long term, much cheaper) to produce a safe and secure environment at the first time of asking than it is to have to revisit and remodel a built environment where the experience of living or working in it has been a negative one from a crime perspective. This suggests that it is possible not only to design crime out of environments (or at any rate to make it hard for crimes to be committed successfully), but also that some designs might actually facilitate crime by failing to recognise and eliminate opportunities for crimes to be committed. We think that this is the case; while there are examples of layouts that have in large measure designed out crime, there are also many examples of layouts that could be said to have designed crime in. This is not, in our experience, because architects, planners, civil engineers and other design professionals are the deliberate assistants of criminals. Rather, it is because they have given too little (or even no) thought to what the crime experience of living in their design is likely to be, and because they often do not acknowledge the resourcefulness and adaptability of individual criminals (Ekblom, 1997b), even when they have given this matter some thought. That said, crime is not the only element that needs to be thought about in the process of urban design, but it is in our view an important and often under-recognised one. Our position is in essence very simple: it ought to be possible to improve the quality of the experience of living in a new development throughout its lifetime by thinking about crime prevention as an integral part of the design process from the outset, and the various chapters of this book have been written in order to contribute to this complex task.

It is important not to generalise too much when talking about these matters, however, because:

1 built environments are very different from each other;
2 the people who occupy them are different from each other in large numbers of ways; and
3 the crimes that are committed in such localities (and the criminals who commit them) are also different from each other, although there is probably more commonality here than there is with the other two propositions.

This last point is of particular significance for this book, because it is important that crime and its relationship with the built environment are not treated as a single entity. One of the most important contributions that Barry Poyner has made to the field is through his careful weighing of the available evidence, and in particular his meticulous approach to distinctions between types of crime. This has led him to suggest that the process of incorporating crime prevention into the design of residential areas is not a single strand of thought but is rather a recognition of the need to develop strategies against four principal crime problems:

- burglary – a strategy is needed to discourage people from trying to break into houses;
- car crime – a strategy for providing a safe place to park cars;
- theft around the home – a strategy for protecting the front of the house, and items in gardens, sheds and garages;
- criminal damage – a strategy to minimise malicious damage to property (Poyner, 2006, p. 99).

He then proceeds to offer a series of principles that can help in the formulation of these strategies (ibid., pp. 99–103), although he is at pains to suggest the following:

> Defining the tasks of design this way around puts the responsibility for thinking about these issues on to the planner or designer. It also opens the way to a more design-oriented approach than a prescriptive approach, giving designers more opportunity for flexibility in developing or adapting solutions that fit well with all other aspects of the design.
>
> (ibid., page 99)

Exactly so. We believe that this approach captures very well what we are trying to say in this introduction. The field does not need more one-size-fits-all solutions, but what it does need is designers of all kinds to think about the kinds of issues that Barry Poyner identifies, in this case in relation to residential environments, from the outset as integral elements of the design process. As part of that process, account should always be taken of the constantly developing understanding of the relationship between crime and the design of the built environment, a process which itself can be greatly enhanced through careful monitoring of the experience of occupying designs (an activity that still seems to take place in only a tiny minority of instances) and open and honest discussion of these experiences.

Before we describe our approach to this task and the structure of the book that has resulted, we want to say a little about the constant companion of crime in the literature, which is the fear of crime. We want to do this here because in large measure this book is not about the fear of crime, although we accept in saying this that many measures that might be put in place in order to reduce the opportunity for crime are also likely to have the effect of reducing public fear of crime; improved street lighting would often be an example of an initiative which could be beneficial in both of these senses. Nevertheless, we think that in a sense crime and the fear of crime are two different but related phenomena, with the latter being in some ways much more complex (and sometimes much more argued about) than the former. So, we acknowledge the need to say at least a few things about this particular phenomenon, before moving on to concentrate on what this book is mainly about: the experience of crime, rather than the fear of crime.

Fear of crime

Fear of crime has probably been around as long as crime itself. And human reactions based upon those fears, as distinct from reactions based upon the direct experience of crime, have probably been around nearly as long (see Schneider and Kitchen, 2002, chapter 3; see also Chesney, 1970, for a graphic exposition of the place of fear of crime in Victorian Britain). In more recent times it has become increasingly fashionable for governments in many parts of the world to undertake programmes targeted specifically at fear of crime, based upon public reactions to this issue, which record levels of fear or worry about crime that are quite disproportionate to its actual experience. What is new here is the idea of large-scale public programmes which specifically seek to address fear of crime, and which in so doing separate it off from activities that seek to restrict the opportunity for crimes to be committed (see, for example, European Crime Prevention Network, 2005) – a distinction that we have previously argued is wholly appropriate (Schneider and Kitchen, 2002, p. 270). In turn, this has given rise to a large-scale critical literature to which we cannot hope to do justice here (but see, for example, Pain, 2000), except to say that the existence of this expanding pool of critical literature reinforces the point that this issue has grown in significance in recent times.

To illustrate the point that the significance of this debate (and certainly its significance in political terms) is a function of expressed fears rather than of actual experience, the 2004/05 British Crime Survey contains some instructive figures:

- Sixty-one per cent of the public thought that crime in the country as a whole had increased over the past two years, with 27 per cent believing that it had risen 'a lot', whereas in fact it had fallen slightly over this period (Nicholas *et al.*, 2005, pp. 17 and 21).
- The percentages of people who expressed a 'high level of worry' about particular types of crime can be compared with the actual rates of victim-isation during the period 2004/05 as follows:

	High level of worry	*Percentage risk of being a victim*
Burglary	12%	2.7%
Car crime	13%	8.2%
Violent crime	16%	3.6%

(ibid., tables 2a and 2d)

So, the overall sense of what was happening to crime in England and Wales was at odds with reality, and for some individual crimes (notably burglary and violent crime), high levels of worry were being expressed by between four and five times as many people as had actually been victims of those crimes.

One of the difficulties in this area is undoubtedly the problem of producing reliable measurements of fear of crime on a consistent basis (Farrall *et al.*, 1997; European Crime Prevention Network, 2005, p. 19). Having reviewed a range of European studies, the European Crime Prevention Network comments as follows:

> Extensive research across EU Member States revealed little in the way of scientifically evaluated examples of studies that measure with any degree of validity the extent or otherwise of fear of crime or feelings of security. There were also few scientifically evaluated examples of measures or initiatives that reduce fear of crime. Research on fear of crime is mainly theoretical.
>
> (European Crime Prevention Network, 2005, Executive Summary, p. 1)

The problems here are not merely about measurement, however, but also seem to be of a more conceptual nature. What exactly is 'fear of crime'? Is fear always and inevitably a bad thing, which whenever evidence of it appears needs where possible to be reduced or eliminated? Do some organisations (for example, commercial organisations seeking to market security products, or police organisations bidding for a bigger slice of scarce public resources) actually have a vested interest in exaggerating fear of crime? These (and many others) are important questions if we are to get under the skin of this particular set of phenomena, and in many ways the answers to them remain controversial. Ditton and Innes (2005), who generally adopt a questioning and indeed sceptical approach to these issues, take a situational view of fear of crime: they argue that sometimes fear is good and sometimes it is bad, depending on the circumstances, which will include differentiating between localities and individuals rather than making broad, sweeping generalisations. Their discussions of these issues, and of some of the attempts undertaken to date to reduce fear, is an illuminating starting point for readers who wish to pursue some of these issues in greater depth.

Another of the difficulties in the area is undoubtedly the problem that much of the mass media reporting of crime and the fear of crime, which has long been believed to have a distorting effect on public views (Ditton and Duffy, 1983), seems to resort too readily to gender stereotyping. This treats gender (and to a lesser extent age) as if there were only one basic pattern of responses: women are more fearful than men (Gilchrist *et al.*, 1998). While in the broadest of senses and in specified circumstances there may be something in this particular stereotype, it seems to hide as much as it reveals. Gilchrist *et al.*, for example, argue on the basis of an empirical study in Scotland that some of the responses from fearful men are more like those from fearful women than those from fearless men; in other words, it is not always gender that is the primary characteristic in determining fear of crime, but instead this appears to be a much more complex process which is affected by a wide range of circumstances, experiences and beliefs (ibid.). There is also a suggestion from recent work (Ditton and Innes, 2005, p. 599) that once account is taken of the tendency of both men and women to lie when responding to questions about fear, the traditional gender stereotype itself might be wrong.

A third area of difficulty is that it is not always clear what people really mean when they say that they are 'very worried' or 'fearful' about crime, or whether they are really talking about fear of crime at all. Leonie Sandercock, for example, argues that a strong strand in expressions of fear of crime is actually fear of difference – as if talking about fear of crime is a socially acceptable way of giving expression to concerns about other people, and especially about how strangers or incomers are bringing about changes to cities, changes that we don't like, by directly or indirectly replacing the familiar with something different. She argues that this deeply conservative stance ignores the fact that this is how cities have often grown and developed over time, and that this sense of the city as a melting pot is actually one of the things that some people find attractive and exciting about cities. Its manifestations include physical changes such as the appearance of gated communities on a large scale in some localities, which can be seen as people deliberately turning their backs on difference and indeed seeking to defend themselves from it. She argues as a consequence that we need to deconstruct what is really being said when people talk about fear of crime, and to tackle the underlying problems of difference that this reveals rather than simply to embark upon policies and practices such as fortification as knee-jerk reactions to these expressions of fear (Sandercock, 2005).

All of this illustrates what an awkward and complex problem expressed fear of crime (and presumably also those fears that remain unexpressed) actually is. Most of the points made above should certainly cause us to stop and think carefully about expressed fear of crime rather than to conclude that we are all submerged by a tidal wave of fear that requires dramatic action. In this sense, it could be argued that in many ways fear of crime is a much more complex notion than is crime itself; after all, a burglary or an assault is usually a specific and tangible thing, whereas someone expressing worries that they might be a victim of something like this is something much more hazy. And yet, we would argue that it is possible to throw the baby out with the bathwater here. It is actually perfectly rational to say that you are afraid of your house being broken into or of being on the receiving end of physical violence, especially when many people's circles of family and friends will include people who have been victims of these kinds of crimes at some time in the past. Similarly, it could be argued that an element of fear of this nature is actually socially beneficial if it encourages people to take sensible precautions that seek to minimise the likelihood of these things happening (Crouch *et al.*, 1999). So, we wouldn't go so far as those who would seek to dismiss the whole idea of fear of crime, or to say that it is really something else entirely, although we certainly take very seriously their important cautionary words about not over-reacting to suggestions that fear of crime is being allowed to become a dominating element in urban discourses. For us, fear of crime really starts to have a meaningful effect when it changes people's behaviour, especially when, through modifying the physical environment (often by doing simple things such as improving lighting or removing overgrown landscaping), it is sometimes possible to make places feel less intimidating and therefore to make them more likely to be used. Of course, we accept in saying this that it is likely in most instances that simple environmental actions such as this will need to be accompanied by extensive dialogue with communities to understand what they feel about 'their' places. Nevertheless, we think it is important not to lose sight of the fact that some localities do induce fear for reasons that are capable of being tackled, and that it is perfectly rational (and, indeed, perfectly believable) for people to express their fears about places of this nature.

Two of the characteristics referred to above – the fact that crime and the fear of crime should be seen as separate but related phenomena, and the fact that when fear of crime begins to affect people's behaviour this justifies appropriate action to tackle these concerns – raise questions about the types of public policy responses to fear of crime that we might expect to see and the ways in which these might differ from responses to crimes themselves. In truth, one might expect to see a very wide spectrum of possible actions here, but one conceptualisation of some of the key points on this spectrum is the so-called 'fear of crime matrix' which has recently been developed in the United Kingdom.[1] A version of this is presented as Figure 1.1. This takes the idea that both crime and the fear of crime can be seen as 'high' or 'low' (although in both cases there is probably a wide variety of positions between these extremes), and then pairs each of these positions with each other creating a matrix of four sets of circumstances. Policy responses that might

1.1 The fear of crime matrix. The small boxes in each of the four quadrants of this diagram give examples of policy responses that may be appropriate to the particular combination of crime and fear of crime.

Source: Adapted from the material on the UK government's Crime Reduction website, at www. crimereduction.gov.uk/fearofcrime0216.htm

be appropriate for each of these circumstances are then identified, although again the range may well be much broader than those illustrated in Figure 1.1. Nonetheless, this might be helpful to make the most basic point, which is that in some situations fear of crime may be a significant problem in its own right (i.e. independent of crime levels), and one that requires a tailored response.

The European Crime Prevention Network, in its study of evaluated projects designed to reduce fear of crime in localities across Europe, concluded that there were so few reliable studies yet available that it was premature to produce lists of good practices that could be expected to be reliably replicated. The Network suggested as a consequence that a combination of interventions was probably more likely to be successful than any single intervention by itself, and offered the following as being likely to be useful as part of approaches of this nature:

- Work to increase community cohesion.
- Work to improve the environment, such as removing signs of neglect and improving lighting.
- Increase partnership working, rather than regarding fear of crime as the responsibility of the police.
- Increase the use of community wardens.

(European Crime Prevention Network, 2005, pp. 46, 47)

The Network also recommended a series of approaches to research in this field, to try to improve the ability in future to draw reliable conclusions about what works in what circumstances:

- Work towards producing a standardised definition of fear of crime, which all researchers should be encouraged to utilise.
- Develop a broad template for evaluating future initiatives to reduce fear of crime so that evaluations can be compared with each other.
- Establish what constitutes an 'acceptable' level of fear of crime so that interventions have the same target threshold. (We suspect that this may need to be in the plural to recognise a range of circumstances; a single common threshold may be an over-ambitious aim.)
- Look specifically at the nature and extent of fear of crime and victims of domestic abuse.
- Look specifically at the relationship between media and fear of crime.

(ibid., pp. 47 and 48)

This research agenda constitutes a huge undertaking which would be likely to take a considerable period of time, not just in doing the work but in brokering acceptance in particular of the methodological standards that constitute the first three points. But it does represent an attempt to try to put some sort of scale to the issue of fear of crime which will help to keep it in perspective (and without forgetting some of the more challenging ideas about what expressions of fear of crime might really represent), and as such it would surely be a desirable agenda to work through if this could be achieved.

Our approach to this book

Our approach is conditioned by two central considerations: the large size of the field, and the practical limitations on how much of it can be covered in depth in a single book. Having already written what we hope is a useful introductory text to the field of planning for crime prevention (Schneider and Kitchen, 2002), on this occasion we wanted to explore in slightly greater depth than is possible in an introductory text some specialist areas that we think are really important. These considerations led us to the view that what we should do on this occasion was to produce a book the core of which consists of two parts. Part One examines the theory, where we introduce what might be seen as the classical theories in the field and also some of the contemporary challenges to these theories. Part Two looks at the practice. We consider in depth five major topics which we believe are of considerable importance to the development of the field. These have quite a strong case study emphasis to them, and in some of these chapters we have concentrated on presenting specific cases rather than general surveys. The five chosen topics are:

- how planning systems across the world are beginning to engage with the crime prevention agenda, because it is through planning systems that most development proposals are mediated;
- the operational experiences of police officers working on planning for crime prevention in Britain, because very little has been written about what the people who work in what is a relatively new field for the police service actually do;
- crime prevention and urban regeneration, because the British experience of moving crime prevention to the centre of the urban regeneration process may have valuable lessons to offer, both as to the management of this as a strategic process and in terms of individual projects;
- the development of anti-terrorism measures in the United States especially after the events of 11 September 2001, which may well turn out to be an important driver of future developments in the field even though (thankfully) the experience of terrorism is on a much smaller and more concentrated scale than is the experience of crime;
- the application of new technologies to the field of planning for crime prevention, because of the scope this offers for performance to become more efficient and more effective.

Clearly, there are numerous specialist topics that relate to the practice of planning for crime prevention that we could have chosen other than these five, and so we do not wish to hide the fact that as well as what we regard as their intrinsic significance, we have chosen these five on the basis of our interest in and our knowledge of them. We hope that readers will share our view that these chapters are about things that really do matter.

The structure of this book

The chapters that follow are derived from the approach that we have set out above:

Part One: The theory

Chapter 2 looks at the 'classical' theories of place-based crime prevention. By contrast, Chapter 3 looks at some emerging phenomena which could be seen as offering some significant challenges to the classical theories: space syntax, new urbanism, the phenomenon of gated communities and the growth of premises liability issues. Together, these chapters seek to offer a strong grounding in key theoretical issues and debates in the field.

Part Two: The practice

Chapter 4 surveys some of the progress that has been made across the world in getting planning systems to engage with crime prevention objectives. We are not aware of another attempt at such a survey, and we wholly acknowledge that our survey is a partial one. We hope that it will begin to develop an understanding of how this issue is developing across the world, and that it will encourage others (perhaps particularly in those parts of the world we have not covered) to write about how this is being tackled in their own particular situations. Chapter 5 looks at the development of the Architectural Liaison service in the British police, and specifically at the experiences of two architectural liaison officers (ALOs: Stephen Town in Bradford, and Peter Knowles in Bedfordshire). Chapter 6 looks at how crime prevention has been incorporated into the process of urban regeneration in the United Kingdom, and presents two specific case studies: a look at the strategic process of doing this in Sheffield; and an examination of an award-winning project, the Blackthorn CASPAR project in Northampton. Chapter 7 explores the various ways in which the need to think much more consciously about protection against terrorism (particularly after the events of 11 September 2001) is impacting upon the built environment, and reflects on the likelihood that this activity will have specific implications for the related field of planning for crime prevention. Lastly in this part, Chapter 8 looks at recent work which has applied the fruits of new technology to the field of planning for crime prevention, in order both to improve knowledge and understanding and to increase operational effectiveness.

Part Three: Conclusions

In our final chapter, Chapter 9, we return to the ground we have covered in the preceding chapters and summarise the conclusions we have drawn in each instance, both about the state of theory in Part One and about the practice issues we have introduced in Part Two. We then use these conclusions to reflect both on the state of development in the field and on a research agenda in relation to some of its most pressing issues.

Concluding remarks

A book written by authors who are respectively American and British is likely, other things being equal, to reflect to a very considerable extent the situation in the United States and the United Kingdom. This book does indeed do so. Since many of the developments that have taken place in the field of planning for crime prevention have been in those two countries, however, we make no apologies for this. But we are also very conscious that circumstances in many parts of the world are not like those in our home countries, and one of the major challenges in the internationalisation of the field is the need to recognise difference, and in particular to acknowledge the importance of cultural acceptability. We do not believe, for example, that successful initiatives from the United States and the United Kingdom can automatically be replicated elsewhere, because of the differing circumstances that would apply, but we do believe that it is possible to transfer lessons across the world by thinking carefully about local circumstances. We hope the material in the chapters that follow encourages readers to do just that.

Part One
The theory

2

Classical theories of place-based crime prevention

Introduction

Classical place-based crime prevention theory is derived from disciplines that span architecture, urban planning, criminology, geography, psychology and sociology (among others) and from on-the-ground experiences that involve juvenile offenders, public and council housing tenants, and the practical problems of police investigations. Working within these disciplines and informed by practice, the scholars and researchers referred to in this chapter developed the family of theories that together form the classical core of today's place-based crime prevention. These theories include defensible space, crime prevention through environmental design (CPTED), situational crime prevention and environmental criminology. In this chapter we review the history and context of the theories' development and consider their application today by law enforcement agencies, criminologists, planners, designers and academics in efforts to organise, understand and resolve criminal events in the built environment. In so doing we discuss problem- and community-oriented policing, law enforcement strategies that have evolved from these, and related theoretical backgrounds. Emerging conceptual frameworks such as space syntax and new urbanism are described in Chapter 3. These latter ideas raise many issues connected to the fundamental place-based crime prevention theories discussed here, and we shall refer back to them as necessary throughout the book.

Organising issues and questions

It is ironic that evidence-based crime prevention approaches developed in the mid- to late twentieth century owe a significant debt to the discredited work of Cesare Lombroso, a nineteenth-century prison physician who documented relationships between physical appearance, criminal disposition and behaviour. While Lombroso's work (1876) was based on flawed assumptions and produced erroneous conclusions, his meticulous scientific methodology nevertheless paved the way for succeeding generations of crime prevention theorists who based their work on observation and data analysis as opposed to a priori approaches.

Although Lombroso's studies influenced the *process* of the research, the fundamental *substantive* notion underpinning the field of place-based crime prevention comes from different sources and is rooted in the notion that the environment influences behaviour. A wealth of research generated by many disciplines supports this clearly observable concept. The great heterogeneity of studies in the field represented by the Environmental Design Research Association (EDRA; http://www.edra.org), established in the United States in 1968, testifies to the resilience of this fundamental principle. Some of this work has focused specifically on understanding relationships between environmental influences and crime, with a concentration on *places* and *settings*, as distinct from scrutinising offenders, police, or the legal and correctional systems (Clarke, 1997). This place- and setting-based focus is the basis for the four major theories that we discuss below: defensible space, crime prevention through environmental design (CPTED), situational crime prevention and environmental criminology.

Strategies budding out of these theories have been adopted by government agencies across the developed world as part of the growing reliance on evidence-based policy making and practice. Some place-based crime prevention theories/strategies are proving to be credible based on scientific evaluations, while the jury is still out on others (Sherman *et al.*, 1997). Many of the applications have come to inform and guide crime prevention and security policy and practice across a wide range of land use categories, infrastructure, and building and estate development practices. This is so even though some scholars argue convincingly that mechanisms for the translation of place-based crime prevention from theory into practice for planners and urban designers are neither standardised nor necessarily efficient (Zahm, 2005).

Nevertheless, there is evidence that place-based theory has influenced – albeit unevenly – day-to-day urban public policy and practice relating to design and building regulation (Schneider and Kitchen, 2002), large scale anti-terrorist design (National Capital Planning Commission, 2002b), protection of microbiological and biomedical facilities (Royse and Johnson, 2002), siting and design of industrial parks, industrial buildings and office facilities (Peiser and Chang, 1998; Nadel, 2004), school security practice (Florida Department of Education, 2003) and courthouse design (Jandura and Campbell, 2004). This is only a very short list of many public and private domains where these theories have been applied on the ground in one form or another.

Despite that, many would argue that these theories only provide us with generic advice relative to explaining and predicting specific criminal events (Office of the Deputy Prime Minister and the Home Office, 2004). Place-based crime prevention theory cannot account for the vast variability of the environment within which criminal events unfold. Every environment differs relative to users, to physical design, and to cultural and socio-economic elements such that a plausible argument is that each is unique (Taylor, 2002).

How, then, can one formulate general principles that apply across a wide range of places? Moreover, we often find ostensibly conflicting advice about places and phenomena relative to crime prevention. For instance, all the theories noted above suggest that surveillance is a good thing, but there is evidence that all surveillance is not equal in reducing crime (Mayhew *et al.*, 1979). Moreover, how much surveillance is enough or too little? Is surveillance as straightforward as Jane Jacobs's prescription of 'eyes on the street' would have us believe (Jacobs, 1961)?

And how do we weigh crime prevention against other desirable aims? For example, when does access control – another crime opportunity strategy advanced by the core theories above – become access prohibition, so lacerating the fabric of democratic societies that the underlying values of open and free connection are irreparably damaged? As we shall discuss in Chapter 3, new urbanist theory suggests that the pendulum should be weighted towards open access, as distinct from access control. While this may be relatively easy to accomplish in new and healthy (greenfield) communities, how is this done in distressed (brownfield) communities which are struggling with access-related crime issues?

The responses to these fundamental questions and conflicts lie in context and balance. Each of the interrelated place-based crime prevention theories has local context-sensitive applications, and each application must be balanced against local physical (and often regional and national), socio-economic, legal, political and cultural concerns. As Colquhoun (2004) points out, understanding the role of context is crucial to urban planners and designers as well as to ordinary citizens, inasmuch as crime is as important in fundamental life choices such as decisions *where* to buy a home as it is in broad-scale public policy choices. The theories we discuss are thus constrained in terms of their power to generalise. On-the-ground strategies must therefore be tailored to local needs, although some similar principles can be seen at work across many contexts. Despite these limitations, without these place-based crime prevention theories we might still be focused solely on the psychological dispositions of offenders and on their socio-economic settings instead of considering what we now know to be important predictors and modifiers of criminal events that relate to the use, management, design and opportunity structure of the built environment.

Defensible space

We begin with defensible space, since it has defined place-based crime prevention practice in many ways. Defensible space is an evocative term used to identify an array of related ideas involving the extension of territorial control and influence, boundary marking with real and symbolic barriers, and the facilitation of surveillance that connect building and site design to crime opportunity reduction. Together these ideas – with multiple subcomponents – comprise the theory of defensible space. It was the first construct of its type to make popular headlines in the United States, has profoundly influenced a generation of public housing designers and policy makers (in particular) in the

United States and the United Kingdom, and has served as the lightning rod for critics disturbed by its ostensibly deterministic (and some argue simplistic) design–behaviour prescriptions. Defensible space is one of the place-based theories at the heart of the British Secured by Design (SBD) scheme (Town *et al.*, 2003), which has significant practical implications for community design and planning in the United Kingdom. We shall discuss this in more detail below and in Chapter 3, especially in relation to the debate between SBD and new urbanist advocates (Town and O'Toole, 2005; Kitchen, 2005).

Defensible space was credited with establishing crime prevention through environmental design (CPTED),[1] but in reality CPTED evolved independently at about the same time as defensible space, although the two have grown together over the years like intertwined vines. This mélange has prompted CPTED's originator, C. Ray Jeffrey (1971, 1977, 1990), to disavow the modern CPTED as quite different from his original concept. However, police rarely distinguish defensible space from CPTED, although in the United States most would more likely recognise CPTED, whereas in the United Kingdom defensible space seems to be more recognised by local authorities, including constables, since it is closely identified with Secured by Design, as noted above. Whatever its pedigree, defensible space evolved out of Oscar Newman's 1960s comparison of two side-by-side public housing projects in St Louis, Missouri, from observations of older St Louis neighbourhoods containing privatised streets, and from research in New York public housing projects (Newman, 1973, 1981). It was augmented by controlled applications in Dayton, Ohio, and Yonkers and the South Bronx, New York (Newman, 1996), and critically assessed in federally supported research conducted at sites across the United States in the 1970s (Rubenstein *et al.*, 1980). Despite its largely residential origin, its applications have been extended across many types of land uses, although there is evidence that it is less effective outside of that realm (Murray, 1994).

The perception and power of ownership: Pruitt-Igoe and Carr Square Village

An architect, planner and critical observer of human behaviour, Newman was fascinated by the power and energy inherent in the command of places by users, even when they were not owners. His fundamental concept is intuitively appealing: places and spaces can be designed and built so as to increase residents' feelings of ownership and control. Since people tend to protect better those areas and things they believe that they own – even if this may be a fiction when it comes to property renters – then places can be fashioned to increase the sense of ownership and induce these territorial feelings. To be sure, this was not a new notion. In the 1930s and 1940s, public housing agencies in the United States speculated that design could play a role in evoking protective and 'social' responses among residents, and they toyed with a number of site design approaches intended to maximise these feelings and behaviours (Vale, 2005; Franck and Mostollar, 1995). Indeed, the concept that the physical residential setting is somehow related to attitudes, beliefs and behaviours, and especially tendencies towards criminality, has a consider-able lineage in US and British urban history and policy development (Hall, 1990).

Newman focused the concept squarely and forcefully on crime *and* design. In his view, places could be designed to be defendable by residents acting on their own protective initiatives which would reduce the likelihood of crime and disorder, especially as perpetrated by 'outsiders'. At its heart, then, defensible space is about creating, shaping, preserving and maintaining proprietary control over one's territory. Allied with this core concept are principles of boundary definition and natural surveillance that we shall discuss further below.

Newman was influenced by Elizabeth Wood's pioneering work with the Chicago Housing Authority, where she surmised that improved site and housing design along with increased surveillance opportunities could enhance security for tenants by boosting chances for informal social control (1961, 1967). Jane Jacobs's (1961) reflections about the importance of vibrant street life, diversity of street uses and the identification of clear boundaries between public and private spaces also significantly influenced Newman's early thinking and philosophy. Indeed, defensible space has been called an operational-isation of Jacobs's themes (Jeffrey and Zahm, 1993). While this notion is accurate, Newman would no doubt bristle at it, inasmuch as he believed that Jacobs did not truly understand the importance of territoriality in relation to the protective implications of space definition and ownership, whether real or symbolic.[2]

Dramatic evidence to support defensible space theory came from observa-tions of public housing authorities in St Louis and New York City. Of particular early interest to Newman was the life cycle of a 2,870-unit high-rise complex called Pruitt-Igoe, constructed in an inner-city St Louis neighbourhood in 1956. It was designed by an award-winning architect following the theory and styles advanced by the International Congress of Modern Architects and by architecture guru Le Corbusier. The intentions were outwardly admirable.[3] One of the chief design aims was to free up as much ground space as possible for communal use by concentrating residents in a series of 33 11-storey towers, thereby allowing 'a river of trees . . . to flow under the buildings' (Newman, 1996, p. 10). Other site layout and building design features, such as skip-stop elevators (elevators that did not stop at every floor), common recreational rooms and galleries, and shared laundry facilities, were meant to encourage collective activity and, presumably, raise public spirit and virtues.[4]

The reality was just the opposite. Soon after being completed, Pruitt-Igoe became a nightmare of crime and disorder. The river of trees became, in Newman's words, a 'sewer of garbage and glass' (1996, p. 10) where crime rates and vandalism soared. The civic concept of shared space devolved into competitive space dominated by gangs and vandals, making law-abiding citizens prisoners of their apartments or pushing them out altogether. Never reaching more than a 60 per cent occupancy rate, Pruitt-Igoe was demolished in stages beginning in 1972, but not before the federal government had spent millions trying to fix its problems.

Directly across the street from Pruitt-Igoe was another, older public housing complex, Carr Square Village, built in 1942. Pruitt-Igoe and Carr Square Village shared the same resident profile: low-income, minority, single-mother households. But they did not share design features as regards density, height and shared entry and corridor spaces. Whereas Pruitt-Igoe's vertical design compacted residents into stacked boxes whose elevation separated residents from their children, Carr Square Village's low-rise site plan achieved the same overall density but permitted closer connections and supervision by parents. Whereas Pruitt-Igoe's floor plan allocated corridors among as many as 20 families, with as many as 150 sharing elevators, entries, lobbies and stairs, Carr Square's smaller, low-rise, row-house design distributed entries and lobbies among only a few families.

To Newman, the design and density differences meant that the Carr Square Village residents could recognise each other and could identify intruders, which was not easy to do in Pruitt-Igoe, given its vast bulk and resident numbers. These features fostered isolation, and their open accessibility to nearby neighbourhoods facilitated anonymity. Who were residents and who were outsiders? Indeed, Jacobs (1961) had argued that a strong predictor for flourishing crime was places where neighbours did not know or meaningfully interact with each other.

Newman was careful to point out the synergistic effect of social context and design: he noted that the combination of design elements and resident profile proved disastrous in Pruitt-Igoe, especially since there was little of the guardianship, child supervision or facility maintenance that one would have found in middle- or upper-class high-rise buildings. Similar findings have been confirmed by other, later studies of different venues, such as schools. For example, a range of work reported by Felson (2002) strongly suggests that smaller secondary schools have much lower crime rates than larger ones, findings largely attributable to the anonymity attendant to size and the difficulty supervising adolescents.

As regards the effects on civic behaviour, Newman suggested that there was a proportional relationship between the number of families sharing space (territory) and the sense of responsibility for that space, such that more sharing meant less caring. Thus, in Carr Square Village it was 'relatively easy for an informal understanding to be reached among the families as to what constituted "acceptable" usage' (Newman, 1996, p. 17). While this finding came as no surprise to sociologists and social psychologists, Newman's empirical connection of physical design, social control and behaviour was ground-breaking.

This is especially so when the results were translated into *criminal* behaviour. In reviewing Pruitt-Igoe and later New York Housing Authority crime data (Newman, 1973), Newman suggested a direct relationship between building height and the occurrence of crime, especially robberies within the 'public' interior spaces, although burglaries were also higher in high-rise buildings than in their lower-rise counterparts. He reached much the same conclusion when he looked at overall project size, although the latter is a social as well as a physical variable inasmuch as it correlated with higher numbers of low-income, single-parent families in the neighbourhood generally.

As other research has since confirmed, the density of poor people in itself is a factor in higher crime rates inasmuch as it tends to concentrate people (particularly teenagers) who, by virtue of other environmental factors, have repeated opportunity for criminal behaviour as well as victimisation (Felson, 2002). Newman emphasised this as an important variable exacerbating Pruitt-Igoe's problems, but stressed that the physical form of the buildings and site layout can nevertheless mitigate (or exacerbate) impacts on low-income, single-parent residents. They are more vulnerable to crime and also more vulnerable to the confounding effects of poor design, which together produce 'results . . . nothing short of disastrous' (Newman, 1996, p. 26). The outcomes play out also in terms of increased fear and community instability.

Mini-neighbourhoods in Dayton's Five Oaks community

Lessons learned in creating defensible space relative to territorial control, access control and boundary marking at Pruitt-Igoe, in New York Housing Authority projects and especially in St Louis's private street neighbourhoods were subsequently translated by Newman (1976) to other areas, most notably Dayton's Five Oaks residential community, a racially diverse neighbourhood close to the city's downtown. Five Oaks was an older area that was in transition from middle-income, predominantly white owner-residents to lower-income black renters, who concentrated primarily in certain sectors.

As distinct from Pruitt-Igoe and Carr Square Village, housing options in Five Oaks were largely confined to one- and two-family structures. But like Pruitt-Igoe, the neighbourhood site had open access to surrounding areas, and especially to the nearby downtown, since its open street network directly connected suburban traffic to the city centre. Analysis of the available crime data showed that vehicular traffic was the main source of neighbourhood problems, and especially traffic linked to drug sales and prostitution. This was the key issue in Newman's analysis of Five Oaks's situation: the lack of access control and boundaries made the entire community completely permeable to outsiders, such that, as in Pruitt-Igoe, residents could not tell who belonged and who did not. Moreover, Newman's research revealed that many residents had little sense of control or proprietorship even though the fundamental residential design was horizontal rather than vertical.

His solution was to slice Five Oaks into pieces and create a group of ten adjacent mini-neighbourhoods linked by pedestrian traffic but disconnected from vehicular traffic at all but one portal to an arterial for each. The net effect was to create many one-way, in and out street systems on relatively short culs-de-sac so that intruders could be observed and stopped as necessary at neighbourhood entrances. Gates to each mini-neighbourhood closed off other traffic movement, except for pedestrians. Short-term crime reduction results traced to this application of defensible space in Five Oaks were substantial, and the implications of the work in relation to the use of permeable versus non-permeable street systems have rippled down the years, impacting urban design theory and practice to the present day, as we shall discuss in Chapter 3.

A subsequent evaluation of Five Oaks has suggested that crime reductions were due more to opportunity reduction factors, such as the elimination of cut-through driving, than to community mobilisation factors where community attitudes are indirectly affected by defensible space or other changes related to the physical design of the environment (Donnelly & Kimble, 1997). Nevertheless, it is arguable that the reduction of cut-through traffic is a significant physical design change. Even so, Newman emphasised that while physical changes to a community may be necessary, they are not sufficient in and of themselves to bring about crime reduction and community building, and should not be applied in 'cookie-cutter' fashion from one community to the next. He stressed that they must be part of a comprehensive programme – a contextual solution – that supports increased citizen participation, policing (guardianship), home ownership and code enforcement (Newman, 1996). This conclusion lends support to situational crime prevention theory, discussed below.

Other components of defensible space theory

Although territoriality is at the heart of Newman's defensible space, there are other important and related elements. These include, as we have noted, access control and boundary marking. Of significance as well are 'natural' surveillance and 'image and milieu'. Natural surveillance is the ability of everyday users to be able to see into and across space by virtue of physical design and site layout, especially at critical junctures (such as where paths lead to building entrances). However, while spatial design and layout may indeed create (or negate) surveillance opportunities, other factors, such as density of use, types of users, temporal issues, and, *central* to Newman's concept, whether neighbours identify surveilled spaces as their own, dictate whether or not spaces will actually be protected and defended against criminal acts. The status of surveillance in crime prevention generally – whether by natural or electronic means – is a central issue that permeates all of the place-based theories and many of the emerging concepts such as space syntax and new urbanism.

Newman's idea of image and milieu focuses on the importance of the appearances of places and the power of stigmatisation that flows from images of residential types, especially low-income, publicly subsidised housing. In many ways, image and milieu anticipate 'broken windows' theory, elaborated by Wilson and Kelling (1983), and some defensible space ideas are replicated in CPTED, whether in the initial formulation by Jeffrey in 1971 or as elaborated by subsequent work (Jeffrey 1977, 1990; Jeffrey and Zahm, 1993). There is also no shortage of critiques of defensible space, which we shall discuss in the context of related and emerging theories of place-based crime prevention in the next chapter.

Crime prevention through environmental design

As an architect, Newman focused his work on the built environment, and especially residential structures and communities, and offered very pragmatic, relatively narrow solutions to crime concerns. Some of his prescriptions seem to prevent or reduce crime in some circumstances, but evidence of wider applicability is lacking or ambiguous (Greenberg and Rohe, 1984; Murray, 1994; Robinson, 1996; Taylor, 2002). The originator of CPTED, C. Ray Jeffrey, was a criminologist who proposed a broad, systems-based approach to the relationship between crime and the environment generally, and provided academic and in some ways much more controversial solutions to controlling criminal events than did Newman. Jeffrey's original notion of crime prevention through environmental design (1971) was based largely on the utilitarian models of philosopher Jeremy Bentham (1789/1907) and on experimental psychology and stimulus–response models developed by Skinner (1938), and was designed as a strongly proactive and positivistic approach to crime. He argued that the established, reactive criminal justice system – policing, courts, prisons – simply did not work, with the self-evident proof being that crime continued to persist as a fundamental societal problem.

Punitive strategies, including those designed to exact revenge and retribution, were ineffective, in his view: they clearly failed to *prevent* crime. Rather, Jeffrey proposed a crime prevention model based on moulding reward and punishment stimulations. Since the physical environment provided pleasurable or painful feedback to individuals such that they learned to change their behaviour to maximise or minimise pleasure or pain as the case might be, changes to the environment therefore held the key to real crime prevention, inasmuch as it could be modified to reward (or punish) offending behaviour. Moreover, each individual reacted and learned differently, so that *general* assumptions about human reactions were not necessarily valid, in his view.

A significantly revised edition of Jeffrey's work (1977) added a strong biological context and systems approach to the original conception by positing that internal *physical* changes in the brain (such as those related to chemical, genetic and neurological factors) were related to and affected by the external physical environment. Thus, the physical brain (as well as the 'mental' – thinking – brain) mediates environmental stimuli and directly affects behaviour. To Jeffrey the processes of the 'physical' brain were an important component which, he believed, could be scientifically tested and verified better than the 'mental' brain, which researchers could study only by depending on verbal responses from subjects, who might or might not be honest.

Although he agreed with many of the strategies of defensible space, Jeffrey contended that the metamorphosis of CPTED largely into a series of target hardening prescriptions had irreversibly changed it. Newman's theory offered concrete, apolitical suggestions and recommendations that attracted government funding, interest from the corporate world and even some support from designers and planners. It ignored the importance of brain processes in mediating environmental stimulus and changing behaviour and, in Jeffrey's view, the dynamic of the interrelated social, behavioural, political and biological systems that affect human behaviour generally, and criminal behaviour specifically. When the US Justice Department and the US Department of Housing and Urban Development dedicated millions of dollars to support CPTED research and applications in the 1970s, and then again in the 1990s,

Jeffrey noted that the CPTED referred to was not *his* CPTED (Jeffrey and Zahm, 1993).

CPTED, as it is known and practised today, is therefore a closer adaptation of Newman's defensible space than of Jeffrey's original concept, even though it blends elements of both. It has evolved over the past two decades and continues to meld with other place-based strategies such as situational crime prevention and environmental criminology, to be discussed below. Much of this evolution comes from the gradual incorporation of CPTED strategies into local building and development codes in the United States, and national policy guidance in Britain, as well as the training of law enforcement practitioners in both nations. A bevy of private consultants have spearheaded efforts to train police agencies in the use of CPTED strategies at local and national levels (Crowe, 1991, 2000). Moreover, CPTED training and awareness have been enormously accelerated by the onslaught of terrorist incidents across the globe since, as we discuss in Chapter 7, many of CPTED's strategies designed to protect against common crime are adaptable to anti-terrorist planning as well. For example, recent publications and training offered by the American Institute of Architects emphasise CPTED as a comprehensive framework for security and anti-terrorist design generally, and for buildings and sites in particular (Demkin, 2003). Some argue for the inclusion of basic CPTED principles in state-mandated comprehensive planning legislation aimed at anti-terrorist design (Schneider, 2003), while many of these have been incorporated, largely as target hardening prescriptions, into design guidelines and physical instal-lations for some major target cities, such as Washington, DC, London (e.g. the 'Ring of Steel') and, increasingly, New York City (Lipton, 2005; National Capital Planning Commission, 2002b).

At its core, the principles of CPTED include:

- natural surveillance;
- access control;
- territorial reinforcement;
- proper placement of land uses.

Outgrowths and related strategies include producing building and site design that facilitate natural surveillance, controlling entry to facilitate the movement of legitimate users and discouraging that of unwanted users, identifying spaces such that users clearly perceive distinctions between public and private realms (and the subtle gradations in between), and the juxtaposition of land uses such that security conflicts are minimised (for example, activities for the elderly generally should not be placed adjacent to those aimed at teenagers) and defences maximised (for example, places where money is collected or stored generally should be located where there is guardianship and surveillance).

Crowe (1997, 2000) and other CPTED consultants and practitioners have expanded the range of CPTED by including space management, scheduling and communication elements that are designed to focus attention on problem areas and to reduce the isolation of users and anonymity, both of which increase user vulnerabilities, as Newman pointed out in relation to certain

2.1 Natural surveillance as a by-product of pedestrianised mall design, as pictured here in central Dublin, Ireland.

public housing designs. Some CPTED scholars and practitioners such as Saville and Cleveland (1998, 2003) point out that CPTED has evolved beyond its 'first-generation' physical focus into a more mature 'second-generation' approach that may use bricks and mortar as a starting point but ends up 'looking at the social aspect of home and neighbourhood – the affective environment' (Saville and Cleveland 1998, p. 1). This broader view connects modern CPTED practitioners directly with situational crime prevention and environmental criminology in terms of CPTED's emphasis on context and setting variables.

CPTED and Secured by Design

In Britain, modern CPTED has been endorsed by the national government and promulgated as policy to local authorities in the context of the Secured by Design (SBD) programme (Department of the Environment, 1994; Town *et al.*, 2003; Office of the Deputy Prime Minister and the Home Office, 2004). Although it involves other government agencies, SBD is fundamentally a police-led initiative aimed at applying place-based crime prevention principles to the built environment. Its application has been documented across Britain in case studies that represent a range of land uses including residential areas, town centres, parking and transportation facilities, retail parks and commercial areas, public institutional uses, recreational and park areas, and mixed-use developments (Office of the Deputy Prime Minister and the Home Office, 2004). Evaluations of SBD versus non-SBD housing in public-sector housing

(Pascoe, 1999), in Gwent, south Wales (Brown, 1999), in West Yorkshire (Armitage, 2000, 2001), in Glasgow (Glasgow Housing Association, 2004) and in case studies (Office of the Deputy Prime Minister and the Home Office, 2004) support its implementation as a means to reduce certain types of crimes and to reduce the fear of crime. This is so despite the suggestion that 'both critics and proponents are still unaware as to precisely why it works' (Cozens *et al.*, 2004).

Some SBD advocates have crossed swords with new urbanist-oriented practitioners and academics by suggesting that new urbanist design solutions turn out to be more expensive (relative to policing costs) inasmuch as they are more likely to produce crime as opposed to SBD-oriented community designs and strategy (Knowles, 2003a, b; Kitchen, 2005). This is a fundamental philosophical divide that will be best resolved through long-term scientific analysis and testing. In the meantime it is likely that planning and design policy advice will remain bifurcated, with police and urban designers taking sides, whereas national policy advice has walked a fine line between the views. The debate has not been as strident in the United States, where there are no national CPTED guidelines and where the structure of federalism has blunted the issue by leaving planning and design guidance to the states and their various jurisdictions. We shall return to this debate in the context of our discussion of emerging concepts of place-based crime prevention in Chapter 3.

Like defensible space, CPTED has many critics. Some, like Taylor (2002), suggest that because the environment is so vast and variable, generalisations about relationships between crime and place are difficult to support empirically. While it is clear that some CPTED applications work *sometimes* in *some* locations relative to *some* specific crimes, there are no magic bullets. This notion is corroborated by evaluations of CPTED applications in the field (Sherman *et al.*, 1997) that find scientific evidence that *some* CPTED applications do indeed prevent *some* crimes. Other researchers who are supportive of CPTED, such as Samuels (2005), nevertheless point out that the CPTED name itself is misleading inasmuch as environmental design cannot really *prevent* crime but rather only mitigate or shape its occurrence.

Still others, such as Zahm (2005), note that the transmission of CPTED theory into practice has been spotty at best, and that planners and urban designers generally have been slow to incorporate CPTED practice into their professional focus on the built environment. Clarke (1997) suggests that while CPTED is a useful theoretical construct, it is too narrow in its primary focus on the physical place in which crimes do (or may) occur, and that concentrating on the crime *setting* or *situation* embraces both the physical and other important dimensions, including the management, use and crime opportunity structure of places. We turn now to that crime prevention theory.

Situational crime prevention

Developed by Ronald V. Clarke, a psychologist and criminologist, and based in part on his experiences with juvenile offenders (like Jeffrey), situational crime prevention is a seeming contradiction in that it is at once broader in scope than defensible space and CPTED, yet narrower in focus inasmuch as it aims to reduce crime by explaining *specific* crimes in *specific* circumstances (Felson, 2002). The essential element of situational crime prevention is the notion of *opportunity*, tempered by concrete strategies intended to reduce, modify or redirect the roles that temptation plays as a part of opportunity. Opportunity is moulded, in Clarke's conception, by five primary factors:

- risk ('How likely is it that I will be caught?');
- effort ('How difficult is it to get to the target'?);
- reward ('How much do I have to gain?');
- provocation ('What pushes me over the edge?');
- shame and guilt ('How excusable are my actions?').

The design and management of the built environment plays an obvious and important role in the risk and effort elements of Clarke's equation such that this theory is properly ensconced among the place-based theory group. Moreover, even though there are undeniable psychological elements to situational crime prevention (emotional triggers, calculations of reward, provocative factors and those driving the formation of guilt and shame), the theory is nevertheless much more directed at the elements shaping the specific crime setting, as distinct from the psychological mood of the perpetrator. Thus, rewards not only are a function of the offender's mental state, but are balanced by the environmental factors – risk and effort – in which they are framed. A valuable racing bicycle left unattended on a deserted street corner presents far more opportunity in terms of reward, and far less risk and effort, than one locked behind a showroom window in a busy shopping district.

Allied with this is the idea that criminals make decisions based on a limited rationality (Cornish and Clarke, 1986; Clarke and Felson, 1993) in which they seek to maximise pleasure and minimise pain (as Bentham, Jeffrey and others have suggested). Criminal decision making may be hasty, ill-informed or influenced by intoxicants, but it is choice making nevertheless (Felson, 2002). Moreover, this process is largely crime specific in that 'decisions leading to one type of crime are very different from those leading to another' (Clarke and Felson, 1993, p. 6). Thus, car thefts are unlike art thefts, and all car thieves are not alike either, inasmuch as there are clear distinctions between, for instance, those who are joyriders and those who steal cars in order to cut them up and market the parts (Clarke, 1999). Similar distinctions can be made within and between most other crimes.

This rational choice model is an outgrowth of situational crime prevention and flows out of a synthesis of studies in sociology, environmental criminology, economics and cognitive psychology (Clarke and Felson, 1993). Situational crime prevention theory is supported by many small scale empirical case studies that concentrate on very specific criminal events, such as cell phone fraud (Clarke *et al.*, 2001), motorcycle theft in Germany (Mayhew *et al.*, 1989), assaults and violence at sports events in Sweden (Bjor *et al.*, 1992), and assaults in crowded nightclubs (Macintyre and Homel, 1997).

Some of this work focuses on environmental components that increase the likelihood (opportunity) for criminal events, such as the design of nightclubs and discos, where increased density on dance floors can lead to unwanted physical contact that can quickly escalate to assaults. Other studies concentrate on non-place-based management strategies that increase risk to offenders, such as the computer validation of cell phone calls, while others aim at strategies to diminish rewards and increase efforts for offenders by adapting product design, such as the redesign of chairs in cybercafés to make purse snatching more difficult (Figure 2.2).

As these examples demonstrate, the aims of situational crime prevention are to 'design safe settings . . . organise effective procedures . . . and develop safe products' (Felson, 2002, pp. 144–145). In situational crime prevention, settings become more prone to criminal activity when they bring together in time and space likely offenders and suitable targets (either property or persons) in the absence of capable guardianship and the presence of people who may act to encourage or promote crime. These are elements of most crimes and comprise the 'conjunction of opportunity' (Office of the Deputy Prime Minister and the Home Office, 2004) and 'crime problem triangle' as depicted in the Center for Problem-Oriented Policing website[5] (see also Felson and Clarke, 1998). The amalgamation of elements helps explain repetitive criminal incidents and those particularly applicable to 'direct contact

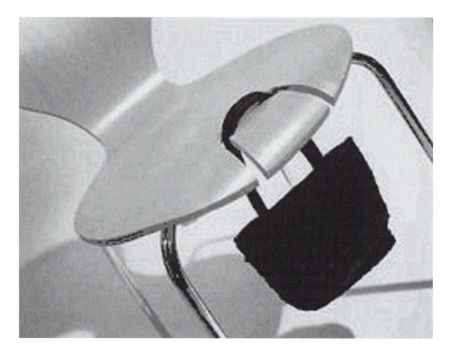

2.2 Stop thief chair.

Source: Courtesy of and created by designers at the Design Against Crime Research Centre, Central Saint Martins College of Art and Design, University of the Arts, London. Image copyright Marcus Wilcocks for DAC Research Centre.

– predatory crime' as suggested by the routine activity approach (Clarke and Felson, 1993; Clarke 1997).

Routine activity theory is directly related to situational crime prevention and is derived largely from geography, demography and human ecology theory, and suggests that crimes are not purely random events but follow patterns that are largely predictable on the basis of the daily, mundane activities of both offenders and victims. Routine activity and crime pattern identification and recognition are also central tenets of environmental criminology, which shares many concepts with situational crime prevention, and will be discussed below as the fourth major place-based crime prevention theory.

Situational crime prevention and community- and problem-oriented policing approaches

Situational crime prevention has greatly influenced community-oriented and problem-oriented policing (POP), as employed by many US and British police agencies. Community-oriented policing (COPS) is an organisational and administrative approach to law enforcement that is designed to put police in closer touch with citizens by emphasising more personal contact between police and citizens (e.g. getting police out of patrol vehicles wherever possible), more police sensitivity to environmental issues and problems that may cause crime, and much more focus on police–community partnerships in crime fighting. In the United States it has become an important model for police agencies and has been supported by significant federal funding, even though it has stirred some controversy inasmuch as it tends to shift emphasis from central police administration to the neighbourhood police officer.[6]

In Britain the Crime and Disorder Act 1998 establishes a similar partnership theme between police, citizens, businesses, organisations and local authorities. This is operationalised through a system of crime and disorder reduction partnerships (CDRPs), augmented by community support officers (CSOs) and neighbourhood wardens.[7] COPS is also an acronym employed in the United Kingdom and other European nations for 'community-opportunity profiling of streets', a toolkit-based system that uses social, managerial and physical factors to provide a CPTED-based rapid crime analysis methodology for sustainable community building.[8] We shall discuss this in more detail in Chapter 4 when looking at its European context.

Problem-oriented policing emphasises the *analysis* of the circumstances that create crimes, which may include a host of factors, including those in the built environment. In this wider context, crimes are seen as symptoms of specific causes. This approach suggests that when police treat symptoms only, they may miss underlying issues that lead to reoccurrences of crime.[9] Environmental examples may include the design of a specific street corner which facilitates drug transactions by allowing sellers to hawk their wares but which also, by building configuration or lighting design, shields purchases from common view or police surveillance. The POP approach uses the 'SARA' model as a framework to describe and categorise the process police use in problem analysis.[10] Ideally, once the crime problem has been analysed,

Table 2.1 Twenty-five techniques of situational crime prevention

Increase the effort	Increase the risks	Reduce the rewards	Reduce provocations	Remove excuses
1 Target harden • Steering column locks and immobilisers • Anti-robbery screens • Tamper-proof packaging	6 Extend guardianship • Take routine precautions: go out in group at night, leave signs of occupancy, carry phone • 'Cocoon' neighbourhood watch	11 Conceal targets • Off-street parking • Gender-neutral phone directories • Unmarked bullion trucks	16 Reduce frustrations and stress • Efficient queues and polite service • Expanded seating • Soothing music/muted lights	21 Set rules • Rental agreements • Harassment codes • Hotel registration
2 Control access to facilities • Entry phones • Electronic card access • Baggage screening	7 Assist natural surveillance • Improved street lighting • Defensible space design • Support whistleblowers	12 Remove targets • Removable car radios • Women's refuges • Pre-paid cards for pay phones	17 Avoid disputes • Separate enclosures for rival soccer fans • Reduce crowding in pubs • Fixed cab fares	22 Post instructions • 'No parking' • 'Private property' • 'Extinguish camp fires'
3 Screen exits • Ticket needed for exit • Export documents • Electronic merchandise tags	8 Reduce anonymity • Taxi driver IDs • 'How's my driving?' decals[a] • School uniforms	13 Identify property • Property marking • Vehicle licensing and parts marking • Cattle branding	18 Reduce emotional arousal • Controls on violent pornography • Enforce good behaviour on soccer field • Prohibit racial slurs	23 Alert conscience • Roadside speed display boards • Signatures for customs declarations • 'Shoplifting is stealing'

4 Deflect offenders	5 Control tools/weapons	9 Utilise place managers	10 Strengthen formal surveillance	14 Disrupt markets	15 Deny benefits	19 Neutralise peer pressure	20 Discourage imitation	24 Assist compliance	25 Control drugs and alcohol
• Street closures	• 'Smart' guns	• CCTV for double-deck buses	• Red-light cameras	• Monitor pawn shops	• Ink merchandise tags	• 'Idiots drink and drive'	• Rapid repair of vandalism	• Easy library checkout	• Breathalysers in pubs
• Separate bathrooms for women	• Disabling stolen cell phones	• Two clerks for convenience stores	• Burglar alarms	• Controls on classified ads	• Graffiti cleaning	• 'It's OK to say no'	• V-chips in TVs	• Public lavatories	• Server intervention
• Disperse pubs	• Restrict spray paint sales to juveniles	• Reward vigilance	• Security guards	• License street vendors	• Speed bumps	• Disperse troublemakers at schools	• Censor details of *modus operandi*	• Litter bins	• Alcohol-free events

Source: Center for Problem-Oriented Policing

 a 'decals' are bumper stickers that are commonly placed on commercial vehicles in the United States, inviting other drivers to report bad driving by the vehicle operator.

situational crime prevention can suggest strategies for *intervention* based upon the fundamental risk, effort, reward, provocation and excuse criteria described above, which together comprise or affect the opportunity framework. Table 2.1 describes 25 intervention strategies based upon this approach.

These are only some examples of strategies growing out of applied situational crime prevention theory. Because of their specificity they are usable by police and public housing officials in a wide variety of circumstances.

Environmental criminology

Like the place-based crime prevention theories discussed above, environmental criminology does not focus on offender dispositions but on the characteristics of the crime event. While related to and influenced by these latter theories, the academic and analytical frameworks of environmental criminology are derived largely from geography, urban planning, mathematics and human ecology, and especially Hawley's work on the importance of the relation of time and human activity patterns (1950). It focuses on uncovering patterns of criminal and victimisation events and has also been referred to as pattern theory. If the end products of situational crime prevention are intervention strategies, such as those detailed in Table 2.1, then environmental criminology provides the broad-scale spatial and temporal crime and victimisation contexts within which these strategies are put into practice.

Like the Clarke formulation already discussed, environmental criminology suggests elements that are essential for a crime to occur. These are an *offender*, a *victim*, a *law* that is broken, and a *place* and *time* where all these elements collide (P. J. Brantingham and P. L. Brantingham, 1981). Day-to-day events and activities create the *activity* and *awareness* spaces of offenders and victims, and define the offenders' search areas for targets (Brantingham and Brantingham, 1993a). Victimisation is therefore related to the mental images (the 'templates') of offenders based on their routine movements in space and time across the urban landscape. Targets (people or property) that criminals encounter in the normal, everyday course of their lives become part of these templates. The templates also include micro-environmental cues. In the case of burglary, for example, such cues might include the perceived ease of entry based on the sturdiness of the door frame, or the risk of being spotted based on the likelihood that neighbours can see from their own widows or yards to the target entry point (natural surveillance).

Environmental cues informing offenders (and victims) may be found at meso (mid-range) and macro (broad-range) levels, which may include neighbourhoods and communities. These cues are also incorporated into their mental templates. Examples for burglars may include the rating of houses based on external façade, landscape features and general maintenance as indicators of prosperity and the likely presence of cash and valuable goods. As noted previously, studies suggest that criminals tend to make rational decisions in the course of their routine activities. For example, commercial robberies tend to be related to the proximity of stores to major roadways, and the increased risk of residential burglary tends to be related to the choice of housing sites that border transitional or distressed neighbourhoods. In both cases, offenders' search times are reduced inasmuch as targets are close to or on their normal journeys to work (Brantingham and Brantingham, 1975; Maguire, 1982; Rengert and Wasilchick, 1985).

Environmental criminology analysis can lead to design solutions tailored to specific crime problems. Thus, in the example of the Five Oaks community cited earlier, most crime was related to the juxtaposition of the neighbourhood vis-à-vis the central city core, where it served as a connecting corridor. The resulting crime pattern, largely comprising street prostitution and drug sales, was classically associated with the open street network, which connected large numbers of targets and offenders. When the neighbourhoods were severed from each other and from the main transit corridor, access and escape were made problematic, and crime rates for vehicular crime such as street prostitution and drug sales were dramatically reduced as neighbours created defensible spaces within mini-neighbourhoods (Donnelly and Kimble, 1997).

Examples of situational and environmental criminology analyses applied at different scales include a report of mitigating pub path-related assaults in Birmingham and Coventry (Poyner, 1983), town centre design solutions aimed at reducing drunk driving in a northern British Columbia mining town (Brantingham *et al.*, 1997), and a study of townhouse site design in Vancouver intended to prevent crime and vandalism by passing juveniles (Rondeau *et al.*, 2005). In each case, patterns of real or potential criminal events were analysed in context with existing (or planned) physical features, and proactive design and management strategies were employed to reduce, mitigate or prevent them. All involved the review of data along *pathways*, at activity *nodes*, along *edges* (or boundaries) and in relation to crime *attractors* or *generators*, signature elements of environmental criminology analysis that have been greatly influenced by spatial and design studies in urban planning and urban design (Lynch, 1960; Chapin, 1974).

The pattern analysis of large data sets of criminal events is set against a dynamic 'backcloth' consisting of physical, social, political, economic and biological factors that frame criminal events (Brantingham and Brantingham, 1991). This broad idea provides the theoretical and operational predicates for modern-day computer-based crime mapping using geographic information systems (GIS). As we shall discuss in Chapter 8, GIS-based crime mapping has been adopted by many law enforcement agencies in the United States and Britain (and throughout the developed world generally) as a fundamental crime analysis tool. It automates an old idea and transforms numbers into dramatic graphic images that convey significantly more information to viewers than bland tabular records.[11]

Environmental criminology has also helped spur the development of forensic sub-disciplines including investigative psychology and geographic crime profiling. Canter's (2003) work in investigative psychology blends environmental criminology with psychological principles using time and place variables as one of five crucial factors that connect victims with offenders. Geographic crime profiling plots potential offender residential locations based on crime event maps. This strategy is rooted in both the 'least effort principle' notion described above in relation to the rationality of burglaries and to the 'nearness' principle, which suggests that many types of offenders operate within a 'comfort' range (activity space) that is close, but not too close, to where they live (Rossmo, 1999). A variety of crime mapping and geographic profiling software has been developed to plot crimes and to locate possible offenders, with the efficacy of the latter being the subject of considerable controversy.[12]

Target hardening and crime displacement issues

Defensible space, CPTED (both 'first' and 'second' generation) and situational crime prevention have been criticised because of their advocacy of 'target-hardening' approaches. Target hardening is a largely intuitive strategy that is probably the oldest crime prevention technique. It aims to impede access to the target (persons or property) by strengthening defences, whether these consist of toughened walls, doors, locks, windows, or installed electronic alarms or shielding devices. The intent is to make targets more resistant and time-consuming to overcome, and thus to entail more risk, effort and energy for would-be attackers.

There is voluminous evidence that target hardening works to mitigate, deflect and even prevent some types of crimes. But as in most other things, this involves balancing resources with sometimes unwanted, even counter-intuitive effects, such as when do-it-yourselfers improvise defensive devices that make them more, rather than less, vulnerable. These 'troublesome trade-offs' (Ekblom, 1997a) may include the ubiquitous risk that target hardening will produce the 'fortress effect' whereby structures or sites are so festooned with bars, locks and barricades that at best their aesthetic value is degraded and at worst their appearance serves only to increase fear and unease among the public.[13]

The aim of target hardening, of course, is to decrease opportunity so much that offenders will be deflected from the target. Where they go next is another matter entirely. This is a fundamental ethical dilemma of place-based crime prevention, inasmuch as it involves a presumption that offenders who are foiled at one target will be displaced to another, more vulnerable one. Where public resources are involved, this may simply mean subsidising one site or community at the expense of another, possibly low-income, already distressed neighbourhood.

But the question of whether offenders who are displaced will *automatically* prey on other targets has been considered, and there is considerable evidence to suggest that offenders are not programmed to switch from one target to the next when thwarted (Hesseling, 1994; Clarke, 1997; Ratcliffe, 2002). Moreover, there is evidence that some place-based crime prevention strategies may produce a 'diffusion of benefits' such that beneficial crime prevention effects spill over onto adjacent areas (Clarke and Weisburd, 1994; Ratcliffe and Makkai, 2004). Much more study needs to be devoted to crime displacement and spillover effects because of the important ethical and public policy implications of these phenomena. Barr and Pease (1990) and Farrell and Pease (2006) suggest that the term 'deflection' should replace displacement since it is less negative and more accurately reflects the notion that crime can be changed, and not merely moved around, through prevention.

Future development of place-based crime prevention theory

The family of place-based crime prevention theory has evolved out of a variety of seemingly unrelated sources: high-rise public housing towers; holistic, environment–organism learning models; the analysis of opportunity structure; rationality and routine behaviour models; and the patterning of crime events across the landscape. Their commonality is the focus on settings – which are usually but not always physical places – and on the manipulation of these settings and places through design and management strategies aimed at reducing the likelihood of crime. Settings and places change in response to broad-scale societal changes, and criminals adapt to these new environments, sometimes more rapidly than we wish (Ekblom, 1997b, 2002).

Broadly speaking, as human settlement, transportation, employment and product development patterns evolve, predation behaviours also adjust. For example, many types of crimes have followed workers from city centres to suburbs, as employment nodes have spread outwards along city edges. In the United States, daytime home burglaries boomed after World War II as women left homes vacant to venture off to work. Evidence of relationships between crime and changes in street patterns is abundant (Taylor, 2002), as is evidence of connections between social disorder and crime rates (Weisburd and Mazerolle, 2000). The large-scale manufacture of concealable, removable, available, valuable, enjoyable and disposable ('CRAVED'; Clarke, 1999) electronic goods beginning in the 1960s helped changed the structure and focus of larceny, theft and burglary across the developed world.

It is arguable that situational crime prevention provides the theoretical glue to link these phenomena. Future theorists should strive to knit together the existing strands, interwoven even as they are. Arguments for this are spurred by the need to respond to what may be the largest driving forces of this and future generations: the costs and availability of energy and the worldwide spread of terrorism. In relation to the first of these realities, new land development policies and regulations in the developed world will almost certainly incorporate resource sustainability and 'smart growth' philosophies that will change living, work and transportation patterns. How these play out in on-the-ground reality in new development is unknown, and the impact they will have on long-term crime patterns is highly speculative, despite the glimmerings of evidence thus far. How these policies are being implemented in existing communities in Britain is clearer (Office of the Deputy Prime Minister and the Home Office, 2004), but we need long-term, comprehensive evaluations of the results. In the United States the picture is not nearly as clear, inasmuch as the spider web of policies and practices among thousands of local jurisdictions is more difficult to tease apart.

As to the second reality, it seems likely that terrorism will have a major impact on the development of new place-based crime prevention theory. This will probably be an unanticipated consequence of the vast amount of resources that both the United States and Britain are devoting to the subject. These funds have mobilised practitioners, consultants and academics in unprecedented ways, and will most likely provide spin-off information and technologies to local-level law enforcement agencies in much the same way that the US space programme has helped produce a host of consumer products. Certainly, more than products will devolve to local police and communities. Inasmuch as most (but not all) terrorist acts are place-based crimes, there is a need to adapt existing theory to this phenomenon, a task made all the more difficult by the statistical issues associated with the relatively small data set and the inexhaustible supply of targets. We will discuss these issues in more detail in Chapter 7, but we foreshadow that discussion by suggesting that terrorism may be the single most important factor driving place-based crime prevention theory for the foreseeable future.

Conclusions

We have shown in this chapter how an array of place-based crime prevention theories – defensible space, CPTED, situational crime prevention and environmental criminology in particular – have emerged to form the core of what we have described as the 'classical' theories. We know quite a bit about the circumstances in which they appear to work, but we also know that relationships among environmental context, intervention and behavioural result(s) are far from straightforward. Indeed, the imperative to keep studying and reporting this relationship remains one of the most pressing needs in the field, especially (we suspect) as interest rolls out from the developed West into much of the rest of the world. This will inevitably encounter a range of variable cultural circumstances, and we suspect that this important variable (the impact of cultural factors) is at present too little understood. But this is not by any means the only challenge that the field faces. There are also several challenges to the classical theories that can be found in existing (and particularly recent) literature, and these are the subject of Chapter 3. We also have significant new opportunities to test empirically basic tenets and strategies of both classical and emerging place-based theories by virtue of the vast quantity of data being generated by computer-based technologies now being applied to crime prevention and crime analysis. As discussed in Chapter 8, these innovations present extraordinary prospects to refine crime prevention theory generally, and to create new models to explain better the complex environment–behaviour connections of crime in developed and developing societies alike.

3

Emerging concepts and trends affecting place-based crime prevention theory and practice

Introduction

Crime prevention practice has often struggled to keep pace with ever-adaptive criminals. It is, therefore, a field undergoing constant change, borrowing liberally from a variety of disciplines, everyday policing and development practice as each evolves. This chapter aims to address some of the challenges that emerging urban design analytical concepts, development trends and real-world events pose to classical place-based crime prevention theory. The confluence of these factors strongly influences on-the-ground crime prevention practice. The first section of the chapter reviews space syntax theory's analysis of crime incidents in urban settings, while the second focuses on reputed crime-preventive effects of a popular urban design trend, the new urbanism. Both space syntax and new urbanism raise questions about key tenets of the classical core theories relative to surveillance, access control, permeability and mixed uses as described in Chapter 2, and these challenges are discussed in this chapter on the basis of the available evidence.

The third and fourth sections look at community gating in the United States and Britain and at premises liability security litigation respectively, two growing trends that have direct impacts on the implementation of place-based crime prevention practices. Community gating is a public act that tends to privatise space, largely in the name of security. It has been used in pre-existing neighbourhoods and is employed increasinly in the United States in many new developments. Premises liability litigation fosters a private, market-driven approach to implementing place-based crime prevention that may ultimately prove more powerful than public interventions.

While space syntax and new urbanism are not *dedicated* place-based crime prevention concepts (in the sense that their crime prevention impacts are arguably spin-offs from their primary foci), they nevertheless provide inter-related ideas that form the basis for police, planning or design applications to deter or prevent criminal behaviour in the built environment. Demonstrably different from each other, all of the above concepts and trends nevertheless contribute significant, sometimes linked, elements to the evolving story of crime prevention in the modern built environment.

Space syntax theory

Origins and intents

Space syntax is a concept of urban morphology that was developed in the 1980s by Hillier and Hanson (1984) and subsequently expanded by Hillier and disciples around the globe. It is a theoretical and analytical approach that provides graphical and mathematical methods of depicting relationships between constructed objects and urban spaces. To accomplish this, space syntax uses a vocabulary of spatial types, syntactic maps, graphs, and measures to represent and analyse quantitatively relationships between buildings and urban spaces.[1] One of its fundamental aims is to capture the extraordinary complexity of city space in such a way that space itself can be measured as a research variable. Scholars have employed its modelling techniques to help explain and predict some crime patterns in urban settings, although this is only one of its intents.

Space syntax argues, among other things, that urban spatial configurations have reciprocally moulding relationships with movement (and especially pedestrianism) which affect land use patterns and urban densities. Moreover, the theory provides a mathematical logic with which to connect *spatial* and *social* information, such as relationships between the flow of pedestrian and vehicular movement and crime in urban areas. A fundamental intent is to uncover the hidden patterns and structures within spaces (Hillier, 1996). In this context it bears a similarity to pattern theory as derived from environmental criminology (although that is specifically focused on crime and space) and to Christopher Alexander's pattern language theory (1977), some of which has also been adopted into new urbanism (as described below).

For space syntax, it is not the substance of urban places (their physical objects such as buildings) that matters most; rather, it is the spaces and linkages among and between them that are crucial. These become the means to connect urban structure with urban function. Space syntax has been hailed by some as a means to 'transform urban design' (Akins, 2003).

Arguments against territoriality

Space syntax techniques have been employed to help predict how space will be used and to advise architects and designers accordingly (see http://www. spacesyntax.com/). As noted above, they have been drawn upon to help explain the distribution of crime in urban areas. For example, Shu (2000) used space syntax to explore connections between property offences such as burglary, vandalism and car crime and the layout of housing developments. His particular focus was on housing layout accessibility relative to open space design, and crime vulnerability. The results of his research led him to argue against Oscar Newman's concept of territoriality in particular and defensible space in general as the means to protect places against crimes. He was particularly dismissive of Newman's suggested reliance on cul-de-sac designs that create 'protective' urban enclaves, as distinct from more permeable street patterns that allow more passers-by to circulate in front of residences. Van Nes (2005) reaches a similar conclusion relative to the general location of burglaries in Haarlem, the Netherlands, but also presents evidence suggesting that 'spatial factors can be overrun by social ones' (p. 4), inasmuch as burglars tend to operate in comfort zones around their home territories, especially as these relate to known escape routes and vulnerable points of entry, despite the predictions derived from space syntax analysis.

Hillier's critique of territoriality begins at a more philosophical level than Shu's. He argues that Newman's defensible space propositions (and specifically, human territoriality) make the connection between behaviour and design too easily, leaping from broad theory to narrow, on-the-site design prescriptions. Hillier suggests that the jump amounts to architectural determinism, inasmuch as it supposes, without much evidence, that structural elements of the built environment 'invade people's minds' (1996, p. 183) and influence behaviour at individual and community levels.[2] He argues that there is little good evidence to support such gross connections between design and behaviour, and that the generalisations about human behaviour linked to spatial elements such as territoriality do not lead us to reliable answers in any case (ibid., p. 67). His remedy is the development of space syntax's micro-analytic theory as a way to understand 'patterns of movement in space . . . the dominant form of space use' (ibid., p. 187). Hillier argues that space syntax is predicated on an empirical, dynamic analysis of urban space, which contrasts with the normative, static view of the world embodied in Newman's theory of defensible space. In essence, he suggests that spatial determinism should replace Newman's architectural determinism.

To be fair, questioning territoriality has a long record in the literature, although the findings are not consistent. For example, MacDonald and Gifford (1989) argue that there is not much evidence that burglaries are prevented by territorial displays. And neither Phelan (1977) nor Bennett and Wright (1984) found much support for territoriality. Despite this, Brown and Bentley (1993) found territoriality to be an important factor in burglars' decision-making processes, and Booth (1981) found the concept of territoriality to be of some, though relatively limited, help in explaining crimes. This is complicated by the fact that Newman's discussions of the interaction of the various elements of defensible space principles really do not describe just how they interact and, indeed, may contain contradictions within themselves (Mawby, 1977). Hillier seizes upon this potential for inconsistency but tends to disregard the possibility that the same problem may apply to space syntax.

The surveillance issue

The crime-preventing efficacy of surveillance is one driving force behind both defensible space and space syntax, and is, as we have seen, an important element in those non-design-based elements of CPTED and environmental criminology. For estate layouts, Shu's research concluded that surveillance was not improved as regards crime prevention in segregated areas such as those created by dead-end streets and associated footpaths, but rather that crimes tended to cluster in these areas instead. This is a recurring argument in other space syntax theory and research (Hillier, 1996; van Nes, 2005). Hillier's analysis of 'New Town X' echoes Shu's conclusions by suggesting that spatial segregation (such as that found in cul-de-sac layouts) does not decrease crime but increases it, especially when compared with long linear routes through housing developments (1998).

Hillier further argues that crime (here burglary) is more likely to occur when 'access is through spaces unrelated to building entrances' (1998, p. 19) and that surveillance by neighbours *along the path to home* is more important than being seen at any one point along the way, or even at home itself. The analysis lumps burglary together with all crimes and makes no attempt at fine-grain analysis relative to types of surveillance, street patterns or local context. British crime survey data contradict his findings about the risks of cul-de-sac safety from burglaries, although there are questions about the 'confounding effects' of income and neighbourhood. (Office of the Deputy Prime Minister and the Home Office, 2004). A recent discussion by Gamman and Pascoe (2004) suggests that space syntax research may have not taken into account the phenomenon of 'leaking' culs-de-sac – especially those drained by footpaths that connect with potentially crime-generating nodes, such as liquor stores – which have long been identified by British architectural liaison officers as problematic areas relative to crime occurrence.

In reality, such places are not privatised enclaves inasmuch as they are indeed permeable to 'outside' pedestrians – some of whom are likely offenders and who are indeed shielded from general public view, especially in the cul-de-sac basin. This design tends to facilitate both hiding *and* easy escape, which may compound the finding that *some* culs-de-sac are more risky than others relative to repeat victimisation (Office of the Deputy Prime Minister and the Home Office, 2004). Moreover, it is an arguable oversimplification of defensible space, especially as it has evolved in modern practice, to suggest that it endorses segregated space as inherently safe or that surveillance is its single defining criterion.

Rather, the central notion of defensibility is that spaces be perceived as 'owned' by residents such that they will control and protect them. This is a very local social/psychological construct that is independent of the design or flow of traffic, although, as Newman suggests, design can certainly facilitate the sense of ownership coupled with the ability and willingness for residents to exert meaningful surveillance.[3] That pathways or even specific places are overlooked is *insufficient* to guarantee their safety. The evidence suggests that there is a great deal of variability in the 'quality' of surveillance as a crime prevention tool that is not necessarily related to the sheer numbers of observers, but may be more relevant to who is observing whom and under what specific, local circumstances (Felson, 2002). These elements are borne out by police experience both in the United States and in Britain.[4]

Strangers

Newman's linkage of 'strangers equals danger' is soundly rejected by Hillier (1996, 1998, 2002), who sees this as a vast oversimplification. As noted previously, he stresses that we cannot easily know the effects of architectural influences on human behaviour, and especially when these are translated into broad social outcomes such as crime. Rather, these outcomes are products of interconnected, intervening variables that cannot be straightforwardly traced to any one source. He argues that the many elements contained within complex independent variables (e.g. architectural design) and dependent variables (e.g. crime) overlap such that it is difficult to know which causes what (1996).

The pattern analysis of space use and movement (behaviours) of co-present individuals provides a 'formula for urban safety'. To Hillier, fear (which may include fear of crime) is the result of a mismatch between people's spatial expectations about the possible presence of others (who are presumed to be protective) and local environmental configurations. In this view, individuals make inferences about the environment rather than from the likely company of other people, to the extent that their fear is out of proportion to the likely occurrence of crime in that area.

In this sense, the environment itself skews perceptions, which is not a novel idea in crime prevention. Relative to the actual occurrence of crime, Hillier provides a complex analysis of 'encounter rates' for people living within a hypothetical housing estate in an effort to prove 'for simple numerical reasons' the general principle that urban safety depends on the 'presence of strangers as well as inhabitants' (1996, p. 192). These suggestions are freighted with complex mathematical intrigue, arguing support for advocates of increased street permeability, and they are germane to new urbanist prescriptions for estate layouts.

Contradictory evidence

Hillier's and other space syntax advocates' largely hypothetical reasoning is hotly disputed by a range of empirical studies showing that increasing the density of strangers and the permeability (also termed accessibility) of space in neighbourhoods leads to increases in certain types of crimes, and specifically opportunistic, property-related crime (Taylor, 2002; Beavon et al., 1994). Even van Nes's generally supportive study found that burglars pay attention to environmental cues such as vulnerable entry points and available escape routes (2005).

P. J. Brantingham and P. L. Brantingham (1981, 1998) argue that areas with gridded networks have higher potential crime rates than areas with organic street design. Simply put, the argument is that such layouts are more predictable, and potential offenders can escape more easily and more rapidly than in areas with culs-de-sac, broken up street networks or winding roads, where it is easier to become confused or lost. Potential offenders who are strangers to the area will probably find it more difficult and problematic to navigate such areas, although burglars who are also neighbours will have a significant advantage. White's research found that neighbourhood permeability (translated as the number of access streets from traffic arteries to the neighbourhood) had a significant effect on burglary rates (1990). Moreover, there are data suggesting that paths between high-activity nodes tend to concentrate criminal offences, as many crimes occur on the main roads that carry significant traffic and have major public transit stops (Brantingham and Brantingham, 1993b). Areas near public transport nodes tend to have higher crime rates than inaccessible areas (Cambridge Police Department, 1997). Newman's work in Five Oaks described in Chapter 2 and empirically reviewed by Donnelly and Kimble (1997) reiterates the point that disruptions in cut-through automobile traffic significantly reduced crime events in that neighbourhood. In addition to auto accessibility, reducing pedestrian movement in certain neighbourhoods may also reduce the occurrence of certain types of burglaries, robberies and assaults (Newman, 1981, 1996).

Relative to street configuration, Bevis and Nutter's study in Minneapolis (1977) argued that dead-ends were the safest streets, a point verbalised as well to the present authors by police in both the United States and Britain on the basis of on-the-job experiences. Block and Block (1995) found, related to liquor-related crimes, that many hot-spot areas are located at major intersections, especially those of grid and diagonal streets.

Other empirical work in the United States suggests further that increased vehicular and pedestrian traffic, especially in mixed-use neighbourhoods, causes 'social cocooning' among residents, making it much more difficult for them to interact among themselves or to sort out neighbors from likely offenders (Taylor and Harrell, 1996; Appleyard, 1980; Baum et al., 1978). The result is less natural surveillance of the street, and increased fear and incivilities. Yang's empirical research on burglary, repeat burglaries and 'near-repeat' burglaries (multiple incidents within a localised area) in a mid-sized American college town (2006) also contradicts the space syntax model, finding, among other things, that increased permeability of street layouts is significantly associated with higher burglary rates. This research takes into account socio-demographic and environmental factors in reaching these conclusions.

Explanations of the divergent findings between space syntax and theories advocating controlled access may lie at two levels, the first being the driving force of different philosophical starting points and the second being crime types and places studied – the local context. Specific urban spaces lend themselves to relatively specific criminal activities in terms of situational opportunity-structures (Clarke, 1997; Felson, 2002). For instance, pickpockets seek crowds, burglars seek obscured entry points to structures, and drug dealers seek street corners with both prospect (open views) and refuge (places to hide) (Appleton, 1975; Fisher and Nasar, 1992). In this sense, at local context level we see that crime prevention applications such as street closures have variable effects depending upon how carefully they target specific crimes (Atlas and LeBlanc, 1994; Lasley, 1998). Neither defensible space nor space syntax models are wholly satisfactory at explaining (or predicting) such focused phenomena. One could plausibly argue that these types of physical and social connections in relation to crime can be best explained by opportunity-based models that take specific management and user variables into account, such as that offered by situational crime prevention theory, rather than by design or pattern-predicting models, such as space syntax or defensible space.

Similarities and differences

Much of the value of space syntax analysis in relation to crime prevention depends on the implied value of surveillance as a deterrence tool. Indeed, space syntax focuses largely on what people see, how they move in regard to what they see and whether they perceive that they are being seen by others. Colquhoun (2004, pp. 72–73) summarises its general findings that relate to crime prevention in terms of the following three conclusions:

- Quieter, less well connected, and isolated spaces are where crime is most likely to take place. Space surveillance, public–private definition and ambiguity are key issues as regards crime opportunity as defined by movement and the built form.
- Fear, crime occurrence and antisocial behaviour patterns are directly related to the spatial relationship of structures to streets and especially the lack of outward-facing dwelling units.
- Clear patterns of movement (and especially pedestrianism) are an effective means of crime control in residential areas.

When we compare these general conclusions to those of the classical crime prevention theories, and especially defensible space and CPTED as described in Chapter 2, we find significant similarities as well as differences. Indeed, one is struck by points held in common. For example, as noted above, space syntax's emphasis on isolation and space anonymity as criminogenic elements clearly resonates with Newman's argument and research findings.

Moreover, CPTED, defensible space and space syntax all place significant value on clear-cut boundaries between public and private spaces, such that the creation of ambiguous spaces should be minimised wherever possible. While surveillance is also a key factor held in common esteem by space syntax and the classical physical design-based core theories, surveillance is married to perceptions of space ownership and control in defensible space and modern CPTED theory, as distinct from space syntax's emphasis on the value of 'co-awareness', which does not translate into real or perceived privatised, owned and protected space.

Key differences tend to stem from this divergence inasmuch as space syntax is guided by the fundamental principle that free-flowing movement through the urban fabric, mixing strangers and inhabitants, is not only architecturally and socially desirable but is therapeutic relative to crime prevention. Through mutual surveillance, the amalgamation provides reassurance to all, especially when this is combined with street-facing residential structures. Such a view comports with Jacobs's philosophy (1961) and with new urbanist design, as described below.

It conflicts, as we have seen, with a significant amount of empirical evidence on the subject, including evidence suggesting that, in general, increased pedestrian traffic means the increased likelihood that motivated offenders will see targets of interest and that this, combined with easy escape routes offered by connected spaces, leads to increased crime. Such evidence has implications for mixed-use design and planning, which tends to attract strangers to residential areas. It also is at some odds with CPTED and defensible space's emphases on the importance of space that is seen to be owned, and therefore protected, as a result of the congruence of design and social factors. In this sense, space that is indeed sheltered from outsiders ('strangers'), either directly or indirectly, is arguably safer.

The variance of space syntax's conclusions from the larger context of reliable research not just in Britain but elsewhere in the world is highlighted by the authors of *Safer Places*, who argue that there is considerable work that needs to be done if the 'divergence' is to be reconciled (Office of the Deputy Prime Minister and the Home Office, 2004, p. 88). Among the suggestions are calls for 'large-scale research studies and . . . persistent and systematic efforts to conduct many individual evaluations of interventions located in diverse environments, with a deliberate effort to synthesise the results' (ibid.). The intent of these would be to reduce the 'knowledge gaps in both risk factors and what works' (ibid.).

We strongly support this view. It is unclear at this time whether this work would result in space syntax taking a defined place among the menu of tools available in the field, or whether it would lead to the conclusion that, although interesting, it is not a fruitful path to follow. Either of these outcomes would be preferable to the existing, ambiguous situation, because at the least it would locate space syntax somewhere in (or out) of the crime prevention field rather than leaving it where it is at present, a floating challenge to orthodoxy which has struggled to garner much independent support.

New urbanism

Origins and intents

First articulated in the mid-twentieth century, new urbanism is a cluster of design and planning ideas encompassing concepts such as 'smart growth', 'liveable communities', 'neo-traditional' development (NTD), 'traditional neighbourhood design' (TND) and 'transit-oriented development' (TOD), each variably influenced by emphases on sustainability. While it has many divergent roots that stretch at least as far back as Howard's Garden City movement, modern new urbanism coalesced in a reaction to modernist design and the manufactured dullness of the American suburbs that were developed after World War II (Kunstler, 1993, 1996; Southworth, 2003) and to the loss of 'authentic' communities destroyed by massive urban renewal programmes as lamented by Jacobs (1961), communities that offered rich and rewarding experiences to many urban ethnic groups (Gans, 1982). Most pointedly, new urbanism rejects the automobile-dominated lifestyle spawned by suburban

American zoning and design practices which distance vital land uses from each other, obviating the possibility that residents can easily walk to shopping, to work, to recreation or even to the homes of friends. As such, new urbanist proponents tend to advocate small-scale, pedestrian-oriented places that are easily accessible yet contain definable boundaries, mixed uses and multimodal transportation options. The Charter of the New Urbanism (1996; http://www. newurbanism.org/pages/532096/) contains a listing of core new-urbanist ideals.

These are heavily undergirded by social principles and laced with nostalgia for the lost community values of bygone eras. As such, they flow from envisioned small-town settings that some scholars argue rarely existed in the United States (Marcuse, 2000). In that sense, a theme of new urbanism (and specifically of the neo-traditional town planning strand) is that a return to past planning and design principles will have healing, civic-value-promoting consequences that, among other things, help reduce or prevent crime. Plater-Zyberk, one of the gurus of new urbanism, has argued: 'We believe that the physical structure of our environment can be managed and that controlling it is the key to solving numerous problems confronting government today – traffic congestion, pollution, financial depletion, social isolation, and yes, even crime' (1993, p. 12).

Such effects, they argue, are the result of open and permeable community layouts that are more compatible with Jane Jacobs's surveillance and community building ideas (1961) and that connect to deep-seated protective instincts of residents. Connected streets are thus to be prized over controlled streets, as emphasised by the Charter's third principle relating to 'Block, Street and Building': 'the revitalisation of urban places depends on safety and security. The design of streets and buildings should reinforce safe environments, but not at the expense of accessibility and openness' (Charter of the New Urbanism at http://www.newurbanism.org/pages/532096/).

Although there are now many communities reputed to be exemplars of the new urbanism, the epitome of the implementation of new urbanist design philosophy is seen in two Florida cities: Seaside, located in the state's coastal panhandle area; and Celebration, situated inland near Disneyworld and Orlando. Both have been subject to considerable publicity in the academic and popular press, and Seaside even merited a visit by the British Deputy Prime Minister, John Prescott, who lauded it as a model for British planning in terms of master planning and urban codes (Prescott, 2003).

A loose coalition of many different (albeit related) viewpoints, new urbanists in the United States nevertheless rally around the theme of shifting the direction of urban and suburban development (Southworth, 2003, p. 211). While some variations apply, the same characterisation would most likely be true in Britain as well, although the British emphasis is driven largely by central government policy emphasising increasing urban densities and inclusiveness, whereas in the United States, new urbanism is more likely suburban oriented (although it has become more urban over the past decade) and driven by private developers, as evidenced by Seaside and Celebration. Moreover, American new urbanism has been fiercely criticised as being greenfield development catering to well-to-do whites who are fleeing poor, black inner cities (Marcuse, 2000). Almost all agree that there is no objective empirical evidence to support new urbanism's claims to prevent crime, and some British police even suggest that new urbanist design increases the number of crimes and, therefore, the costs of policing (Knowles, 2003b).

Resistance to new urbanism

New urbanism, like space syntax, grew largely out of architectural principles and the ways in which architects envision space. This has proved problematic for other professionals, such as landscape architects and urban planners, whose views and/or empirically based methods are not always accounted for in new urbanist thinking or designs.[5] Nevertheless, many planners and landscape architects on both sides of the Atlantic could now be characterised as converts. Challenges to new urbanist design orthodoxy have been increasingly voiced by some ideologues and scholars in the United States (O'Toole, 2001; Marcuse, 2000; Southworth, 2003) and by police in Britain who question its crime-preventing abilities (Town and O'Toole, 2005; Knowles, 2003b). Indeed, the controversy relative to the reputed criminogenic qualities of new urbanist design is a subject of growing scrutiny by crime prevention planning scholars as it highlights, among other things, fundamental issues relating to the field's empirical and normative foundations (Kitchen, 2005; Schneider and Kitchen, 2002).

This controversy has centred on two elements of new urbanist design advice. First and foremost is the focus on permeability of community layouts (much like space syntax theory) and second the focus on mixed uses. New urbanist orthodoxy contends that gridiron street layouts are to be preferred over cul-de-sac or broken-up street patterns, and that layouts that push cars to secondary importance – and indeed to parking lots in the backs of buildings where possible – allow residents and strangers to meet and interact without the added interference of vehicles. This in turn, it is claimed, increases the physical likelihood not only that people (especially neighbours) will be able to watch over each other but that they will be more responsive to criminal acts perpetrated on one another. Thus, as in space syntax, permeability and protective surveillance are inextricably bound together.

Second, and arguably related to permeability, is the issue of mixed land uses. Mixing land uses (primarily combining residential with commercial uses) is advocated as a means of providing diversity to neighbourhoods that by virtue of homogeneous use would otherwise be abandoned and unguarded during certain hours. In this context, the notion is that integrating businesses with residences helps reclaim streets and encourages pedestrianism, which increases 'eyes on the street' as advocated by Jacobs (1961) and thereby makes them safer. Newman also advocates the *careful* juxtaposition of different land uses as a means of decreasing the isolation and anonymity of some residential areas (1973).

In Britain the debate among new urbanist design advocates and their critics, especially relative to permeability, has been heightened by a web of conflicting or ambiguous planning advice from the government vis-à-vis that offered by the police-based crime prevention scheme 'Secured by Design' (as discussed in Chapters 4 and 5). SBD emphasises target hardening and controlled access, based on Oscar Newman's defensible space models as described in Chapter 2. Kitchen (2005) has chronicled this colloquy, which has now crossed the Atlantic via the Internet and has occasioned a series of lively electronic exchanges between informed partisans as well as average citizens (see, for example, http://www.planetizen.com/node/107). At the heart of the debate are differing ideological and cultural orientations among the design and police factions, variably supported by empirical evidence.

Contradictory evidence

Permeability

Relative to permeability, blanket gridiron design prescriptions have long been shown to have negative effects, documented by evidence. For example, Ben-Joseph (1995) found that unrestricted grid street networks have higher rates of pedestrian and automotive accidents. Bothwell *et al.* (1998) acknowledge that traditional neighbourhood design (TND) may indeed lead to more crimes that are dependent on accessibility, but they argue that this problem is offset by increased social controls attendant to closer interaction of neighbours. This balance has not been tested, to our knowledge.

However, what have been scrutinised in considerable degree are burglary patterns. Burglary is arguably the best example of an environmental design-related offence that is related to street permeability, and a long line of research connects burglary incidents with street types and incident locations. Table 3.1 depicts the stream of generally consistent research relating to street types and incidents of burglary, with the exception of the two most recent studies by Hillier, and Hillier and Shu. Table 3.2 suggests that burglaries tend to be related to corner locations and to highway accessibility. Taken together, the research depicted here supports the contention that residences and commercial areas are more at risk when they are more exposed to external traffic.

A recent study concerning burglary patterns is Yang's multi-year research (2006) on environmental factors influencing more than 3,000 residential burglaries. These factors include permeability, mixed land uses, adjacency and housing density. The study identifies permeability as 'the level of intrusion difficulty' for an area and uses the following variables to define it further:

- distance to closest major arteries;
- street layout patterns;
- street types around parcels;
- distance to public transportation;
- corner location;
- block length;
- connectivity index (a ratio of roadway segments to intersections or culs-de-sac).

Table 3.1 Research on the relationship between street type(s) and burglary incidents

Street type(s)	Conclusion(s)	Source
Traditional street pattern (grid) or hierarchical street pattern	A strong correlation between layout type and crime: traditional street patterns the best and the most 'modern' hierarchical layouts the worst.	Hillier (2004)
Through street, cul-de-sac, integrated (more movement potential) or segregated (less movement potential)	Culs-de-sac may be preferred by burglars, as they deter passers-by and reduce natural surveillance.	Hillier and Shu (1999)
Culs-de-sac, quiet residential street, commercial street,busy residential street, back road/ local traffic	The most victimised locations are houses located on a busy residential street or on a back road with local traffic only.	Rengert and Hakim (1998)
Major thoroughfare or small neighbourhood street	Low-crime neighbourhoods were more likely to have small one-way and two-lane neighbourhood streets.	Greenberg and Rohe (1984)
Major thoroughfare or small neighbourhood street	Low-crime neighbourhoods tended to have fewer major streets and more small, neighbourhood streets than high-crime neighbourhoods.	Greenberg and Rohe (1982)
Major or minor streets	There were higher rates of commercial burglaries in facilities along major streets.	Nasar (1981)
Dead-end, culs de sac, 'L' type, 'T' type, and through-traffic streets	There is a noticeable pattern of lower residential burglary rates in housing located on blocks with lower accessibility.	Bevis and Nutter (1977)

Street layout patterns are identified using the template shown in Figure 3.1, which identifies a general evolution of street designs. The analysis uses matched sites (controlled for social and demographic factors), and the data are plotted using geographic information systems (GIS). Statistical analysis of the results demonstrates that, within the city study area, the incidence of

Table 3.2 Research on the relationship between burglary incidence and location/ distance to highways or downtown areas

Location/distance	Conclusion	Source
Located on dead-end street	Houses located on dead end street are less likely to be burglarised.	Hakim *et al.* (2001)
Corner location	Houses at corner locations are more likely to be burglarised.	Hakim *et al.* (2001)
Distance from highway exit	Houses close to a highway exit are more likely to be burglarised. Within 0.25 mile, 0.25–0.5 miles, 0.5–1 mile, >1 mile.	Hakim *et al.* (2001)
Corner location	There were higher rates of commercial burglaries in facilities on corner lots.	Nasar (1981)
Distance to major thoroughfare	There were higher rates of commercial burglaries in facilities near major thoroughfares, <0.5 mile or >0.5 mile.	Nasar (1981)
Distance to downtown	There were no significant effects of commercial burglary related to the distance from downtown.	Nasar (1981)

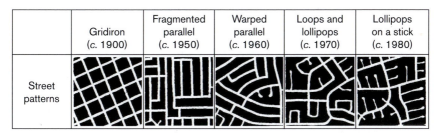

	Gridiron (*c.* 1900)	Fragmented parallel (*c.* 1950)	Warped parallel (*c.* 1960)	Loops and lollipops (*c.* 1970)	Lollipops on a stick (*c.* 1980)
Street patterns					

3.1 Street patterns.

Source: Southworth and Owens (1993)

first-time burglaries is highly correlated with permeable street patterns. Indeed, the street pattern most statistically associated with burglarised residences is the gridiron layout. The relationships between fragmented parallels, warped parallels, loops and lollipops, and lollipops on a stick designs are not statistically significant. Figure 3.2 illustrates the distribution of burglarised sites and control sites among street layout patterns, for first-time burglaries.

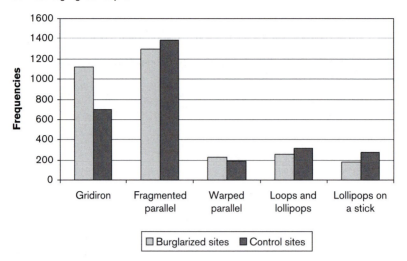

3.2 Street layouts and burglaries.

Source: Yang (2006)

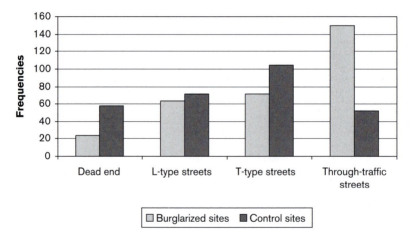

3.3 Street types and burglaries.

Source: Yang (2006)

When one drills down to specific street types, as in Figure 3.3, the following pattern emerges: through-traffic streets are far more vulnerable to residential burglaries than are other types of streets, and especially T-type and dead-end. Yang's data reveal, however, that there is no clear relationship between incidents and L-type streets, which contradicts earlier findings (Bevis and Nutter, 1977). The study further suggests, in line with other research, that corner house lots tend to be the most at risk for first-time burglaries (Brantingham and Brantingham, 1993a) by virtue of their relatively easy accessibility and the multiplicity of escape routes.

When the issue of repeat burglary (the multiple victimisation of the *same* household) is considered, Yang's research demonstrates that multiple burglaries tend to be located close to major transportation arteries and public transportation, and are situated in neighbourhoods with high permeability (connectivity). She notes that 'single-family households located in areas with grid networks are more likely to be victims of multiple burglary than households in areas with other types of street layout' (p. 119). This is so despite the fact that the 'protective' effects of the reduced access street patterns (fragmented, warped, etc.) are not found, which is consistent with other research suggesting the same effects (Osborn, *et al.*, 1996).

In considering incidents of *near*-repeat burglaries (defined as burglary cases whose occurrences are close in both time and space, such that an area is at higher risk than would be expected by random distribution), Yang found that a previous burglary is the best predictor of a future burglary not only for the *same* household (Pease, 1998) but also for homes nearby. Moreover, near-repeat burglaries tend to cluster in areas close to transportation arteries, on shorter blocks, and in neighbourhoods with high connectivity (permeability) ratings. Thus, grid street networks are consistently associated with (but do not necessarily cause) higher rates of all types of residential burglaries in the case study.

Mixed land uses and crime

While mixing of land uses is valued by new urbanists and by planners generally as a means to invigorate economically and socially otherwise homogeneous areas, and has been supported by some as a means of reducing crime (Jacobs, 1961; Newman, 1973), there are multiple studies that suggest it is not totally benign. Greenberg *et al.* (1982) and Greenberg and Rohe (1984) found that homogeneous residential neighbourhoods had lower rates of crime than those that combined land uses, and Dietrick's research (1977) noted that residential burglary occurred more frequently near commercial areas. A recent study by Wilcox and Quisenberry (2004) claims that the presence of businesses in neighbourhoods tends to increase burglaries, though this effect is mediated by physical disorder and by levels of relative residential stability. In this context, mixing playgrounds into residential areas tends to increase burglary risk regardless of neighbourhood social-structural characteristics. A considerable body of research has shown that the value of your neighbour's property and what happens on it are elements in crime incidence relating to such factors as target and spatial attractiveness (Rhodes and Conly, 1981), presence and accessibility of potential and motivated offenders (P. L. Brantingham and P. J. Brantingham, 1981), median house values of adjacent properties (Katzman, 1981), and the criminogenic effects of certain land uses (P. L. Brantingham and P. J. Brantingham, 1981; Block and Block, 1995). Some research has gone as far as suggesting the likely penetration depth of burglars from various adjacent land uses into residential neighbourhoods (Luedtke & Associates, 1970; Buck *et al.*, 1993).

Yang's in-depth research of multi-year burglary patterns (2006) found that at both the census block and major street block level, burglarised home sites of all types (first time, repeat and near-repeat) were much more likely to be found in mixed-use rated sites than those at matched control sites. Moreover, when one looks at the major street block level and the *relative* land use mix (a ratio of non-residential to residential units), there is a statistically significant correlation of burglary to land use mix.

There is, therefore, a growing body of evidence arguing that land use heterogeneity has a price relative to the incidence of certain types of crime. Whether that cost is outweighed by other factors that make urban living interesting and exciting and ultimately worthwhile is not the issue here. Individuals must make those choices. The issue is whether they, as designers or users, bring this knowledge to the table when making their decisions.

The new urbanism and crime prevention

Poyner's (1983) remark that research studies that produce good evidence are much preferable to those that look good or offer no real guidance for crime prevention purposes is to the point here. The studies presented above suggest, in essence, that performance is more important in crime prevention than formulaic style. Such is the case, we argue, relative to new urbanist design inasmuch as its rhetoric and aesthetically pleasing results have not, to date, demonstrated much crime prevention substance based on evidence. Whether that will change as more new urbanist communities are built and are subject to long-term evaluation is speculative, especially since to date there has been very little longitudinal evaluation of new urbanist communities in terms of their experiences of crime. Presently, the number of such communities on the ground is paltry compared to the strong influence new urbanist ideas have had on urban designers and planners. Thus, there has been little connection between idealism and empiricism when it comes to the development of workable crime prevention solutions. This leads some to argue that new urbanism is design determinism not unlike that attributed to Newman by his critics. Southworth (2003, p. 214) suggests that not only are the blanket prescriptions of new urbanist design refuted by decades of environment–behaviour research, but they are simplistic when one considers the extraordinarily complex reality of urban life.[6]

How could we not want urban design to inoculate us against bad things, including crime, and to heal the wounds that are attendant to such deep sociopathologies? But the urban complexity that Southworth portrays, and that we know from our own experience in cities, argues against simple solutions. The likelihood that neighbours and, to a lesser extent, strangers will intervene to deter or prevent crimes depends on many factors that cannot neatly be predicted by street layout or architectural models, since design and humans interact in ways that are still too numerous to catalogue or subtle to know, given present insights or technology. As regards both permeability and mixed uses, seen as generators of increased surveillance, probably the best we can do, given the available evidence, is to say that, all things being equal, increased accessibility means the likelihood of increased crime, and especially opportunistic property crimes. To know that is not to say that we must stop building attractive and liveable communities pursuant to models offered by new urbanism, but rather that we should know what trade-offs we may be making in the process. Thus, if people are not informed of the possible consequences of their residential choices, at the very least they should not be actively misled by over-enthusiastic designers into believing that, like the snake oil of bygone days, new urbanism (or any other broadly based design ideology) will prevent crime and heal society's ills.

Gated communities

Issues and origins

Modern-day community gating is fraught with a large and growing array of issues that include (besides the fear of crime) broad-scale urban design and transportation implications, questions about real estate values, concerns about immigration and the relocation of ethnic groups, ideological and cultural questions related to social and spatial segregation, and related worry about the increasing privatisation of space in some Western nations, especially the United States and Britain. Other concerns include crime displacement, as well as social equity and inclusiveness issues. While these are all important concerns, to be sure, they are, for the most part, beyond the scope of this section. Rather, we are concerned primarily with the case for and against modern community gating as a viable crime prevention tool based on the available evidence.

Though seen in many shapes and types, community gating is a form of target hardening at the far end of the access control scale. For our purposes, we define a gated community as sharing a number of physical characteristics, which include:

- an area composed primarily (but not exclusively) of residential units that is fenced, walled or otherwise bounded from neighbouring land;
- filtered entry using structural, mechanical, electronic or human guardianship access control elements (or some combination of these);
- privatised internal gathering areas and circulation systems, which may include roads, pavements and footpaths.[7]

Although most of the communities that fit this definition were designed from the outset to be gated enclaves, there are a growing number of retrofit gated communities in the United States and South Africa, made largely in response to perceived security threats from adjacent areas (Landman, 2003). Residents of new and retrofit areas usually share informal social affinities and can be bound by a bewildering array of formal (legal) agreements which govern housing design and landscaping details but also include arrangements to maintain and repair perimeter structures with special emphasis on the entry points – the gates themselves – which tend to be the most problematic (and expensive) elements. In many gated American examples, walls and fences do not completely encircle the community but rather provide extravagant entrance portals flanked by equally impressive but abbreviated edges, with the balance of the boundaries left to minor structural or landscape elements, such as low hedges. As such, they have largely symbolic security effects, which may nevertheless make residents feel elite and happy. In other communities and neighbourhoods, walls completely surround residents in a hardened embrace that cinches the security zone. Indeed, there is significant evidence that a prime reason that many people select gated living is to enhance their safety and security, although there are certainly many other reasons (Blakely and Snyder, 1997; Blandy *et al.*, 2003).

Though recently rediscovered by the popular press, gated communities certainly are not new. They have been found from time immemorial across the width and breadth of human cultures (Kostof, 1991, 1992; Schneider and Kitchen, 2002), although gating arguably has reached its modern zenith in North American and South African cities and suburbs. First built in the United States to protect settlers from attacks by the native population (Reps, 1965), they were later adapted as a means to insulate wealthy families from the outside world and they have since spread across all income classes, especially in the American South and West (see Figures 3.4–3.6).

Their use is spreading across Britain as well, and Blandy (2005) notes that a survey of English planning authorities reported approximately 1,000 gated communities in 2003–2004, mostly in the London metropolitan area and the south-east of England. Other studies show growing numbers of gated communities in Portugal, Bulgaria, Brazil, Argentina and China (Brunn *et al.*, 2004). In the United States the number of gated communities burgeons each year, as developers compete with each other to match market demand. Estimates based on US Census data suggest that almost 6 per cent of American households (about 7 million) are located in restricted access developments of one type or another, with 4 million of those in communities that are *only* accessible through gates, entry codes, key cards or through guarded entry points (American Housing Survey, 2002). This is a vast increase over the numbers estimated by Blakely and Snyder only a few years earlier. Moreover, gating spans income ranges, as illustrated by Figure 3.4, which shows a low- to moderate-income gated mobile home park in Florida, and Figure 3.5, which depicts a Florida gated community on the other end of the income spectrum. Figure 3.6 shows a range of gated communities around Gainesville, Florida, which were all photographed during the same day in 2003. The interesting thing about this selection is that all the gates were open at the time the photographs were taken, so in this very practical sense they were symbolic rather than physical barriers, at any rate at that time of day.

Crime prevention

If, as we have said earlier in the chapter, increased urban permeability is associated with increased crime, then does it necessarily follow that reducing access through community gating or street closures will decrease crime rates? The question implies causality, and the answer is complicated by the sparse amount of empirical research directed specifically at gated communities, which

3.4 Gated mobile home park in Winter Garden, Florida.

Source: Courtesy of Jeff Davis

3.5 Gated upper-class neighbourhood in Gainesville, Florida.

is wholly unbalanced by the large amount of ideological rhetoric on the subject. While there are two studies that focus directly on this point (Atlas and LeBlanc, 1994; Donnelly and Kimble, 1997), most evaluations of gating deal with other issues, such as the fear of crime, or economic, land use, social, transportation or social segregation concerns. More research has concentrated on the effects of street and alley closures, which as access control measures are important components of gating but are by no means the only components. Nevertheless, the results of that work are instructive, if only to point in the direction of the need for further research in the area.

3.6 Gated communities, Gainesville, Florida. The extent to which the gates of 'gated communities' actually represent significant physical barriers to entry is variable, as these four photographs of different gated communities around Gainesville demonstrate. All the photographs were taken in a single late morning/early afternoon session in the autumn of 2003, and in all four instances the gates were fully open at that time of day, offering no physical barrier to entrance.

Contradictory evidence

Blakely and Snyder (1997) argue that although residents may feel safer in gated communities, there were no real decreases in crime rates. This finding is supported by a reassessment of street closures in Hartford, Connecticut (Fowler and Mangione, 1986). Helsley and Strange (1999) argue that while gating may have strategic, localised effects in crime prevention, it may actually increase crime rates if it negatively affects local employment, all other things being equal. These suggestions are variably challenged by a broad evaluation conducted for the US Department of Justice's Community Oriented Policing Program (COPS), which compared 11 studies of street and alley closures and reviewed their effectiveness in relation to crime reduction and prevention (Clarke, 2003). The studies were from American, British and Canadian sites, and included a variety of neighbourhood types (from distressed, low-income areas to affluent high-income communities). The evaluation recorded the crimes targeted by closures and their results, and identified, in some cases, positive and negative crime diffusion effects. The evaluation rated the quality of the research designs used for the 11 studies from 'weak' to 'strong' depending on whether the studies compared pre- and post-intervention crime rates and whether control groups were used. Of the 11 studies, five were rated as strong research designs, three weak and three as adequate.

Strong designs that also showed marked and almost immediate crime reduction results included the Donnelly and Kimble study (1997) of the Five Oaks, Ohio, neighbourhood described in Chapter 2, studies of an inner-city Los Angeles neighbourhood where 14 streets were closed (Vernon and Lasley, 1992; Lasley 1998), two London studies (Finsbury Park and Streatham) which focused on the impacts of street closures on street prostitution and cruising (Matthews, 1997), and research in Liverpool that very positively connected alley-gating with burglary reduction (Bowers *et al.*, unpublished). The London studies report 'large' reductions in prostitution and cruising, along with variably lower rates of burglaries and conveyance-related crimes attributed to closures. Both studies also reported increased levels of citizen comfort and satisfaction levels following the interventions. The Los Angeles study documented an immediate reduction in serious crimes (murders and shootings) following the street closures in a drug-infested neighbourhood. When the streets were reopened following the Rodney King riots, crime levels bounded up again.

Almost all the 'adequate' and 'weak' studies Clarke evaluated show lowered violent crime rates (homicides, assaults, shootings) or reduced property crimes (burglary, larceny, auto thefts). One produced a vexing but realistic result. An intervention in Vancouver, British Columbia – where street diverters were installed to prevent cruising for prostitution – revealed that the crimes were quickly displaced to other adjacent areas, since the prostitutes and their customers adapted to the street changes. Moreover, the prostitutes used the diverters to increase business, since they slowed down traffic in the area. This illustrates the adaptability of offenders, as emphasised by Ekblom (1997b, 1999) and the critical importance of carefully fitting interventions to the local context, with on-site evaluation and refinement. For the most part, however, none of the other ten studies report evidence of crime displacement, and some even suggested that street or alley closures helped spread positive effects by 'diffusing benefits' in adjacent areas (Clarke and Weisburd, 1994, p. 169).

Conclusions given the evidence base

A range of caveats apply to the studies described above. First, with one exception (Vancouver), all present positive findings relative to the impact of street and alley closing on crime prevention. But, as Clarke cautions, negative reports are rarely presented in the literature. In 9 out of the 11 cases, access control interventions were accompanied by reinforcing activities such as increased guardianship, more press attention and heightened neighbourhood sensitivity. Thus, it is difficult if not impossible to untangle the confounding effects of the other interventions. This reiterates the point made by Hillier in relation to the efficacy of defensible space applications, which also obviously applies across the breadth of modern crime prevention. Most of the studies were conducted over relatively short time periods and only one, a study done in St Louis, reviewed five years of data. The useful impacts of crime prevention tend to decay quickly, and this is borne out by evidence from the Vancouver, Hartford and Los Angeles studies showing that offending reoccurs quickly after criminals adapt to changes made or when the intervention is rescinded.

Thus, though there is some evidence that street and alley closures may affect some targeted crimes in some specific neighbourhoods, the impacts are likely to be short-term unless the intervention effect is bolstered over time, most likely by guardianship or concerted neighbourhood action. Given the limited and inconclusive studies that we have about closing streets and gating communities, there is still not a viable case to be made in one direction or the other regarding crime prevention efficacy over extended periods. Whether the short-term positive effects of street and alley closures balance the costs of mounting and sustaining such action must be determined at a local level through a local negotiation process that assesses the impacts of (and on) adjacent neighbourhoods, available resources, local political will and crime incidence. This is especially germane where large-scale gated enclaves are proposed within existing urban areas, since the impacts of these can ripple through the structural and physical fabric of the entire city (Blakely and Snyder, 1997).

Indeed, even the evidence concerning fear of crime and gating is inconclusive. Some studies suggest that neighbours' sense of security in some higher-income gated communities is higher (Fowler and Mangione, 1986; Blakely and Snyder, 1997; Wilson-Doenges, 2000), whereas others suggest that there is no difference or that neighbours in adjacent areas may be more fearful that displaced crime will affect them (Clarke, 2003). Moreover, most of the studies on both sides of the issue fail to distinguish between fear of crime and the personal sense of security, an important difference that taps into whether survey respondents provide emotionally charged or intellectually based answers (Yin, 1980; LaGrange and Ferraro, 1989). We shall not attempt to broach this large and rapidly growing body of research on crime fear or personal security further, other than to say that it is a wholly relevant sphere of further enquiry, since we know that fear and security are the fundamental factors driving people to seek out gated communities or closed streets in the first place. The question is whether gated living measures up to its security promises (and hopes) or whether, as the present evidence points out, its real crime prevention benefits are ephemeral, at best.

Premises liability

Issues and definitions

Access control through gating, and street or alley closures, are direct examples of physical and management crime opportunity reduction strategies, derived equally from defensible space and CPTED. They are frequently *public* acts, though they may be initiated by private actors and certainly may involve private benefits. We argue that premises liability litigation has produced a new, essentially *private*, approach to implementing place-based crime prevention strategies. This approach can augment place-based crime prevention efforts by public authorities (planners and police), and may even surpass it, given its trajectory. Indeed, at one time premises liability cases based on negligent security were the largest single growth area of American tort litigation (Kaminsky, 1995), with assaults and sexual batteries being the preponderant crimes reported in lawsuits (Leavitt *et al.*, 1997; Bates, 2005)

Premises liability has a long and complex history within English and US law, encompassing a vast amount of case law that we will not recount here. Rather, we use a broad-brush approach that targets important points relating to place-based crime prevention planning. In this context, we define premises liability as an area of tort law dealing with civil wrongs or injuries (Black, 1968) that places a responsibility on those who possess property (whether land or premises) for certain injuries sustained by those present on those premises. Legal questions as to the meaning of 'possession' and the status of the injured party (most likely the plaintiff) are important.

Possession usually implies some level of occupation and control of the premises, which could, for example, apply to owners and managers of apartments, one of innumerable relationships that are found in this context but one that is applicable to our discussion of place-based crimes. Whether the injured party is an 'invitee' (generally someone who has a business relationship with the owner or possessor), a 'licensee' (e.g. a social guest with no commercial relationship) or a 'trespasser' (a person uninvited to the premises) is a central issue that roughly calibrates the owners' degree of responsibility, with invitees being owed the highest duty of care, followed by licensees and, at the bottom of the heap, trespassers, who are nevertheless owed some level of responsibility under US and English law (Hanson, 1998).

In the United States property owners can be liable for negligence if they do not institute appropriate security measures that give 'reasonable' protection against criminal attack. Bates's analysis of 1,176 security negligence claims over a ten-year period found that the most common allegations were that property owners failed to provide adequate security where the crime took place, and that they failed to follow their own security guidelines and procedures (2005). To prevail in US courts, plaintiffs must establish by a preponderance of evidence that the defendant owed a duty to the plaintiff to provide reasonable security, that the duty was breached and that this lapse caused the injury, which was foreseeable (Kennedy and Hupp, 1998).

While it is by no means simple to prove all these elements in court, changes in society, culture and economics have generally synchronised with the evolution of civil law such that presumptions of non-liability that traditionally accrued to property owners (with some exceptions) have moderated in the United States, providing more opportunities for plaintiffs (Gordon and Brill, 1996). Of course, the great majority of premises liability incidents are 'slip and fall'-type cases, and have no security implications. However, a growing proportion of cases involve negligence security premises issues (characterised as a 'sub-species of premises liability law'; see Dain and Brennan, 2003) and, in US courts at least, owners have been found liable for an increasing range of security-related injuries at such places as ATM machines (cash points), car parks, apartment building lobbies, hotel complexes, convenience stores and shopping malls (Kennedy, 1993; Gordon and Brill, 1996; Kennedy and Hupp, 1998; Bates, 2005). The likelihood of the number of these cases growing has increased in recent years, given gradual changes in the law, society and increases of terrorist activity in Britain and the United States.

Nourishing the growth of premises security liability

This trend was pushed along by growing crime rates (both real and perceived) between the 1960s and the 1990s that pushed victimisation issues onto the front pages of the popular press and brought them to the attention of academics (Pease, 1998; Felson, 2002). While these rates have generally declined in the past decade, there is evidence that the fear of crime persists long after the reality has passed (Schneider and Kitchen, 2002). In Britain and even more so in the United States, social and cultural changes in the 1960s and 1970s, including the civil and women's rights revolutions, gave more people the confidence that they could pursue criminal *and* civil remedies for injuries they sustained (Wallace, 1998). This movement was given further impetus in the United States by several notable cases, which included one that was highly publicised in the mid-1970s in which a celebrity recovered a large award from an innkeeper for blatant security lapses that contributed to her vulnerability to a sexual assault (Giordano, 1997).

This same period corresponds with the evolution of empirically based crime prevention theories and applications, such as those described in Chapter 2. Courts now had theories such as CPTED to apply to case circumstances and could search out standards of care based on rational, if inconsistent, practice. Environmental and place management elements such as site design, lighting, natural surveillance and guardianship were increasingly considered within the context of the foreseeability of injurious acts, as noted above (Gordon and Brill, 1996; Kennedy and Hupp, 1998). Moreover, a legal concept took root that considered premises liability claims within a 'totality of circumstances' framework. This notion corresponds with the holistic view of the criminal event suggested by modern CPTED theory and by situational crime prevention, where offences are considered within the overall context of physical design, management and use elements since they are often the product of many, interrelated factors.

This view is at odds with the traditional legal view in the United States, which suggested that foreseeability of events was based largely on the occurrence of prior similar events. The practical result of this posture is that offenders were allowed 'a free bite of the apple' inasmuch as present civil liability for an injury is based largely on the incidence of a similar crime in the past at the same location. For instance, under a strict interpretation of this rule, in order to prove liability for an assault in a car park, a plaintiff would have to show that owners had knowledge of a previous, similar assault in the same car park. The legal and crime prevention trend, however, is away from this seemingly logical but constricted thinking as more information about environment, context and management of places flows into the process. Indeed, the fundamental principle that has evolved is that property owners must maintain *reasonably* safe premises in proportion to the crime risk, with 'reasonableness' determined by the specific risk and security circumstances, within a framework of common and accepted practice. Prior events may be considered as part of the risk factors, but they are certainly not the only ones.

Future trends

With the threat of legal action for security negligence becoming both theoretically and practically real, owners and managers have increased resources in terms of knowledge and expertise at their command to defend their own economic interests by implementing, either in initial designs or at the retrofit stage, place-based crime prevention strategies. Whether and to what extent they use these resources, at least in the United States, is at present unknown; however, we speculate that the growth in the consultant and related information industries certainly means there is a market.

For example, there are a burgeoning number of Internet listings of premises security consultants, where only a few years ago there were almost none. One webpage alone lists 15 experts who are available across the United States for such courtroom consultancy purposes.[8] Specialised publications for property owners and managers, such as the *Premises Liability Report*, now present detailed accounts of cases from around the United States, mostly garnered from appellate court records (the most fertile source of case data) and recounting grisly injuries suffered by patrons and, in so doing, cataloguing a broad array of security negligence cases that have recently passed through state dockets or been noted in the popular press.[9] Training in premises security liability is now offered by professional associations, as exemplified by the American Institute of Architects' and the American Society of Landscape Architects' provision of a range of seminars and continuing education programmes focused on CPTED applications for crime and terrorism prevention.

For all development professionals, and especially attorneys and those in the risk management industry, premises security liability issues have assumed a special significance as a result of the attacks on the United States on 11 September 2001. As an outgrowth of the attacks, many legal and associated insurance questions have emerged around the central issues of whether terrorism is foreseeable and, if so, how to assess the risk of attack at any one structure, place or mode of transportation. At the time of writing, lawsuits are still in progress to determine the liability of the Port Authority of New York and New Jersey relative to the 1993 bombing of the World Trade Center ('WTC I'litigation). Baker and Merriam argue that this litigation provides a powerful example of how 'negligent security law for ordinary criminal activity may be extended to determine liability for terrorist attacks' (2004, p. 6). Liability for the 2001 attacks (WTC II litigation) has been legally restricted by the federal government against airlines, airports and some governmental agencies and otherwise reduced by the Federal Victims Compensation Fund.[10] The Terrorist Risk Insurance Act 2002 (TRIA) further stabilised the market by, among other things, making the federal government a reinsurer for 'certified' terrorist acts (American Academy of Actuaries, 2004). However, significant legal issues remain to be resolved relating to the standards of care that apply to the owners of premises (whether public or private), given the totality of circumstances of terrorist attacks (especially their foreseeability) and the exercise of reasonable care in preventing injury. These issues will probably be contested in this field for many years, although they are unlikely to change the general legal direction of premises liability litigation for the vast majority of cases. We suspect, however, that they will continue to heighten interest in empirical, place-based crime prevention theory and applications as evidenced by the rediscovery of the field by many federal agencies, by academics and by the loss prevention industry in the United States following the first major terrorist attack, that in Oklahoma City in 1996 (Schneider, 2003).

If the United States is a model for other nations, it is likely that Britain will also follow the path of market-driven implementation of place-based crime prevention strategies, though at a different pace (Cozens *et al.*, 2001, 2004). There is some evidence of this in Secured by Design awards given to developers, who use the award for marketing purposes, although there is less evidence from the premises security standpoint at present. Nevertheless, for both nations, the trend of holding property owners, managers, tenants, lessors, architects and engineers more accountable for problems that take place on their premises, coupled with the threat of civil liability growing out of terrorist attacks (Baker and Merriam, 2004), makes it more likely that place-based crime prevention measures will increasingly be incorporated into the early design of developments or in retrofits. As a privately initiated strategy based on the risk of being held to account for negligence, it may become one of the most effective ways of insinuating place-based crime prevention strategies into the design and management of urban structures and spaces, and we argue that it may possibly even surpass public efforts in this regard.

Conclusions

The first section of this chapter has argued that although there are points of agreement between space syntax, new urbanism and classical place-based crime prevention theory (especially defensible space and CPTED), there are fundamental and problematic differences as well. Space syntax is problematic because its application to the field of crime prevention has produced results which to a considerable extent do not fit with what we know from many other studies in the field. It is possible, of course, that this makes it a leader in the field; but it is also possible that it makes its value questionable. We need to try to understand which of these two propositions is correct. New urbanism is challenging because whatever the arguments for it relative to urban design quality, its crime prevention value is yet to be demonstrated, and in terms of at least one basic issue – its insistence on the importance of permeable layouts – this argument remains questionable from a crime prevention perspective. Part of the problem here is that there is very little hard evidence based upon longitudinal studies of new urbanist projects, and without this we are in the territory of rhetoric often advanced by true believers (both ways). We need in this case to see the information base improved considerably, so that if developers are going to continue to construct new urbanist layouts there is a reasonable level of reliable knowledge about what the crime experience is likely to be for owners and tenants.

The second and third sections looked at two phenomena which we see as being of growing importance. Gating of communities, especially in new construction but also as a retrofitting activity, has been expanding very rapidly in parts of the United States (in particular), and there is no evidence that this is about to stop. Clearly, there are many dimensions to debates about gating, but what stands out from a crime prevention perspective is that this fashion trend (for this, in part at any rate, is what we think it is) has not grown on the back of clear evidence that it actually works; and indeed, the truth is that we do not know what the long-term experience of gating will be, although there is evidence that some benefits may be experienced in the short run. Long-term crime prevention evidence is lacking. On a different dimension, we believe that long-term study will show that gating is not a sustainable or socially beneficial urban policy, even though some segments of society may reap limited benefits. As another incarnation of crime prevention policy, premises liability litigation, on the other hand, seems likely to be a growing phenomenon, where in a very practical sense the evidence that it works (in the form of court awards against landlords and others) will drive its continued expansion. We expect this not only to continue to grow in the United States, but also to transfer to other (probably inherently less litigious) jurisdictions.

What links all these examinations is a concern for what the available evidence actually tells us, and in at least two of these instances (the growing influence of new urbanist thinking, and the continued increase in the number of gated communities) a worry that the lives of millions of people who have bought into developments based upon these phenomena – in the belief that among other things this will protect them from crime – have been influenced by an expectation which is not grounded in much reliable empirical evidence. It may turn out to be the case that in both instances the crime prevention benefits are real and long-lasting, and that this is at least in part attributable to the design principles that have been applied here rather than to other intervening variables; if so, all well and good. But the real need here is to strengthen both the evidence base that applies to decision making of this nature and its effective communication to people considering buying into these concepts. Indeed, in different ways this idea applies to all of the phenomena we have examined in this chapter, so that they can take their appropriate positions in the lexicon of place-based crime prevention ideas and so that we can understand more effectively exactly what challenges they do pose to the classical theories in this field.

Part Two
The practice

4

A global perspective on integrating crime prevention into planning systems

Introduction

Our focus in this book is on the role of attempts to manipulate the physical environment in order to reduce crime and the opportunity to commit crime. Since in most modern industrialised societies, proposals to engage in development are mediated through planning systems, we want to focus in this chapter on the ways in which and the extent to which the crime prevention agenda is being addressed via planning processes.

We know of no systematic study that enables an overview to be taken of the extent to which and the ways in which this issue is being addressed across the world, nor indeed do we believe that there is even a general acceptance that planning systems can contribute usefully to crime prevention. This chapter can therefore be seen as a small start down this road, but we are very conscious that we are covering only a limited number of all the possible situations in this material. We have chosen to look here at four situations:

- the position in the European Union;
- the position in African cities;
- the position in the United Kingdom (and, specifically, in England);
- the position in the United States.

We tackle the first two in a fairly broad-brush manner by utilising recent studies, but the third and fourth are examined for two particular reasons. The first, of course, is that they are the systems best known to us. The second is that they offer two very different kinds of models, even though in many ways their subject matter is essentially the same. The British system has a very strong top-down, central policy direction to it, whereas the US system lacks this almost entirely but could be described as 'let a thousand flowers bloom' – in other words, it provides plenty of scope for local initiatives. We precede this analysis with a brief review of how crime prevention has impinged on planning literature.

Crime prevention in the planning literature

The short answer to the implied question in this subtitle is 'not much and not until relatively recently'. In essence, both crime prevention and planning have long and full literatures, but the connections between the two have not tended to be very strong until fairly recently (Zahm, 2005). Many of the key pieces of literature in the crime prevention field have been introduced in Chapter 2 of this book, where we discuss what we have called the 'classical' theories of place-based crime prevention. As far as the planning literature is concerned, readers who wish to see how crime prevention might figure in its key theoretical debates can look at Brooks (2002). Brooks attempts to distil what can at times be esoteric debates about planning theory into readable sets of propositions about matters that planning practitioners can readily relate to from their practice experience. As if to underline the point we make above, neither 'crime prevention' nor 'public safety' is to be found in the index to the book by Brooks, not, we think, because of omissions on the part of its author, but because planning theory has scarcely addressed this issue. What Brooks does do, however, is to talk about what the focus of planning activity in the United States in the twentieth century has been, picking up on some work by the Strategic Marketing Committee of the Association of Collegiate Schools of Planning (ibid., pp. 11–13). This argues, among other things, that planning deals in particular with some of the most pressing issues – some would say, the wicked issues – that confront us in human settlements. We would argue that the experience of crime (and, more controversially, the fear of crime, which we have discussed in Chapter 1 of this book) should certainly count as one of these, and we think that there is by now a substantial accumulation of evidence which supports this view. Box 4.1 presents one British example of a study of this nature which makes this point strongly.

Two things are particularly noticeable about the data in Box 4.1 for present purposes. The first is that the desire to see a low level of crime tops the list of factors that respondents said characterised somewhere which was a good place to live, with almost two-thirds of respondents identifying this particular factor. The second point is that a low level of crime not merely tops the list, but tops it by a considerable margin; it is 17 percentage points above the factor in second place, and by the time that readers get down to fifth place on the list, that factor is scoring considerably less than half the score achieved by a low level of crime.

So, if planning does indeed deal with some of the most pressing issues that confront us in human settlements, then it certainly *ought* to be dealing with issues to do with the experience of crime, given how highly these rank among people in terms of what constitutes a good place to live. Nevertheless, we were very conscious in our previous book on this subject (Schneider and Kitchen, 2002) that the connection between the planning process and the scope for reducing the opportunity to commit crime was one that had not been made strongly by the planning communities in either the United States or Britain, and we suspected that this was also true in relation to much of the rest of the world. Indeed, our desire to establish this relationship and to get the planning

---

Box 4.1 The most important things that make somewhere a good place to live

These are the top ten responses to attempts by the public to identify the things that make somewhere a good place to live, in rank order, according to the English Best Value User Satisfaction Survey, 2003/04. The dominance among the public views recorded here of being in a relatively crime-free situation is clear from this table.

1	Low level of crime	66% of respondents
2	Health services	47%
3	Clean streets	37%
4	Affordable housing	36%
5	Shopping facilities	29%
6	Education provision	28%
7=	Public transport	26%
7=	Low level of traffic congestion	26%
9	Parks and open spaces	25%
10=	Job prospects	21%
10=	Road and pavement repairs	21%

Source: Summarised from Office of the Deputy Prime Minister (2005b, p. 11).

---

community to appreciate its potential significance was one of our primary motives for writing that book, which reviews the extant literature up to that point fairly comprehensively. The situation has improved a little since then, as the study in this chapter of how the British planning system has formally embraced crime prevention will demonstrate, but nevertheless we think that the dearth of recognition in the planning literature of crime prevention remains a significant issue, which in turn inevitably impacts upon the training of planners, among other things.

Part of this problem is that much of what is in the planning and related literature is negative in its tone and content in terms of the relationship between planning and crime prevention. Three examples, from three different points in time, will serve to make this point. First, the seminal work of Jane Jacobs, extolling the virtues of the parts of Greenwich Village in New York she knew (including the natural 'eyes on the street' provided by human activity, which has been much argued over in crime prevention terms ever since; see Gratz, 2003), and bemoaning their absence in much of the new urban development that she saw, is actually subtitled *The Failure of Town Planning* (Jacobs, 1961). Second, Alice Coleman's study of the experience of living in post-war housing estates, mainly in London, explores the relationship between the signs of social malaise that she itemises and the design and layout of those estates (Coleman, 1990). The point about this is that it looks at housing estates that were designed and laid out in 'the planning era' (that is, during the period when development proposals were fully reviewed by local planning authorities with extensive powers to refuse them if they felt they were inappropriate or inadequate), and it argues that crime opportunities were actually designed into these areas by the approaches adopted by the design process at the time. So, far from the planning system contributing effectively to crime prevention here, the argument is that it actually assisted in the creation of the problem. Third, and most recently, the Office of the Deputy Prime Minister in the United Kingdom, in setting out what it sees as the primary purposes of the planning system, says the following:

> Planning shapes the places where people live and work and the country we live in. Good planning ensures that we get the right development, in the right place and at the right time. It makes a positive difference to people's lives and helps to deliver homes, jobs and better opportunities for all, while protecting and enhancing the natural and historic environment, and conserving the countryside and open spaces that are vital resources for everyone. But poor planning can result in a legacy for current and future generations of run-down town centres, unsafe and dilapidated housing, crime and disorder, and the loss of our finest countryside to development.
>
> (Office of the Deputy Prime Minister, 2005a, paragraph 1)

So, the legacy of poor planning in the past is presented here as including unsafe housing and crime and disorder. And there can be little doubt that this analysis is correct; the failure of the planning literature to explore the relationship between planning processes and the opportunity to commit crime is matched by the failure of planning practice in too many instances to contribute to the creation of development where the experience of crime is at a low level – the very thing that, as we have seen from Box 4.1, is prized more than anything else by people in terms of what makes somewhere a good place to live.

That said, the cupboard is not completely bare in terms of the extent to which planning and related literature has begun to engage with crime prevention, even if it is neither as full nor as positive as we would wish to see. We review some of this specifically later in this chapter in the context of the British case, and we have also examined much of this material in Chapter 2 in the context of what we have chosen to describe as the classical approaches to planning for crime prevention. Nevertheless, we believe that one of the reasons why planning as a process has struggled to come to terms with the idea that it can contribute positively to crime prevention is that the general planning literature has either struggled with or substantially ignored this relationship. In one sense it is not surprising that if the available academic and professional literature is sparse, then practice is also likely to be limited, since it will not have much material on which to draw; and so one of the challenges for subsequent years is the need to improve this situation. This applies not only to the developed world but also to those areas of the world still experiencing urbanisation on a large scale. The difference here is that at present most of the available literature is drawn from First World experience, and it should not be assumed that it will transplant easily and automatically into Third World situations. Thus, we would suggest that particular attention needs to be paid in the development of a stronger literature to the very different contexts that exist across the world. This all suggests that a large agenda exists in this area, but we hope that this book makes at least an initial contribution to it.

Planning for crime prevention in the European Union

As far as the position in Europe is concerned, a recent trans-European project has demonstrated by how much it varies from country to country (Oxley *et al.*, 2005). Its summary of the position is as follows:

> Quickly identified was the wide-ranging level of basic awareness and implementation of CPTED practices amongst the participating countries. In some countries, crime reduction measures have, or are about to become, part of the planning and building regulations, for example Netherlands and the UK, whereas some other partner countries were just becoming aware of the way some changes in society and speculative development could quickly lead to increases in opportunistic crime, for example Estonia and Poland.
>
> (ibid., p. 7)

It seems clear from the review of practice in individual countries (ibid., pp. 14–22) that the United Kingdom, the Netherlands and Germany in their different ways have many policy strands that relate the planning process and crime prevention, particularly in relation to housing developments (see also Town *et al.*, 2003). In terms of a governmental intention that the planning process will play a leading role in this area, however, the United Kingdom appears to have the most formalised system, which is one of the reasons why this case is examined in more detail later in this chapter. One of the trans-European projects that has been developing in this context is the emergence of a European pre-standard for the reduction of crime and the fear of crime by urban planning and building design, the urban planning component of which was published in 2003 (CEN, 2003). This is based upon six propositions drawn from a review of the extant literature, from research and from project evaluations and agreed by a technical committee (ibid., pp. 5 and 6). These propositions are summarised in Box 4.2. We would argue that they are broadly consistent with the nine key propositions we advanced in our previous book in this field as a basis for making progress (Schneider and Kitchen, 2002, pp. 292–303), to which we return in Chapter 9 of this book. They led the technical committee to think in terms of both contents (what might work?) and processes (how might it be put into effect?) in drafting the pre-standard. Inevitably, something like this is bound to be stated in relatively general terms, relating as it does to a wide range of circumstances, but the essence of the guidance it offers is helpfully summarised by Colquhoun (2004, pp. 296–303).

Box 4.2 The key propositions in the European pre-standard on urban planning and crime prevention

The six propositions agreed by the technical committee preparing the pre-standard are as follows:

1 Urban planning can have an impact both on different types of crime and on the fear of crime by influencing the conduct, attitudes, choices and feelings of the key players in these processes, such as offenders, victims, residents and police.
2 There are specific types of crimes with environmental dimensions which can be seen as being amenable to urban planning activities, such as burglary and vandalism.
3 Crime and fear of crime are different phenomena.
4 Fear of crime is an important issue, but if it is to be tackled meaningfully, attempts have to be made to separate it out from a much broader set of feelings people have about the whole of their living space and about the degree to which they feel deprived of a good social and physical environment in which to live.
5 A more secure and safer city or neighbourhood can be achieved through a strategic approach to these issues aiming at the physical and social environment.
6 Policymakers and practitioners should never focus on planning and design only. Every newly built neighbourhood, public space or building needs good maintenance. Planning/design and maintenance are thus two sides of the same coin.

Source: Summarised from CEN (European Committee for Standardization), 2003, *Prevention of Crime: Urban Planning and Design*, Part 2: *Urban Planning*, ENV 14383–2, CEN Management Centre, Brussels, pp. 5 and 6.

The pre-standard identifies 15 types of strategies that could be applied, or that are at least worth thinking about, grouped under three broad headings: planning strategies, urban design strategies and management strategies (CEN, 2003, pp. 15–17). These are summarised in Box 4.3. It is important to see this as a menu from which combinations can be chosen that are appropriate to the particular circumstances being addressed rather than to regard it as a list offering single solutions, because very often a preferred approach will need to include elements from all three – planning, urban design and management. Certainly one of the ways in which this kind of thinking can be taken forward in future is through the accumulation of evidence about which of these appear to work best in which particular sets of circumstances.

Although the pre-standard represents the agreed findings of a technical committee, it is not without controversy. For example, as we have already

---

Box 4.3 Crime prevention strategies where the planning process can contribute

The text of ENV 14383–2 identifies 15 strategies in three broad group-ings in this context.

1 *Planning strategies*
   • respecting existing social and physical structures;
   • creating liveliness (blending functions and attractive street layout);
   • mixed status (blending socio-economic groups, avoiding isolation and segregation);
   • urban density (creating sense of neighbourliness, avoiding waste-land and desolate areas).

2 *Urban design strategies*
   • visibility (overview, lighting);
   • accessibility (orientation, space to move, alternative routes, limiting access for non-authorised people);
   • territoriality (human scale, clear zoning, compartmentalisation);
   • attractiveness (colour, materials, lighting, noise, smell, street furniture);
   • robustness (doors, windows, street furniture).

3 *Management strategies*
   • target hardening/removal;
   • maintenance;
   • surveillance (patrolling, camera monitoring);
   • rules (for the conduct of the public in public places);
   • providing infrastructure for particular groups (e.g. youth, homeless, drug addicts);
   • communication (of preventive measures and behaviour rules to the public).

Source: Summarised from CEN (European Committee for Standard-ization) 2003, *Prevention of Crime: Urban Planning and Design*, Part 2: *Urban Planning*, ENV 14383–2, CEN Management Centre, Brussels, pp. 15–17.

---

noted, perhaps the most contested territory in the field is the issue of acces-sibility, and particularly the permeability of layouts. The guidance summarised in Box 4.3 could be said to represent a somewhat uneasy compromise between the various positions taken up on this issue, a stance largely replicated by the slightly later British guidance (Office of the Deputy Prime Minister and the Home Office, 2004, pp. 16–19). Similarly, its emphasis on clear zoning could well be seen as unhelpful by advocates of mixed use approaches. In these senses, this guidance needs to be seen as a work in progress rather than as the finished article. Its primary value may well turn out to be the role it plays in drawing attention to the relationship between planning and crime prevention in those EU member states where relatively little has, as yet, been done in this field.

There are other instances of initiatives being taken forward under a trans-European banner, as well as this process of assembling the European pre-standard.[1] One such initiative is Crime Opportunity Profiling of Streets (COPS), which is essentially about looking at the problem of crime and disorder in terms of the opportunity presented for crimes to be committed, not just by reference to an individual site but by taking into account the street or area within which it is located. It is described as follows:

> Crime Opportunity Profiling is a systematic and detailed study of a street and the built environment interfaces with the street in commercial districts which suffer from street crime and other problems associated with the consequences of a drug market. A Crime Opportunity Profile (COP) identifies a whole raft of built environment features that offer opportunities to commit crime or generate fear of crime and also features that provide sites for drug-taking and drug-dealing and other antisocial behaviour.
>
> Importantly, a COP report suggests practical solutions to the problems identified using situational crime prevention techniques and crime prevention through environmental design practices. The delivery of the solutions relies heavily on the willingness of the problem owners to do something about them and the support of multi-agency partnerships committed to the process and to that end must be seen as an essential part of an overall strategy to prevent street crime and disorder.
>
> (Beckford in Oxley *et al.*, 2005, p. 189)

Much of the work to develop this technique was originally carried out in the London Borough of Camden, and it is being offered to the wider European practice community as an example of a process that has worked well in a particular location and may have the potential to work well elsewhere. This illustrates one of the real advantages of transnational approaches, which is that it is possible to look at how experience from one locality might be capable of offering lessons to elsewhere, thereby shortening the process of learning. The brief survey in this chapter has shown that the pace of development of planning for crime prevention across the European Union is very variable, but certainly for the countries at the lower end of this range it offers a framework for making more rapid progress than they would be able to do by themselves; and maybe the COPS initiative will prove to be an example of this process at work.

Planning for crime prevention in African cities

Crime appears to be a serious problem in Africa, and particularly in African cities, not merely in an absolute sense (although many of the data needed to establish the position reliably are not available) but also because the experience and the fear of crime appear to be holding back necessary development (United Nations Office on Drugs and Crime, 2005). In particular, much of Africa exhibits many of the characteristics that internationally would be seen as being associated with high levels of crime. Key elements here are:

- income inequality, with large numbers of very poor people to whom the loss of properties of various kinds as a result of criminal activity can have a devastating impact, and who may also be tempted to commit crimes as a way of helping to overcome some of the problems of poverty;
- a youthful population, including many young people not enrolled on educational courses and not employed; and this is a major issue, because experience across the world has shown that teenage and young adult males are among the groups with high offending rates;
- rapid rates of urbanisation, which means that many urban areas have unstable populations and thus lack some of the social structures which can help to create norms about acceptable behaviour;
- poorly resourced criminal justice systems, so that the likelihood of detection and punishment for crime is small and the prospect for the rehabilitation of criminals is poor;
- the proliferation of firearms, exacerbated in many areas by the continuation of armed conflict (ibid.).

It is perhaps hardly surprising, therefore, that in recent years some more systematic attempts to tackle the problems of urban crime and violence have commenced, and we look briefly here at a small selection of these and at the role within them of environmentally related measures.

The Safer Cities Programme of UN-HABITAT was launched in 1996 at the request of a group of African city mayors who were concerned about the problems of crime and violence being experienced in their cities (UN-HABITAT, undated, p. 2). In summary, the Safer Cities Programme aims to support the following types of activities:

- strengthening the capacity of local authorities to address urban safety issues and reduce delinquency and insecurity;
- promoting crime prevention issues, usually implemented on a multiple partner basis;
- encouraging city networks in order to exchange experiences;
- preparing and implementing capacity-building programmes, and bringing in qualified and experienced partners from elsewhere to help;
- targeting three main action areas in particular: groups at risk, developing situational crime prevention approaches, and reform of the criminal justice system (UN-HABITAT, 2005, p. 27).

As can be seen from this list, the approach adopted is wide-ranging, but it is interesting to see from the perspectives of the present book that the development of environmentally based approaches to crime prevention (in the form of situational crime prevention; see Chapter 2) is clearly identified as one of the three action areas targeted for development. What is also clear from this list is the importance attached to capacity-building initiatives and to putting in place systems and procedures that enable crime prevention initiatives to be effective. These issues are of particular significance in the context of this present chapter because of two potential difficulties in the developing world around the ability of cities to incorporate crime prevention into their planning activities: the inherent strengths of their planning systems themselves, and then the human capacities available to them. The experience of First World cities has tended to be that getting planning systems to take crime prevention seriously as part of their responsibilities has been a relative latecomer, when it has happened at all, so that even where strong planning systems exist (and this is by no means always the case in the developed world), they have not tended to see contributing to crime prevention as being high up their agenda, at any rate until relatively recently. As we have noted, this has in turn limited the intellectual resources available in this field to the planning profession at large. In addition, planning systems depend critically on human capacity for their effective operation, and thus having the right numbers of people in post with appropriate skills (Kitchen, 2007) is fundamental to their success. So, while inevitably this is likely to be quite a long-term process, the emphasis in the UN-HABITAT Safer Cities Programme on building capacity and on improving systems is of considerable importance. It is wholly appropriate that these are seen as being among the primary objectives for the programme, since developing capacity and building a culture of crime prevention that is deeply embedded in the process of governance are the main ways in which the ability to tackle crime as a local 'quality of life' issue is likely to grow (UN-HABITAT, 2005, p. 27). This process is likely to be taken considerably further by the scheduled appearance in 2007 of the sixth issue of UN-HABITAT's 'Global Report', which takes as its focus 'Enhancing Urban Safety and Security'.

Since 1997 the Safer Cities Programme has initiated projects in several African cities, and that process is now being rolled out in other parts of the developing world as well. The broad Safer Cities methodology consists of seven stages, although the ways these are applied depend on local circumstances. The seven stages are diagnosis; building coalitions of stakeholders; strategy; plan of action; implement; institutionalise; and monitor and evaluate continuously. The main African cities that have seen projects established are Johannesburg and Durban (South Africa), Dar es Salaam (Tanzania), Abidjan (Côte d'Ivoire), Antananarivo (Madagascar), Dakar (Senegal), Nairobi (Kenya) and Yaoundé (Cameroon). We will look briefly here at the Durban and the Nairobi cases.

One of the interesting aspects of the work on the Durban project has been that some of the funding for it has been provided by the Dutch embassy. This links well with the previous section of this chapter, where we have shown that one of the most active processes of governance in the European Union in embracing planning for crime prevention has been the Dutch system. The approach in Durban has had a strong strategic element to it, with the new eThekwini Municipality Safety and Crime Prevention Strategy being adopted by the city council in 2003 as part of a five-year strategic plan of action. The three key elements of the strategy are effective policing and crime prevention, targeted 'social' crime prevention (such as violence against women and victim support), and the adoption of CPTED approaches (crime prevention through environmental design, which we discussed in Chapter 2). This is all overseen by a partnership which brings the key players together, in the form of the Safer Cities Steering Committee, which consists of councillors, public officials, police and business representatives. As well as 'process'-type initiatives, it has also been involved with specific urban renewal projects in various part of the city, which has been helped by the fact that the council has adopted an area-based management approach to the delivery of services; and so the approach here is to try to integrate crime prevention and safety issues into the work of mainstream services.[2]

The Nairobi Safer Cities project was launched in 2001, and it has some similarities with the Durban project. Again, the emphasis was very much on adopting a strategic approach, with the city council approving the basic strategy in April 2004 and then final agreement being reached via two City Residents Conventions on Urban Safety on an Urban Pact on Safety and on a two-year Action Plan. Specific initiatives have included training programmes for key stakeholders, the establishment of an interdepartmental committee within the city council chaired by the Deputy Town Clerk to ensure that the strategy is fully taken into account in corporate and departmental activities, pilot activities in crime 'hot spots' and targeted at key social issues such as violence against women and youth at risk, and the establishment of an annual Residents Crime Prevention and Urban Safety Week as a means of ensuring that initiatives remain in the public eye.[3]

It is, of course, very early days to judge projects of this nature, when their timescale is inevitably quite long-term and when they are trying to change processes and perceptions rather than just looking for quick fixes. For present purposes, the important point is that initiatives of this nature are under way in African cities, and that the authorities in Africa do see environmental activities as part of a broader fight against crime and the creation of a greater sense of the city as a safe place in which to live.

Crime prevention and the English planning system

As a factor which the English[4] planning system is explicitly expected to take into account, crime prevention is a relatively late arrival on the scene. The Acts of Parliament which established the English planning system in its contemporary form date back to 1947, but the first formal guidance from the government about the relationship between planning and crime prevention did not appear until DoE Circular 5/94 (Department of the Environment, 1994). This was notable mainly for the emphasis it placed on consultation with police architectural liaison officers (ALOs) or equivalent rather than for solid advice about how planners should handle crime prevention issues in their everyday work; in effect, it established the police via their architectural liaison officers as legitimate consultees within the planning process, but it did not take much further forward understanding of how the planning process could contribute to crime prevention. Since that point, crime prevention, public safety and the contribution that attention to these matters can make to the achievement of sustainable communities have risen rapidly up the planning agenda as issues for consideration. There are four key stages in this process, which will be discussed in more detail below. More or less in parallel, the 43 police forces of England and Wales were generating their own capacity in this field, through the establishment of an ALO service in each force to handle crime prevention issues in relation to the management of the development process, and we shall look in more detail at the work of police ALOs in Chapter 5. More or less in parallel, the police service also developed its national Secured by Design (SBD) scheme, which provided a set of key principles as a basis for the work of ALOs (see, for example, Colquhoun, 2004, pp. 202–212). There is some research evidence that in its own terms Secured by Design has been successful (see Armitage, 2000; Topping and Pascoe, 2000; Cozens *et al.*, 2004), although it is less clear which elements of the SBD package are the most effective ones. Nevertheless, what this clearly shows is that the police service was developing some appropriate tools to help it in its new relationships with the planning process, alongside the steps taken between 1994 and 2005 to bring crime prevention into the centre of planning.

The first such step after the issue of Circular 5/94 was the passage of the Crime and Disorder Act 1998. This had two impacts in particular on the planning process, one of which was probably more noticed at the time by the planning community than the other. The high-profile element was the requirement for the creation of Crime and Disorder Reduction Partnerships between local authorities, the police and other key players to identify and tackle problems in this field, which are now operational in various forms in local authority areas across England. There is some doubt about how effective these have been, however. For example, Gilling (2005) suggests that the achievements that are truly attributable to partnership working may be somewhat less than the impressive partnership infrastructure that has been created. In many areas this particular type of partnership has been incorporated into the broader partnership structure that drives the urban regeneration process in the locality. Sheffield is an example of this kind, where the 1998 Act partnership flourishes under the auspices of the city's Local Strategic Partnership (Sheffield First for Safety, 2002; Sheffield First Partnership, 2005), and we will look at this particular case in more detail in Chapter 6 of this book, where we take a less pessimistic view than Gilling does. The reason for this type of development in partnership working is that, in parallel with the rise of crime prevention up the planning agenda, there has been a recognition of its significance as part of more holistic approaches to urban regeneration than the property development focus of much regeneration activity in the 1980s and early 1990s (see, for example, Social Exclusion Unit, 2001).

The less immediately recognised element of the 1998 Act was the new duty imposed on local planning authorities by its section 17 to take account of and to do all they reasonably can to reduce crime and disorder in their work. The feedback from planners at the time seemed to suggest that the level of awareness of the significance of this new duty was relatively low (Kitchen, 2002), and this was reflected in an early review of its impact on development control decision making, which detected little evidence in planning appeal decisions of this factor (Wright, 2001). There was, however, some evidence beginning to emerge to the effect that this new responsibility was having an impact on recent development plan work (Williams and Wood, 2001), and further momentum is expected to develop over the next few years as a new round of development plan making is ushered in by the provisions of the Planning and Compulsory Purchase Act 2004.

The second key step in the process of moving crime prevention into the mainstream of planning thinking was the appearance of the Urban Policy White Paper in 2000 (Department of the Environment, Transport and the Regions, 2000) following on from the work of the Urban Task Force chaired by Lord Rogers (Urban Task Force, 1999). This latter document (ibid., p. 127) emphasised in particular the importance of 'designing out crime' through the application of philosophies closely associated with new urbanism (which we discuss in Chapter 3; see also Duany, 2003), and this by implication raised important questions about how the planning system should approach its new task, because, as we have already noted, this kind of urban design advice contradicts in some important ways the approach adopted by the police via their national Secured by Design scheme (Kitchen, 2002, 2005). The Urban Policy White Paper did not go far into this difficult territory, but it did recognise the need to address the question of the guidance given by the government on crime prevention and the British planning system by making two key commitments. The first was to review DoE Circular 5/94, which was widely seen as already having been overtaken by events. The second was that crime prevention should become a key objective for planning (Department of the Environment, Transport and the Regions, 2000, p. 120). So, in the six years since the appearance of Circular 5/94 the importance attached by the government to the contribution that planning could make to crime prevention had grown significantly, as was confirmed by these two commitments.

The third step in the establishment of crime prevention in the planning lexicon was the publication in 2004 of *Safer Places: The Planning System and Crime Prevention*, the government's new advice on planning for crime prevention, some four years after the commitment in the Urban Policy White Paper to review the extant guidance (Office of the Deputy Prime Minister and the Home Office, 2004). The amount of time this process took might be seen as a commentary on the difficulty of this task, although it was not made any easier by the existence of relevant but not always consistent guidance in government policy documents in fields such as housing, urban design and highways. The differences of views about how this agenda should be tackled, which were partly based upon evidence but seemed to have at least as much to do with ideological standpoints, came to the surface in the process of preparing the new guidance (see, for example, Knowles, 2003a). In addition, there had been a flurry of new literature in the interim period reflecting the growing interest in the field (see, for example, Schneider and Kitchen, 2002; Town *et al.*, 2003; Colquhoun, 2004) to complement some of the more traditional literature (see, for example, Newman, 1973; Jeffrey, 1977; Poyner, 1983; Coleman, 1990; Brantingham and Brantingham, 1991; Poyner and Webb, 1991; Clarke, 1997).

While the new guidance was undoubtedly aware of the major controversies in the field (and even attempted in its Annex 2 some reconciliation of some of the available evidence surrounding them; Office of the Deputy Prime Minister and the Home Office, 2004, pp. 87–90), it cannot be said that it resolved them. So, for example, what went into the process was both urban design advice stressing the value of permeable approaches to housing layouts (see, for example, DTLR and CABE, 2001, pp. 24–31) and advice on the other hand from reviews of the available research to the effect that permeable layouts consistently demonstrate higher crime rates than do less permeable layouts (see, for example, Taylor, 2002, p. 419). What came out of the process was guidance which appears to acknowledge both perspectives, without suggesting how they might be reconciled in individual circumstances (Office of the Deputy Prime Minister and the Home Office, 2004, pp. 16–19). Nevertheless, the new guidance undoubtedly raised the profile of planning for crime prevention, via a substantial document containing among other things several thought-provoking case studies.

The most recent step in the process has been the issue by the government of Planning Policy Statement 1 (PPS1: Office of the Deputy Prime Minister, 2005a). This key document takes as its central theme the proposition that the primary task of the planning system is to deliver sustainable development. To this end, it identifies five tasks for the planning system, the fifth of which is 'ensuring that development supports existing communities and contributes to the creation of safe, sustainable, liveable and mixed communities with good access to jobs and key services for all members of the community' (ibid., paragraph 5). So, the role of the planning system in helping to achieve public safety (building on an older tradition in this field; see, for example, Ekblom *et al.*, 1996; Oc and Tiesdell, 1997) is clearly established here among the main tasks that the planning system is expected to tackle in seeking to achieve sustainable development. PPS1 links clearly to the good practice advice given in *Safer Places*, and together these two pieces of work discharged the two major commitments the government made in this area in the Urban Policy White Paper of 2000. They also complete the journey from the first recognition that planning has a role to play in this field in DoE Circular 5/94 to the establishment of this major role by early 2005, although, as noted above, it could still be argued that this left some of the key issues in the field unresolved and therefore provided guidance to planners, police ALOs and other interested parties that was of limited value. Emerging government policy also continues to ask difficult questions of this enhanced process of planning for crime prevention. For example, a government consultation paper on a revised version of PPS3 (the government's planning policy statement on housing: Office of the Deputy Prime Minister, 2005c) issued in December 2005 continues government policy pressure to raise significantly the densities achieved by new housing developments. But it does not ask whether this process of raising housing densities creates new challenges for planning for crime prevention, which we would suggest it will; and indeed, since its only reference to this issue is to its guidance in *Safer Places*, it seems to be suggesting that this covers the ground, even though few if any of the case studies in that document seem to be based upon longitudinal experience of making higher housing densities work. This example, along with the point about the ambiguity of some of the guidance, suggests that, while planning for crime prevention was a much more formally established process in England by the end of 2005 than it had been ten years previously, this should still be seen as a work in progress rather than as something fully developed and understood.

Of course, government decreeing that things should be so is an important matter in its own right, but of itself it does not make things happen. In this particular instance, the most critical element in helping the planning system to engage effectively with this relatively new agenda is the series of working relationships established up and down the country between planners and their local police force ALOs. This relationship could potentially have four elements to it, although to date the first of these has almost certainly been the most significant numerically:

* consultation on planning applications as part of the development control process;
* work on planning policies and supplementary guidance documents as part of the development plan-making process;
* collaboration on individual environmental or area-based improvement projects where crime prevention is a significant element in the project design;
* taking forward the partnership process in the regeneration field, especially where Crime and Disorder Reduction Partnerships established under the 1998 Act have been incorporated into the Local Strategic Partnership structure which drives the regeneration process.

We will look in more detail at examples of work in some of these areas in Chapters 5 and 6 of this book, and in particular Chapter 5 introduces some recent evidence about ALO–planner working relationships.

Crime prevention and planning systems in the United States

In a previous comparison of practice in the United Kingdom and the United States (Kitchen and Schneider, 2005) we argued that the most visible difference between the two was the absence from the United States of any equivalent of the very formal, top-down structure for incorporating crime prevention issues into planning and related activities in Britain that we have described above. We attributed this primarily to the clear division established in the US Constitution between federal matters and those that are the responsibilities of states, with planning for crime prevention quite clearly being seen to be an issue of more localised significance rather than something which is at heart a federal matter. That said, it is an oversimplification to conclude that there has been no federal interest in the field whatsoever. For example, the Department of Housing and Urban Development (HUD) was one of the parties that took an early interest in the work of Oscar Newman, and that interest can be seen in its housing redevelopment and funding policies and practices, and particularly in the published statement of its former Secretary, Henry Cisneros (Cisneros, 1995). There are other examples also of federal interest in the field (Schneider and Kitchen, 2002, chapter 5), and over and above this there have been many examples of nationally funded research in the field that has been extremely valuable in summarising what is emerging from practice and in suggesting ways forward (see, for example, Sherman *et al.*, 1997; Taylor, 1999), often produced under the auspices of the US Department of Justice. So, it is not accurate to say that there has been no federal involvement in planning for crime prevention in the United States, but it certainly is the case that the major involvement has been at more localised levels.

The strength of a system that we have described above as 'let a thousand flowers bloom' is the opportunity it provides for local initiative, and indeed innovation; and there are many examples of this in the United States which involve the development of processes or of projects (for an extended discussion of this, see Schneider and Kitchen, 2002, chapters 5 and 6). More than anything else, what seems to be required in the US system is concerned individuals who are prepared to push to get things done in their localities and then to keep pushing so that momentum is maintained.

One of the problems that local initiatives in the field of planning for crime prevention have often faced in the United States is the very strong feeling in some quarters of the private sector (which is often articulated both locally and nationally) that this is simply creating more red tape and increasing the cost of doing business. So, one of the major challenges here is the need to convince stakeholders that planning for crime prevention is not simply making the process of regulation still bigger but is introducing something which is beneficial to all parties. To date, this has obviously been more successful in some parts of the United States than in others, but, as we will argue in Chapter 7, we think that the recent pressure to establish effective anti-terrorism measures (with strong support from the federal government) is having the effect of advancing this cause more rapidly than in all probability would have otherwise been the case.

It is also clear that things can change over time. For example, Schneider (2003) argues that Florida's Safe Neighborhood Act does begin to acknowl-edge the value of place-based crime prevention activities, but that the funding and implementation of that Act have not enabled this promise to be realised. In other words, getting the approach written into state legislation may be a necessary condition of progress, but, as this example shows, it is not a suffi-cient condition if it is not followed up in appropriate ways. So, the American system offers considerable potential for innovation at the local level, but it also puts many barriers in the way of innovation happening. This explains why the range in the United States is so broad, from examples that can be seen internationally as leading the way to many areas where nothing at all appears to be happening.

At the top end of this range may well be the process of embedding principles of place-based crime prevention in the city zoning ordinances of Tempe, Arizona, so that officials can stop, or 'red-tag', construction that does not conform (Schneider and Kitchen, 2002, pp. 147–150). This is a power of some significance in a locality that has been experiencing considerable growth in recent years. It has the effect of putting planning for crime prevention here more clearly in the same boat as the work of (for example) the fire marshal, where construction work that does not accord with fire prevention principles can be stopped. The latter situation is, of course, common but the former is certainly not. Indeed, we believe that the situation in Tempe may well be unique in the United States; and in turn we suspect that there are few, if any, examples similar to this across the world. Of course, it may be asked why nowhere else appears (at any rate, as yet) to have copied the example of Tempe, but the point is that in the US system things like this can happen if enough people believe in them and can get together at the right points in time to make them happen. So, if this works for Tempe, whether or not anywhere else has copied this initiative makes no practical difference as far as local interests are concerned.

One of the other reasons why a considerable variety of experience exists in the United States is that it exhibits a very considerable variety of circumstances. For example, the large-scale growth in parts of the South and the West in recent years has given rise to the phenomenon of gated communities (which we have discussed in more detail in Chapter 3 of this book), which can be seen as a market-led application of at least some of the principles of CPTED; safety, or at least the appearance of safety, sells. What we mean by this is that this has occurred not because local planning or police professionals have demanded it but because developers have provided gated communities on a large scale and purchasers have bought into the phenomenon. There is room for argument about which is the chicken and which is the egg here, but what is difficult to argue against is the sheer scale of the activity over the past decade or so, notwithstanding the negative and socially divisive elements of some gated developments (see our discussion in Chapter 3). So, here is an example of one type of development that can be seen as taking into account at least some of the principles of planning for crime prevention which has happened without much public regulation at all; rather, it has happened essentially because developers have harnessed both a reaction to some of the adverse elements of city living and a strong marketing tool.

As noted above, and as we shall argue later, in Chapter 7, it may well be the case that the most recent phenomenon that will shape American practice in this field is the process of planning to take account of the threat of terrorist attacks, particularly in the wake of the events of 11 September 2001. In particular, we suspect that this may well galvanise areas that were at the end of the spectrum where very little was being done to take the field more seriously. At the same time, while areas are always likely to look around at what others are doing and to try to learn from those experiences, we see little sign in the United States of the 'one-size-fits-all' mentality that can be one of the biggest weaknesses of top-down systems. The trick here, we suspect, is going to be to build in protection against terrorist attacks without creating fortresses, without destroying the aesthetics of public spaces and buildings, and without eroding basic civil liberties; and achieving this delicate balance will be a challenge indeed.

Conclusions

We are dealing here with a relationship (that between place-based crime prevention and the planning system) that is still in a relatively early phase of development, and that has a long way to go before it is an accepted and understood part of everyday planning practice across the developed world. We suspect that this is even more true of the developing world, although our brief review of cases in African cities under the auspices of the UN-HABITAT Safer Cities Programme shows that this process has begun. In much of the developing world, though, planning systems themselves are in their infancy, and clearly the first stage in what we are arguing for here must in these circumstances be to get effective planning systems in place. Even then, there would undoubtedly be a distance to go before such systems would see tackling crime prevention as a major issue for them. This status (i.e. the limited extent to which planning systems see a role for themselves in addressing crime prevention) is reflected in the, as yet, quite limited literature that has specifically gone down this road. It is also reflected in the brief survey of experiences in Europe and in the United States contained in this chapter, which shows that in these areas there is a huge amount of variation in practice. Variation is not in principle a bad thing, of course, because it enables innovation to take place; and from innovation should come the opportunity to learn. In many instances, however, it is clear that very little if anything is being done to use the planning system to help with the process of crime prevention, and in these instances we would suggest that there is a need to think carefully about how this situation might be changed.

Some of this is inevitably about formal structures of governance, and we think this is really a question of finding ways of tackling these issues which suit both the machinery and the culture of governance to be found in various parts of the world. The British system, for example, which is fairly formal, quite strongly top-down, and has a key role for central government in formulating policy advice but with a great deal of local discretion about how that gets implemented, certainly would not suit everywhere, and in any event, as we have demonstrated in this chapter, there is a long way to go before it can be declared a success. In particular, the British system has formal structures in place, but it has not resolved all the outstanding issues and it has not won the battle for hearts and minds – the generals have lined up the troops for battle, but have then issued conflicting orders about the direction in which they should be marching. Thus, the British system is not a model for everywhere, but is simply one among many possible ways of proceeding. Issues of governance are really about finding appropriate ways of addressing these issues in the local context, because the essence of effective place-based crime prevention is its emphasis on specific places.

A second dimension to the process of encouraging planning systems to engage with the crime prevention agenda is around a knowledge of what works well in what circumstances. As we have argued previously (Schneider and Kitchen, 2002), while we certainly know some things about this, there is much else that we cannot say with certainty, and much also that is clouded by rhetoric or by belief rather than being driven by dispassionate analysis. Poyner (1983, p. 2) said very much the same thing in his review of the extant literature two decades previously, so it could be argued that in this sense things are not changing quickly enough. While ideas can and do move around the world at an ever more rapid rate, abetted by modern technology, we also think that it is important to recognise that cultural differences may be one of the elements which help to explain why ideas that seem to work well in one set of circumstances do not appear to transplant readily to others. We think this difficulty of transplanting particular approaches emphasises the importance of context in this field, both in the immediate and local sense of understanding how the site in question relates to its surroundings and also in the much broader sense of understanding how societies work, including their processes of governance and their cultural norms. We also think that it emphasises the importance of honest evaluation and open reporting on the success or otherwise of initiatives, both for the direct benefit of immediate participants and for the wider contribution evaluation and reporting can make to general learning about what works, what doesn't, and in what circumstances. The development of ideas in this field has not yet reached maturity; in truth, it has only just begun, and practitioners and researchers alike have an obligation to contribute to this process on a continuing basis as best they can.

A third element in this process is conceivably the most important of all, and that is in the commitments made by planners and the police both to the development of understanding of the field and to the development of effective working relationships with each other. Both of us have observed many instances of police and planners trying to work with their fellow professional opposite numbers, and both of us have seen what a large difference is made to these processes by the personal attitudes of their participants. Basically, these sorts of relationships can be made to work if people respect each other's contributions as fellow professionals, understand where the other is coming from in terms of aspirations, professional cultures and working practices, are able to agree as much as possible about shared objectives, and are prepared to listen to the points the other makes without approaching them with a closed mind. Working relationships can also be strengthened not only by a discussion of the differences that may exist (for example, a planner who is heavily influenced by new urbanist thinking about permeable layouts needs to be able to explain the benefits that are seen as flowing from them as compared with alternative approaches, and at the same time to be willing to address the elements of them that are likely to be seen as problematic from a crime prevention perspective), but also by joint visits to look at what has happened when previous projects have been implemented, including talking to people who live or work in the vicinity about their experiences. Because very few police or planning professionals are used to working with each other, as compared with their extensive experiences of working with other groups of professionals in society, we think that the training of both groups also needs to take more account of the requirements of multi-professional working and specifically of the development of police–planner relationships. This matters hugely, because more than anything else the success of attempts to embed crime prevention in planning systems and processes is likely to depend on the ability of police and planning professionals to work with each other in order to make this happen.

Fundamentally, we think that planning systems ought to be encouraged to embrace crime prevention because of the central role they play in regulating development; and it is surely both more effective and more efficient to think about crime prevention when initiating development than to have to tackle it as a retrofitting activity. Our review of the development of practice in this field suggests to us that there are five broad categories of activity where planning systems can assist with the process of crime prevention. How this operates in a particular locality will depend on local circumstances, including in particular the culture of governance, but some or all of these five elements are likely to be found in planning systems that are committed to making this kind of contribution:

1 Writing appropriate policies into plans and associated guidance documents.
2 Dealing with applications for planning permission from a series of starting points, which include the value of action at this stage that is designed to ensure that crime prevention is built into development proposals; and the plan-making activity at (1) is likely to be of particular importance in this context because it provides the foundation for the control of development.
3 Getting involved in projects which are designed through the manipulation of the physical environment to make the experience of crime in a locality both less common and less threatening. Many of these may well be carried forward via formal partnership mechanisms, be these regeneration or other kinds of partnerships.
4 Encouraging formal and unbiased monitoring, review and reporting of experience on the ground, to contribute to learning at all levels; and supporting the need for empirically based evaluations of crime prevention initiatives.
5 Given the particular role that planning systems tend to play in local public consultation/participation initiatives, ensuring that activities around crime prevention and the experience of crime are a continuing part of dialogue with planning stakeholders.

The mix of these five elements will vary according to local circumstances and according to the stage of development of planning systems themselves. As yet, it is probably true to say that there are very few planning systems across the world that are very active in all five of these areas. Nonetheless, we feel that this is a useful model for planning systems to look at if they want to try to identify the kinds of activities to engage in to integrate crime prevention fully into their ongoing activities. We also feel that it offers a means whereby progress down this road is capable of being measured, and future work looking at the development of systems could usefully take a framework of this nature as a starting point for evaluating what is being achieved in these terms.

5

Some UK police perspectives on the process of planning for crime prevention

Introduction

Chapter 4 has already demonstrated that, while urban and regional planning systems have been around in much of the developed world for many years now, the notion that these can be used effectively to address crime prevention issues and the associated idea that this means that police officers have to interface with the planning system are both much more recent. As we noted in Chapter 4, the first UK government guidance to planners that they should consult police architectural liaison officers (ALOs) in relation to development proposals is as recent as 1994 (Department of the Environment, 1994); and even then the speed of response to this new relationship among planning authorities across the country clearly varied (Williams and Wood, 2001; Kitchen 2002). So, the contribution of the police service to the process of planning for crime prevention via the planning service (as distinct from all the other crime prevention activities in which police forces have a leading role) is a relatively recent arrival on the planning stage.

As well as being a recent development, this is also an innovation which has received very little attention in the academic literature. So, for example, Cozens et al. (2004), in reviewing how the police's Secured by Design scheme has contributed to residential new-build in Britain, summarise the available research by suggesting that although in the round SBD appears to work, we do not know which elements of it are the most effective, and in particular we know very little about what police architectural liaison officers actually do when applying the scheme to an individual project. What we are trying to do in this chapter, therefore, is to understand a little more about the operational experiences of police specialists who liaise with planning systems over development issues. We do this by concentrating on two case study officers; we have kept the number down in what is (at any rate in the academic literature of the field) to the best of our knowledge a first attempt at this task so that we can present these experiences in sufficient detail. Clearly, a useful research task for the future is to compare and contrast these UK experiences with those in other countries.

Our approach to this task is an empirical one: we have worked with the officers in question over a period of time and in a variety of ways, including encouraging them to write for us about their experiences of working with planners and the planning system, and this chapter records and compares their perceptions of these experiences. We make no claims to representativeness in our choice of case study officers (which we hardly could in any event when working with only two officers), other than in the most general sense that these officers are doing a job that is also done by many other officers in other parts of the United Kingdom. We have chosen officers who we know do have opinions about these matters and about the processes of working with planners; so in a sense we are aware that we have chosen two of the 'movers and shakers' in the ALO community, rather than people who would not see themselves in these terms. In both cases the officers in question have agreed that the text that follows is an appropriate reflection of their own working experiences.

Before we present our material on the operational experiences of our two ALOs, we describe and discuss the operating contexts within which they work, and we also present some recent research data on ALO–planner relationships. After looking in detail at our two cases, we offer some reflective conclusions which might be helpful in the development of the ALO role in future. As noted above, we are conscious that, to the best of our knowledge, nothing like this has been attempted in the literature before, and so we hope that, as well as being of value in its own right in throwing some light on this work, it will encourage others to write about these experiences, so that our understanding of how this relatively new police function works and relates to planning systems can be improved.

The Police Architectural Liaison Service in Britain

At the time of writing, there are 43 police forces (and police authorities) in England and Wales, each of which has an architectural liaison service or equivalent. Their operational basis is the national police Secured by Design scheme (Schneider and Kitchen, 2002, pp. 220–231; Colquhoun, 2004, pp. 202–209), which would be readily recognised internationally as a CPTED-based package (see Chapter 2), although recently it has been re-presented to make it consistent with the government's national good practice guidance (Office of the Deputy Prime Minister and the Home Office, 2004). In our opinion, this diluted version is less distinctive than it was, less clearly based on the accumulated operational experiences of ALOs, and less helpful as a consequence as a source of advice about planning for crime prevention. We believe that this change is a mistake, and that SBD should revert to what ought to be the strength of its brand, which is its grounding in the operational experiences of ALOs.

In terms of ALOs working with local planning authorities on development proposals that constitute applications for planning permission or on policies in development plans, there are a huge variety of operational circumstances to be found. There are approximately 400 local planning authorities in England

and Wales, and so, on average, each force ALO team has to work with about nine or ten planning authorities. But around this average there are large differences. For example, the Metropolitan Police have to work with 32 London boroughs (excluding the Corporation of the City of London), whereas the Bedfordshire Police have to work with only four district councils. Similarly, there are different approaches to how ALO teams are structured, so that in some instances an ALO team works as a single team with all its local planning authorities, whereas in other instances individual ALOs work with individual local planning authorities on a continuous basis, sometimes even having a desk and spending considerable time during each working week in the offices of the local planning authority. This latter model seems to be growing in importance; for example, at the time of writing, the Metropolitan Police are strengthening their ALO service and working towards having identified ALOs allocated to work with each of the 32 London boroughs. Finally, there is sometimes also a degree of functional specialisation within ALO teams. For example, the Bradford ALO team has an officer who specialises in the particular problems associated with school buildings, which results in officers in the other four districts covered by the West Yorkshire Police seeking his advice from time to time about problems of this nature.

It is probably fair to say that, when looked at in the context of all the things that a modern police force does, the ALO service is small and relatively new, and its activities are rather different from many other police tasks. These characteristics raise questions about how it is seen within the police service, for example in terms of personal career development, and how it fits into a police culture where the glamorous and high-profile activities tend to involve 'catching the bad guys' rather than doing the kind of things that ALOs do. We would also suggest that senior managements in police forces have not always fully understood the potential of ALO work to contribute both to human happiness and to the minimisation of opportunities to commit crime, perhaps partly because the performance measures that apply to the police service do not tend to emphasise factors such as these; one might compare, for example, the sizeable resources often put into a team established to tackle a major crime incident with the small-scale resources put into the police contribution to the design of a housing estate so as to reduce the opportunity for crime throughout its life, and reflect on the costs (in terms of staff resources) and the benefits (in terms of the contribution to human happiness) of each. Indeed, one might even factor into this equation the benefits of contemporary ALO work in terms of the future saving of police resources as a result of designs which generate little crime, since there is a relationship between current design decisions and the future costs of policing (Knowles, 2003b). There is also an issue around how police officers used to exercising a considerable degree of discretion in operational roles with which they are familiar can develop both the knowledge and the confidence to behave in similar ways in a field with which they are not familiar when they move into ALO roles, which may well include challenging planners on matters where they would probably expect those planners to have quite a high level of expertise. That said, we are aware of several experienced ALOs who do exercise considerable discretion regularly and who seem to relish the degree of independence of operation they have created; and so it is clear that this transition can be made. These points all suggest that there are some important questions to be asked about how the ALO service fits within the police service as a whole, not just in terms of formal structures but also by reference to issues such as culture, training, career paths and the location of management responsibility. It is probably not too fanciful to suggest that the ALO service is still regarded in some police forces at least as something of a 'Cinderella' service.

There are also, at the time of writing, some important larger-scale issues under consideration which have the potential to affect the ALO service significantly. One of these is the process known as 'civilianisation' (the use of staff from outside the police service to undertake tasks previously seen as police tasks). Not all ALOs are serving police officers (although our two case study officers are), and the Greater Manchester force (for example) has been making a virtue out of employing what it sees as people with appropriate professional backgrounds in this role. One of the important issues raised by the use of 'civilian professionals' in the ALO role, however, is the question of how their work relates to the range of police experience with crime prevention, not least because for many of the other participants in the development process the reason why they are being encouraged to take seriously the views of ALOs is precisely because these are seen as being drawn from that background of police experience. A second large-scale issue is the possibility of the reorganisation of the structure of the police service into a smaller number of larger forces, which would clearly have implications *inter alia* for the operation of the ALO service. And a third (and possibly related) issue is the idea that the ALO service might be incorporated into a single national crime prevention service, with obvious issues around how a nationally run service would relate to an activity which is essentially about what happens on specific sites or in specific localities. These broader issues are being debated at the time that this chapter is being written, and as a consequence they form part of the context for the specific case studies that follow alongside the material above that has introduced the current structure of the ALO service.

Working relationships between ALOs and planners

There is some recent evidence about the development of working relationships between ALOs and planners, and we review this evidence here because it helps to provide a context for the following presentation of the work of our two case study officers. This study (Morton and Kitchen, 2005) concentrates on three issues:

- attitudes to the contents of the government's guidance about planning for crime prevention in *Safer Places* (Office of the Deputy Prime Minister and the Home Office, 2004);
- experiences of the development control process; and
- experiences of development plan-making activities.

Table 5.1 Working relationships between planners and police architectural liaison officers

Question	Percentage of positive answers in sample	
	Police ALOs	Planners
1 Is it important for the police to be involved in the preparation of local planning policy?	98	84
2 Have ALOs actually been involved in the preparation of local planning policy?	58	–
3 Are the police adequately trained and qualified to input into the preparation of local planning policy?	56	61
4 Are the current policies in development plans adequate in terms of planning for crime prevention?	28	57
5 Do you have regular meetings with your opposite number(s) to discuss planning applications?	47	30
6 Are ALO comments on applications given considerable weight by planning officers?	60	65
7 Is the ALO fully integrated into the overall planning process?	67	37

Source: Morton and Kitchen (2005).

Note: The study results come from a sample of responses from 59% of police forces in England and 36% of the local planning authorities in the areas of the police forces that responded to the survey, undertaken in late 2004/early 2005.

We do not cover the first of these points here, but the main points emerging from this study in respect of the second and the third of these items are summarised in Table 5.1. It would be fair to say that the data in Table 5.1 show a working relationship that is still in the process of developing. There are some positive elements in the responses – notably the finding that 65 per cent of planners and 60 per cent of police ALOs think that ALO comments on planning applications are given considerable weight by planning officers. But there are also some quite negative elements – notably the large gap between the desirability of police involvement in the preparation of planning policy and the reality of experience up to that point, and also the finding that only just over half of police respondents think that they are adequately trained for this task. There are also some significant differences between the responses of police ALOs and planners: ALOs are only half as satisfied as planners with the current policies in development plans about planning for crime prevention, planners do not seem to think that they meet as regularly with ALOs as their opposite numbers do, and ALOs are far more likely than planners to see themselves as being fully integrated into the planning process. At the very least, these areas of difficulty and of difference represent an agenda that needs to be explored as part of the development of working relationships between police ALOs and planners in England.

In summary, then, crime prevention has been formally embedded into the English planning system, as we have shown in Chapter 4, but some of the key tensions about what planners and police ALOs should be seeking to agree with developers and their agents in negotiations over development proposals remain unresolved. In addition, there is a distance still to be travelled in terms of the development of working relationships between planners and police ALOs before it could really be said that good working relations are being turned into an effective operational reality across the country. Some of this is almost certainly about the development of something that is relatively new: planners have not generally been used to working alongside police professionals, as compared (say) with their long practice at working with other development professionals, and especially those who act as agents for developers; and thus they need to learn the skills of doing this effectively. Similarly, police ALOs need to understand and to learn how to work within the planning process. In particular, the evidence seems to suggest that ALOs are more comfortable with and more experienced at working on individual cases in the context of the development control process rather than at framing policies in development plans that then provide both the basis for future development control work and the guidance to developers about what they should be doing. We would suggest that this is a balance that needs to change in favour of a greater commitment to plan-making activities, and we discuss this point in more detail below.

The above comments have important implications for the training of both planners and police ALOs, and it seems from Table 5.1 that many ALOs do recognise problems of this nature. But some of the development that needs to occur is surely about what the system is actually trying to achieve, and it is not entirely surprising that since national policy guidance has not resolved all of this (for example, as we have shown in Chapter 4, the differences of view about permeable layouts remain), then difficulties will be experienced at the local level as well. Two other findings illustrate this very well. The first is that both police ALOs and planners were asked (just under a year after it had been published) whether they had actually read the new national policy advice in *Safer Places*; 86 per cent of ALOs responded positively, but only 38 per cent of planners did likewise. This is a large and troubling difference. It is clearly problematic in terms of the ability of the national policy advice to influence the thinking and behaviour of planners if only just over one in three of them had read it. Indeed, it probably suggests that, at any rate as far as the planning community is concerned, the publication of advice by itself is not enough; if the government wants that advice to be taken seriously by planners, then it must put more effort into the dissemination process, rather than assuming that planners will automatically read and act on these words. The other significant finding in this context is that 51 per cent of police ALOs said that the design of housing layouts usually fell short of their advice, which suggests that in a large number of cases they feel the need to intervene to try to get such submissions for planning permission changed. It could be argued that this is very late in the day to intervene to seek changes, and that what would be evidence of a successful process would be a much smaller level of dissatisfaction with submitted applications, either because police advice had been sought beforehand or because developers and their agents had taken more notice of the published guidance. Indeed, one of the primary purposes of publishing guidance is that it should encourage developers to consider these matters for themselves before planning applications are submitted, so that there is less need for intervention at that stage. This is the argument noted above for more effective ALO engagement with the development plan-making process, since it is via development plans that the basic policies that developers are expected to take into account get expressed. So, there is clearly still a long way to go before it could be said that the system is working satisfactorily.

Stephen Town – ALO, Bradford

Stephen has been the ALO working specifically in Bradford since 2000, having previously done a lot of ALO work as a crime prevention officer within the West Yorkshire police force from 1995 onwards. This longevity of responsibility gives him a range of perspectives on the operation of the planning process (and the attitudes and behaviour of individual planners in this context) as well as the experience of seeing through to completion and then being able to assess reactions to projects that have quite a long timescale. He is an example of a serving police officer who was injured in the line of duty and who then chose to move into crime prevention and then ALO work, but who through experience and perception has seen for himself many things about the relationships between built form and the opportunity for crime and has tried to learn from these experiences in a variety of ways. He talks in particular about his 'Oscar Newman moment' as part of his practice experience – a recognition in respect of a particular case in Bradford (the difficulties being experienced by the Mallard Court development; see Figure 5.1) of the importance of defensible space.

Bradford is one of the cities in the West Yorkshire conurbation, and the local authority area (the Metropolitan District of Bradford) runs from very typical inner-city areas reflecting the city's nineteenth-century industrialisation in the woollen industry to very attractive suburban residential areas in the foothills of the Pennines and the Yorkshire Dales. Bradford's social mix includes one of England's larger ethnic minority communities, mainly comprising people who originate from the Indian subcontinent. The consequence of all of this is that Bradford presents a range of development situations, including refurbishment projects in relation to housing from various periods as well as new-build; but although there are local new-build pressures in parts of Bradford, this is not the part of the country or the region where they tend to be at their most intense. There are five Metropolitan Districts in West Yorkshire (the area covered by

5.1 Mallard Court, Bradford.

a *(top) Relatively modern development which has been boarded up and covered in graffiti, undoubtedly in substantial part because it is fronted by large areas of communal space which are easy to access and very poorly overlooked; they feel like no one's responsibility.*

b *(bottom) Space laid out for car parking flowing immediately into the footpath system, thereby facilitating access to the rear of adjacent properties. The sense that no one owns this space is illustrated by the fact that it has become a dumping ground, in this case for an unwanted sofa.*

5.1   Mallard Court, Bradford (continued).

c   *A vivid illustration of one of the problems at Mallard Court, with a hole punched in the hedge which facilitates intrusion from the adjacent street.*

d   *What many people would regard as a dangerous space, with overgrown landscaping, poor lighting and very little effective overlooking.*

the West Yorkshire Police), and ALOs work individually in three of the districts, with the Force ALO covering the other two districts that lack an ALO. As noted above, there is also an element of functional specialisation here; the example has already been given of one of Stephen's colleagues who specialises in school buildings and whose specialist knowledge is used by other ALOs. In this context, Stephen has played an important external role on behalf both of the force and of his broader region in matters such as responding to consultations on the draft of the government's publication *Safer Places.* Stephen's external profile within the ALO community at large is quite high, partly as a consequence of activities of this nature but partly also because on an individual level he has committed himself to learning and to networking. One very significant output from this latter suite of activities has been his joint work with the University of Salford, carried out with the help of European Union funding, on general guidance for the design of residential areas from a crime prevention perspective (Town *et al.*, 2003).

A major project with which Stephen has been particularly associated, and which has received considerable national as well as local attention (see Office of the Deputy Prime Minister and the Home Office, 2004, pp. 58 and 59; Colquhoun, 2004, pp. 210–212), has been the regeneration of the Royds Estate. Figure 5.2 contains a set of photographs illustrating some of the main projects in the regeneration of the Royds Estate. The Royds Estate by the mid-1990s was a run-down area of local authority housing experiencing major

5.2 The eight photographs in this figure show a selection of the works undertaken to help make the Royds Estate a safer place, with, in particular, strong boundary treatments, the clear delineation of spaces, and the creation of a stronger sense of place.

Reproduced by permission of West Yorkshire Police.

5.2 continued

5.2 continued

5.2 continued

5.2 continued

physical and social problems and very high levels of crime; the burglary rate in 1995, at 138 forced entries per 1,000 houses, was seven times the then current national average (Office of the Deputy Prime Minister and the Home Office, 2004, p. 58). The approach adopted, after an intensive programme of consultation with local residents, was to identify the main physical contributors to this high burglary rate and to tackle them. So, private space was created and defined with metal railings and gates where previously it was not clear who owned or was responsible for that space; rear alleys, garage courts and unused public open space behind buildings were removed, with the space being incorporated into rear gardens; and several segregated footpath connections away from the road network which created a multiplicity of access and egress points were closed. New development in the area aimed to create small and identifiable communities, to promote social cohesion and to reinforce neighbourliness, and to assist with the ready identification of strangers. The principles of Secured by Design as they stood at the time were applied to the existing housing stock, typically through the provision of in-curtilage parking where possible, boundary treatments which clearly delineate public and private space, and new windows and doors with high security specifications. The new uses that were introduced to the area were those that emerged from resident consultation as being uses that were both needed and wanted (such as, for example, a new local health centre; see Figure 5.3), and the opportunity was taken to locate these uses on what was formerly anonymous space.

5.3 New local health centre, Royds Estate, Bradford

a and **b** *Two views of the new local health centre on the Royds Estate. Crime prevention features include the relatively small windows, the roofs (which are difficult to access) and the perimeter fencing supported by landscaping. Readers will form their own views about the architecture of the building, but we would argue that these features do not produce a building that looks like either a fortress or an eyesore.*

The outcome of this package of measures has been dramatic:

> As well as the clear environmental improvements, the programme had social impacts creating employment for young people and improving access to the job market for residents by providing experience and training. It also provided the first use of performance-related standards for door and window design based on attack resistance.
>
> The creation of defensible space and the clear definition and robust separation of private and public space provides residents, among other advantages, with the confidence to challenge strangers and, if necessary, call the police.
>
> The ALO reports that there has not been a single forcible entry on any of the refurbished properties. Including the properties in the Royds regeneration area that have not been refurbished, the last 5 years have seen a fall of 69% in dwelling burglary and 58% in all burglary.
>
> (ibid., p. 59)

The Royds project has been important not just in its own right – and the outcome reported above is surely an impressive one in terms of the improved quality of life for the residents of the Royds Estate that it has brought about – but also, in Stephen's view, in establishing the credibility of the police contribution to the planning and development process both in the eyes of Bradford's planners and with senior officers in the West Yorkshire Police. He reports the fact that in his early days as an ALO he did come across views among some of Bradford's planners to the effect that the planning process and crime prevention had little relationship with each other, that their urban design preferences should be unsullied by crime prevention considerations, and that the police could not be expected to add very much to an activity as sophisticated as planning (what he reports one planning officer describing as 'dancing to Plod's tune'). We suspect that this range of attitudes, alongside views from other planners that were much more positive, was not uncommon within the planning community at that time. As one of us has reported elsewhere (Kitchen, 2002), the British planning community was not especially quick to respond to the new challenges being set by the government in respect of its potential contribution to crime prevention, and it was also not always very receptive to questions from this direction that challenged its urban design presumptions and preferences. Stephen has written separately about the urban design preferences of planners and their tendency to see these as the overriding issues (Town and O'Toole, 2005). We think this situation has improved in recent years, but the available evidence suggests that it is still far from ideal (Kitchen, 2005; Morton and Kitchen, 2005). Thus, Stephen's report that he came across a range of views among planners, some of which were much more unhelpful than others, probably mirrors the experiences of many other ALOs. Given this, it is easy to see why a successful project such as the Royds would have been helpful in establishing the credibility of an ALO and of what he had to offer among a group of planners that included several that needed to be convinced both about the role that planning could play in crime prevention and about the value of a police contribution in this context.

The process of interaction between Stephen Town, as the Bradford ALO, and Bradford's planners does appear to have improved over the years, however, even if at times this has obviously been a bumpy ride. We can examine the consequences of this in two ways. One of these involves looking at projects in Bradford on the ground to see where relatively modern developments undertaken via planning processes with no police input of this kind have experienced subsequent difficulties in terms of crime and antisocial behaviour. The other is to look at the development of planning policy, because Stephen Town has understood the importance of the message about the need to have appropriate development plan policies in place in a plan-led system (see Chapter 4) and has worked with his planning colleagues to produce an example of this in Bradford which we think represents contemporary best practice.

One of Stephen's primary concerns has been the extent to which development carried out in the relatively recent past has created opportunities for crime. The example of Mallard Court (Figure 5.1) has already been cited. This is an instance where a relatively modern development has been ruined by the problems arising from the lack of any effective stewardship of communal space – we use the concept of 'stewardship' here to include ownership, control, supervision and influence – and by the lack of effective boundary definition. When Stephen took us to look at this site we were approached by residents from the neighbouring estate (of rather older housing, which had itself at one point in time been regarded as being problematic), who said that in their opinion the properties on the Mallard Court site should be demolished because they were dragging down their estate! Another site we went with Stephen to look at was Gondal Court (see Figure 5.4), which illustrates the difficulties that can arise from through-access arrangements which inevitably bring people into the locality who are there because they are walking through

5.4 The problems of through access: Gondal Court, Bradford. These two pictures show a heavily vandalised public building (a children's nursery) which has become in effect a public liability, undoubtedly assisted by the ready through access past the site.

5.5 Ready access to the rear of properties: Gondal Court, Bradford. The rear alley problem at Gondal Court is very obvious from this picture, which shows how it offers ready access to the rear of the adjacent properties.

it rather than needing to be in it; and who also have a variety of possible escape routes if their intentions are criminal. Gondal Court also illustrates a very common problem with much modern development, which is the provision of rear access that undoubtedly facilitates intrusion, as local residents have experienced (see Figure 5.5). The solution to a problem of this nature that occurred to us on-site seems to be to incorporate that alley into the rear gardens of the houses and, if this creates a problem with domestic and garden refuse, to design a refuse store at the front of the house. If done carefully, this need not become an urban design problem. These are two cases which arise from relatively recent developments; arguably, crime was designed into them rather than out of them. They also represent a valuable learning opportunity for planners and others, and Stephen reports the benefits of discussing these issues with planners not as theoretical issues of urban design but as practical problems best understood on the site.

On the positive side, we asked Stephen to take us to a relatively recent residential development where there had been a significant ALO input and which seemed to him to work reasonably well, and he took us to Javelin Close. This is a modern mid-market, mainly private development of just over 100 houses and apartments which achieves a gross density of 36 dwellings per hectare, where boundary treatments are strong and clear, the definition of public and private spaces is unambiguous, and where considerable care has gone into the location of what can be a difficult use, which is a children's play space. Figure 5.6 shows two views of the Javelin Close development.

5.6 *Javelin Close, Bradford.*

a (top) General view of the housing. It is very noticeable that even at this kind of density it is possible to achieve front drives to houses which are long enough to provide off-road car parking.

b (bottom) The careful location of the children's play space, with its very well overlooked short access path from one of the estate's main roads.

Clearly, readers will have their own views about the design of a residential area such as this, but what was clear on-site was that it had proved popular in the marketplace and that there were no visible signs of antisocial behaviour (such as graffiti or vandalism) or of crime problems such as burglary or break-ins to cars. Access to the development is on a restricted basis, with no through-routes for vehicles (the residential streets are all culs-de-sac) and very few footpaths other than those along the streets. The impression the development gives on walking through it is that this is a private space that is cared for by its residents, and the evidence of children playing in the streets during our visit supports this perception. The crime record appears to confirm the view that this is a safe place with little experience of crime, because very little crime has been reported.

The Crime Pattern Analysis for the 12 months from 12 December 2004 to 12 December 2005 shows the five recorded crimes for the area of the development were as follows:

- 'burglary other' – 3 (these are thefts from wooden garden sheds located near a footpath);
- 'taken without the owner's consent' – 1 (a car was stolen and then dumped);
- 'damage to a building' – 1 (this appears to be part of a domestic dispute).

So, this represents a very low level of crime when looked at in comparison to the situation in Bradford as a whole, and in particular it is noticeable that there are no instances here of houses being broken into. The thefts from garden sheds may be environmentally related in the sense that these are located near a footpath, but in most instances these will be on a small scale and may reflect a low level of security in the treatment of garden shed doors or windows rather than anything else. Overall, then, this would seem to suggest that the advice of the ALO in this instance has proved beneficial in creating for the residents of Javelin Close a living environment where the experience of crime is a minor one.

The process of working on appropriate planning policy documentation for Bradford on planning for crime prevention started in May 2000, and resulted by late 2005 in a policy which is now part of the adopted development plan for Bradford (Unitary Development Plan Policy D4, which is reproduced as Box 5.1), and a draft of an associated supplementary planning document which provides more detailed guidance. Most of the work done during this period was on the latter document, which is on a much larger scale than a single development plan policy. We asked Stephen to produce a chronicle for us of his work on these documents, and the main elements of this are summarised below. It shows that the process could only be described as stop–start, and that it was heavily influenced by the presence (or absence) of supportive members of staff:

- *May 2000* – work on the supplementary planning document started in partnership with a supportive member of staff from Planning.

Box 5.1 The Bradford UDP policy on planning for crime prevention

Crime prevention through improved design

Crime and the fear of crime affect the way people use and enjoy the places where they live, work and use for recreation. The design of the built environment can play a very significant part in reducing crime and disorder and cutting down the fear of crime.

Section 17 of the Crime and Disorder Act 1998 makes it a duty for a local authority to exercise its various functions with due regard to the likely effect of the exercise of those functions, and the need to do all that it reasonably can to prevent crime and disorder in its area.

Safety and tackling the fear of crime is a priority for the Council and is a key element in Bradford's Vision 2020. A Crime and Disorder Reduction Strategy which seeks to tackle the key crime and disorder problems facing communities in the District has been produced by the Bradford Crime and Disorder Reduction Partnership, which involves the Council, police and other key bodies. One of the key aims of the strategy is to create a safe environment for all those living, working, shopping, playing and investing in the District. The strategy identifies six key priorities for action. Planning has an important role to play in furthering the aims of the Strategy. For example, tackling house and commercial burglary and tackling the fear of crime and improving the quality of life for all communities.

Successful crime prevention often depends on a wide range of measures in which the planning process can assist in 'designing out crime' at the outset of the design process. Revised PPG12 draws attention to the need to include measures for crime prevention in the social considerations of a development plan (para. 4.14), emphasising the role of better urban design. Circular 5/94, 'Planning Out Crime', states that crime prevention is capable of being a material consideration in determining planning applications and sets out advice on the planning considerations relating to crime prevention. It advises that development plans should establish principles for the design, layout and landscaping of new development which aim to make crime more difficult to commit, increase the risk of detection and provide people with a safer, more secure environment. However, any solution should remain sensitive to local circumstances and there should be a balanced approach to design which attempts to reconcile the visual quality of a development with the needs of crime prevention. Developments can be made more secure without resorting to razor wire, grilles, bars, unsightly types of fencing and other visually intrusive security measures, if safety and security are considered at an early stage of the design process.

Policy D4: Development proposals should be designed to ensure a safe and secure environment and reduce the opportunities for crime

Developers will need to ensure that crime prevention is considered as an integral part of the initial design of any development and not as an afterthought. Development should incorporate the principles of 'Secured by Design'. In particular, they will need to demonstrate how their development proposal has addressed the following issues, with regard to designing out crime:

- Natural surveillance of public and semi-private spaces, in particular entrances to a development, paths, play spaces, open spaces and car parks.
- Defensible space and the clear definition, differentiation and robust separation of public, private and semi-private space, so that all spaces are clearly defined and adequately protected in terms of their use and ownership.
- Lighting of the development, in particular streets and paths.
- Design and layout of pedestrian, cycle and vehicular routes into and within the site, including how these integrate with existing patterns.
- Landscaping and planting (in particular, hiding places and dark or secluded areas should not be created).

The design and layout of access opportunities is of fundamental importance to designing out crime and needs careful consideration to avoid the creation of opportunities for crime. The 'Places Streets and Movement: A Companion Guide to Design Bulletin 32 − Residential Roads and Footpaths' provides advice on security issues in relation to the design of routes and connections. It emphasises that, while clear and direct routes through an area for all forms of movement are desirable, they should not undermine the 'defensible space' of particular neighbourhoods.

Developers should, at the earliest stage, seek advice from the Bradford area Police Architectural Liaison Officer on designing out crime. A guide is currently being prepared by West Yorkshire Police in partnership with West Yorkshire Planning Authorities setting out detailed advice on designing out crime, to assist developers.

Source: Stephen Town, Bradford ALO.

- *May 2001* − considerable progress had been made with the guidance document, but the supportive member of Planning staff left and no replacement support was forthcoming for two years.
- *April 2003* − the ALO was successful in a bid for funding to the Neighbourhood Renewal Fund to enable a senior member of Planning

staff to be seconded to work with the police to complete the guidance document.

- *September 2003* – a draft joint document was completed.
- *December 2003* – a range of responses to the draft had been made by various arms of Planning, which illustrated a clear difference between a negative response from policy staff and a more supportive view from development control staff. As a consequence, a meeting was held at police headquarters involving around 20 members of planning staff to agree what was going to be done to move the document forward, and it was agreed that a sub-group from Planning would work with Stephen to agree a common line on it.
- *May 2004* – the sub-group reached agreement on the text, after examining it line by line.
- *January 2005* – after further internal delays, during which the difficulties with policy staff resurfaced, the new Head of the Planning Service reviewed the position and agreed about the importance of finalising the guidance document as a Supplementary Planning Document.
- *October 2005* – Unitary Development Plan Policy D4 was adopted as part of the updated Unitary Development Plan for Bradford, and the associated Supplementary Planning Document on planning for crime prevention in Bradford agreed as a basis for public consultation, which was scheduled to begin in January 2006.
- *First half of 2006* – the public consultation process was delayed as internal disagreements within the planning service resurfaced in the wake of the departure of its head.

This is clearly the story of a process which has experienced some difficulties, and it is possible to see at least two places in this narrative where it would have been easy to give up in the absence of a degree of tenacity. Our experience is that work on crafting policy can often be like this: the process of getting everyone who needs to agree to do so is often far from straightforward, and similarly there is no guarantee that difficulties thought to have been resolved will not resurface if the opportunity presents itself. It may well be that this helps to explain Stephen's observation that the ALO community has not proved itself to be very effective at assembling planning policy, and that it also helps to explain why ALOs often seem to be more comfortable working on individual development cases than on broad policies. In particular, if ALOs lack confidence and knowledge, this seems much more likely to be a problem when it comes to a process of crafting policy such as that described above than it would be when dealing with an individual case as a one-off.

The Bradford documentation can also be compared with similar planning policy documents from other localities about planning for crime prevention, including those that have gained the highest profile in England in recent years. Probably the most quoted example of this kind is the Dudley Supplementary Planning Guidance (Dudley Metropolitan Borough Council, 2002). As compared with Stephen Town's work in Bradford, the Dudley document has involved a substantial degree of compromise of some of the basic principles of the Secured by Design scheme in order to get it accepted. For example, it argues that 'Streets and spaces should be highly connected, well-overlooked and busy' (ibid., p. 16), and justifies this stance as follows:

> A connected network of streets contributes to personal safety and security of properties by encouraging pedestrian activity which helps to provide natural surveillance and a degree of self-policing. The degree of connectivity in a new development is often the key to its success. Areas that are well connected to other areas increase the opportunity and choice of users to socially interact, which assists in the development of neighbourhood identity and affinity.
>
> (ibid.)

In so far as we have been able to understand the justification for a statement such as this in a document of this nature, it appears to be that this is what the planners wanted to see from an urban design perspective, and the ALO negotiating this particular document was willing to accept it as the price for getting the document agreed and as a means of raising the profile of his work. But the price paid for this compromise in terms of policy consistency and support from the available research (Kitchen, 2005) is a high one. In its essence, the above quotation reflects the new urbanist concern to achieve permeability that we have discussed in Chapter 3, rather than SBD's concern to restrict unnecessary through-movement. Nevertheless, the Dudley document in turn was instrumental in the later appearance of a Supplementary Planning Guidance document agreed between the Northamptonshire planning authorities and the Northamptonshire Police (Northamptonshire Planning Authorities and Northamptonshire Police, 2004), which openly acknowledges the Dudley parentage and which reproduces this particular stance (ibid., p. 8). So, there is clearly some evidence from these two examples of police forces which have struggled to apply their own SBD scheme (or, at any rate, SBD as it was before the appearance of *Safer Places*) in planning policy documents.

The Bradford documentation does not take this stance at all, but instead sticks with the basic principle of limiting access opportunities to the minimum necessary. It is possible, however, that some of Bradford's planners may well have been influenced by the fact that the high-profile examples from other authorities were of this nature. In this sense the Bradford documentation can be seen as a clear alternative to the Dudley and the Northamptonshire examples, rather than as something following in their footsteps; and as a set, these examples illustrate the differential willingness of ALOs to compromise basic CPTED principles in the face of planners heavily influenced by new urbanist thinking about access and movement (see, for example, Rudlin and Falk, 1999). We believe that the Bradford guidance is much more likely in the long run to serve its citizens well than will the Dudley and the Northamptonshire guidance, because we believe that the research evidence about the effect of permeability on neighbourhood crime rates is clear. This is effectively summarised in a review of the evidence about which elements of CPTED appear to work by Taylor (2002) as follows:

Neighbourhood permeability is a case in point. I pick this case because it is one of the community-level design features most reliably linked to crime rates, and the connections operate consistently in the same direction across studies: more permeability, more crime. Several studies across several decades link neighbourhood property crime rates with permeability versus inaccessibility of neighbourhood layout. Neighbourhoods with smaller streets or more one-way streets or fewer entrance streets or with more turnings have lower property crime rates.

(ibid., p. 419)

Faced with this, it seems extraordinary that two documents on planning for crime prevention endorsed by their local police forces can take the views that the Dudley and Northamptonshire examples do, since on this matter at least they are clearly out of step with the available research, whereas the Bradford documentation is more closely in tune with the broad thrust of that research. But what these exchanges also illustrate is the variable willingness of ALOs to compromise on basic principles, with in some instances the process of reaching agreement appearing to be more important than the content of what has been agreed. Stephen Town's willingness to stick to what he believes is right has clearly been an important element in the tenacity needed to steer the Bradford planning policy documentation to the position reached at the end of 2005, and in this we believe that his experience offers valuable lessons to other ALOs embarking down the road of working with their planners on the preparation of planning policy.

Peter Knowles – ALO, Bedfordshire

Peter Knowles has been the ALO in Bedfordshire since the mid-1990s, having moved into this role from other duties in the force when the opportunity presented itself to do so. As such, he has to deal with four district councils as local planning authorities, plus potentially a fifth in Bedfordshire County Council, although in practice its role in the development control process is so limited that he has very little contact with the county council. Bedfordshire is one of the counties in the area around London (the southernmost part of the county is around 30 miles (50 kilometres) north of London) that has experienced large-scale development pressures in recent years, and will continue to do so as part of the government's drive to distribute the region's expected population growth. So, he has considerable experience both of public reactions to relatively recent development and of the policing issues that arise therein, and also of dealing with development proposals, developers and their agents, and planners in the four district councils.

It would probably be fair to say that Peter is one of the more outspoken of the ALOs working today in England, both nationally in terms of what he feels about policy developments and locally in terms of the operation of the planning process in Bedfordshire at both levels, albeit with the very strong support of his own line manager. We shall discuss below his involvement in national policy issues, but we focus first on the development of working relationships between the Bedfordshire Police ALO service and the Bedfordshire local planning authorities.

Peter describes this relationship, in taking a broad overview of it, as being very variable, from in one instance being nearly at breakdown to in another instance working much better and producing positive outcomes as a result. One characteristic of the process in Bedfordshire, which we are not aware of happening on any scale anywhere else, is that the Bedfordshire ALO service has been willing on matters that it regards as being important both to talk to local councillors about areas of major disagreement with planners and to make use of the local media to publicise issues of concern. In the former instance, that has meant that planners who have written reports about planning applications for their planning committees, reports that in their view have recorded police views (but in the ALO's opinion have taken insufficient notice of them), have found that when their reports have been discussed at com-mittee, some members of that committee had already received a separate police briefing about the issue. This has clearly been seen as problematic by some of the planners in question, because they have regarded it as a challenge to what they see as officer–officer working relationships; although it seems to us, looking at this practice from the outside, that it is a legitimate part of the democratic process, if used sparingly in relation to important issues that have a proper place on the public agenda where planning and police views cannot be reconciled. Nevertheless, it seems that different attitudes to this practice contributed to the reported difficulties in working relationships between two of the Bedfordshire local planning authorities (in particular) and the ALO service.

This may be one distinctive, and locally controversial, aspect of practice in Bedfordshire, although the vast majority of cases were not handled in this manner but instead involved a regular pattern of liaison between the ALO service, planners and (sometimes) developers and their agents without involving elected members. What became clear from this experience was the need to have at least a common and agreed series of starting points for discussions of this nature, rather than having to start afresh each time, which in turn needed to be embedded formally in the planning system if they were to have maximum impact. The agreed way forward, therefore, was for the local planning authorities and the police together with their partners to get together in the form of the Bedfordshire Community Safety Working Group, and to commission a document which was capable of being adopted by the local planning authorities as a Supplementary Planning Document (that is, it would be formally tied to the development plan) to give guidance to developers about the expectations of the local planning authorities and the police in the field of planning for crime prevention. The commission to draft the document was given to the same consultants who had worked on the draft of *Safer Places* for the Office of the Deputy Prime Minister (ODPM) and the Home Office (Llewellyn Davies), and the document itself appeared as a draft for consultation purposes in May 2005 (Llewellyn Davies, 2005). After a general introduction about the field of planning for crime prevention, there are three elements of this document that are of particular interest for the purposes of this present book:

- a series of protocols about design principles;
- a protocol about the consultation process;
- some case studies which utilise Bedfordshire development sites.

This chapter looks at the first two of these elements in some detail.

The design protocols cover the following ground:

- dwelling position;
- permeability;
- parking;
- commercial and non-residential development;
- closed-circuit TV (CCTV)

The major points made in each of these protocols are summarised in Box 5.2.

Bearing in mind the controversial nature of the subject matter, perhaps the most noteworthy element of the protocols is the explicit treatment of the subject of permeability, where the text recognises both the intrinsic need for connectivity and the desire not to see safety or amenity compromised by that provision. There is clearly an element of compromise in what has been written here (and it is not too difficult to imagine the difficulties involved in reaching this level of agreement!), but the critical point to note is that, to an extent at least, these two elements do need to be brought together, because new residential development needs both connectivity and safety. So, maybe the Bedfordshire example can be seen as one attempt to explore this balance (ibid., pp. 10–13).

The sixth protocol in the draft Bedfordshire document is about process. Part of this commits the local planning authorities in their work on development plans to incorporate appropriate polices on planning for crime prevention, in consultation with the Bedfordshire Police (ibid., p. 17). This is a matter of huge significance in a plan-led system, because what it means in practice is that the process of development control will be guided by the policies in the development plan. As a consequence, if the planning system is to test meaningfully whether development proposals in seeking planning permission have taken proper account of crime prevention issues, there need to be appropriate policies in the development plan that provide the starting point for the process. Conversely, the ability of the planning process to make these sorts of issues stick with developers would be adversely affected by the absence of development plan policies of this nature. The other major element of this protocol on process relates to development control. Here, the central issue is that the Bedfordshire Police ALO service does not have the resources to look at every planning application, and so needs to be selective in what it does; and this is true even though it is the case that very few of the applications at the most minor end of the spectrum will raise serious crime prevention issues. From the viewpoint of the local planning authorities, they are under considerable

Box 5.2 The Bedfordshire design protocols on planning for crime prevention

1 *Dwelling position*
1.1 Public and private spaces should be clearly distinguished.
1.2 Avoid conflicts between public and private spaces, particularly from buildings 'turning their backs' or 'dead frontages' created by fences or blank walls.
1.3 Orient dwellings to enable surveillance.

2 *Permeability*
2.1 While places should be well connected, community safety or residential amenity should not be unacceptably compromised by connectivity.
2.2 There should be a clearly defined need or benefit for the existence of all routes – which should be thought about at both the macro scale (i.e. as part of a 'walkable neighbourhood') and at the micro scale (i.e. by looking at their impact on particular sites and buildings).
2.3 Permeability needs to be designed in an appropriate manner, with block/grid structures which create 'active frontages' (defined as 'a frontage with several primary accesses, windows which overlook the street and little or no blank façades') and a regular movement framework that focuses people and vehicles on to a small number of principal routes without creating opportunities for rear access from alley and streets. It is usually desirable to avoid through-routes in new housing areas.
2.4 There needs to be minimal opportunity for unplanned routes to develop.

3 *Parking*
3.1 A blend of options needs to be applied to meet the scale of design.
3.2 Parking areas need to be integrated with the design to create ownership.
3.3 If courtyard parking is proposed, designs need to create the impression that the area is private and access needs to be restricted.
3.4 The design should address management, lighting, surveillance and access.

4 *Commercial and non-residential development*
4.1 Consider the scale of development and devise solutions appropriate to that scale.
4.2 Reinforce the distinction between the public front of the building and the private back.

5 *CCTV*
5.1 Where appropriate, consider the use of CCTV.

Source: Summarised from Llewellyn Davies (2005, pp. 8–17).

pressure from the government to improve their development control performance in terms of speed of decision making, and so, while being comfortable with the principle of police consultation on planning applications, they want to see a system in place that will not have the effect in practice of slowing the whole process down. The upshot of this is the agreements that are summarised in Box 5.3, which identify classes of planning applications where police consultation will be automatic (on the basis that these are likely to encompass the most problematic cases), but which also give the ALO service the right to look at other applications identified from weekly lists provided they do this expeditiously (ibid., pp. 18–20).

The issue that the agreement in Box 5.3 is seeking to deal with relates to a common problem in the British system, because at present the police ALO service is not generally resourced to a level that would enable it to deal with every planning application submitted. Just to put a scale on this, in England alone in the local government year 2003/04 675,000 planning applications were submitted, a rise of just under 20 per cent over the position in 2000/01

Box 5.3 The Bedfordshire protocol on police consultation on planning applications

The agreement on police consultation on planning applications in Bedfordshire has two elements:

1 *Consultation will always take place* on applications that fall into the following categories:
   - housing developments comprising ten dwellings or more;
   - major commercial office, industrial, retail or leisure schemes;
   - development involving new neighbourhood or district community facilities;
   - proposals which include significant areas of open space/landscaping proposed as part of the development;
   - developments incorporating significant off-street car parking provision;
   - proposals involving transport interchanges or other significant highway infrastructure improvements such as cycle lanes and new or improved footpaths;
   - applications for class A3 food and drink uses (i.e. restaurants, hot food take-aways and similar uses).

2 *In addition, weekly lists of planning applications received* will be sent by each District Council to the police, and the police will have one week from receipt of lists to notify the authority concerned about any further planning applications they wish to see.

Source: Llewellyn Davies (2005, pp. 18–20).

(Addison & Associates with Arup, 2004). If these were evenly distributed across all police forces, ALO teams if they were to review all of them would need to see in excess of 15,000 applications per team; and ALO teams are not generally resourced at this level. Thus, agreements of the kind reached in Bedfordshire seem likely increasingly to be part of the British system, balancing a desire to make effective use of ALO inputs with the need to improve the efficiency of the development control process.

It seems most unlikely that the series of agreements recorded above will eliminate all the tensions that appear to have existed in police–planner relationships in Bedfordshire, since the expression of different points of view from time to time must surely be expected to be a continuing part of any consultative process, albeit one that developing understandings between police and planners about what they are jointly trying to achieve should reduce in frequency. But at least the protocols about design considerations and about process provide a framework within which each of the parties can operate in full knowledge of what the other parties are committed to, and this should ensure that as and when disagreements arise, these are about genuine matters of substance which do need to be sorted out by face-to-face discussions.

Importantly, the protocols cover not merely what planners and the police will do when dealing with each other, but also what they will do when dealing with third parties such as developers, for example in pre-application discussions. The aim here is to ensure that, as far as possible, what gets submitted to the planning system for formal consideration has already taken account of these guidelines and that, as a consequence, less time has to be spent dealing with applications needing major renegotiation. In addition, since the thrust of the guidance given by planners and by the police should be the same, the hope is that these protocols will help to avoid too many cases arising where in effect the local planning authority and the ALO are on different sides of the argument. The proof of something like this, of course, is in its operation over a period of time, and as yet it is too soon to comment on this, but on the face of it this framework ought to be a helpful contribution to improved police–planner working relationships.

As far as Peter's involvement in national policy issues is concerned, there are two examples of this that we wish to explore here. The first of these was his willingness during the process of work on what became the ODPM's and the Home Office's *Safer Places* document to express his concern publicly about the extent to which the work was reflecting what he saw as the ODPM's urban design agenda rather than a crime prevention agenda based upon the practical experience of operating the Secured by Design scheme (Knowles, 2003a). Along with Stephen Town and a small number of other people, Peter then played a role in helping to improve the draft document, at a time when he felt that the police representatives participating in the consultative arrangements had not done what they should have been doing in those terms. The fact that there was some disquiet in police circles about these issues, and the fact that this disquiet had surfaced in the form of the paper written by Peter, would have come as a surprise in some quarters, but arguably it helped to play a part in the process of improving the draft ODPM/Home Office document.

Peter's primary concern in these processes was the extent to which he saw new urbanist ideas as creating living environments which increased the likelihood of crime being committed. The dimension of this which he chose to pursue publicly was the question of the added costs of policing that would arise as a result (Knowles, 2003b). The thrust of this argument was that, on the basis of crime statistics drawn from a 10 per cent sample of housing units in Bedfordshire, the number of police officers needed over a year to deal with the incidents that could be expected to arise in a notional new housing estate of 4,500 dwellings would rise from 9 if the estate had been planned using Secured by Design to 26 if the principles of new urbanism had been applied. This in turn would raise the annual policing bill from £270,000 in the former instance to £780,000 in the latter instance, representing an additional charge on the public purse of £510,000 (ibid.). Perhaps predictably, this generated an explosion of criticism on new urbanist websites, concentrating mainly on the argument that the attribution of the schemes under review to new urbanism was incorrect – although it probably also added considerably to the number of visits made to this paper on the Bedfordshire Police website (Kitchen, 2005, note 9). What was largely missed in this barrage of criticism was the simple point that there is a relationship between the approach adopted to the design and layout of a housing estate from a crime prevention perspective and the future cost to the public purse of policing that estate, over and above the more obvious issue of the impact that the future crime record would have on the quality of residents' lives.

It was clear from the present authors' exchanges with Peter about these matters that what he was concerned about here was the widespread impact he has experienced of new urbanist ideas on the views and proposals of developers, architects and planners, rather than the (inevitably much smaller) number of fully card-carrying new urbanist developments being constructed. He reports, for example, very frequently seeing housing layouts based upon the principle of permeability, and he also reports discussions with planners which started as far as they were concerned from the desirability of this approach from an urban design perspective, without any awareness whatsoever of what the available research shows about the propensity of permeable layouts to facilitate crime as compared with less permeable approaches. Much of his concern about this was that he saw developers, architects and planners adopting a 'taking it for granted' view of these matters, which in his view condemned future occupants of houses to an experience of crime which was likely to be more frequent than was necessary, and which was something of which they were likely to be totally unaware at the time they bought the property in question since no one would be advertising this dimension of the layout. These concerns can be linked back to the discussion reported above of the issue of permeability in the draft Bedfordshire community safety design guide, and also to the expectation that Bedfordshire in the coming years will see large-scale population growth.

These concerns were also reflected in the site visits we undertook with Peter to look at projects and at issues. We looked in particular at two identically sized grid squares of property on the eastern edge of the small town of

Biggleswade in Bedfordshire which were characterised by housing from different periods with different road patterns. Area A consisted mainly of quite densely developed housing built on a series of through-routes, whereas Area B consisted of more modern housing built at a lower density, organised mainly around a series of culs-de-sac. The reported crime records over the two-year period up to our visit (in September 2005) are strikingly different both in terms of their scale and (following Poyner, 2006) their pattern; not all crimes are the same.

	Area A		*Area B*	
Burglary	92	(15.5%)	3	(4%)
Auto crime	112	(19%)	20	(25%)
Damage/arson	118	(20%)	16	(20%)
Public disorder	270	(45.5%)	41	(51%)
Total number of crimes	592		80	

(NB. These figures have been calculated from relatively small dots on a map, and may therefore contain minor arithmetical errors. It is their scale that is significant, rather than their precision.)

There are, of course, many factors that contribute to the crime rate experienced by residential areas, including in particular their socio-economic composition and their density, and there is no suggestion here that the differences in layout as between these two areas are the sole explanation for the very considerable differences noted above. But this difference is so large – Area A experienced crime over the two-year period on a scale approximately 7.5 times greater than did Area B – that it seems highly likely that layout was a significant contributor to it. The patterns of crime in the two instances are also significantly different, with burglary being a much smaller element relatively speaking in the case of Area B than Area A; indeed, it appears that it is this much lower figure for burglary that causes the shares attributed to auto crime and to public disorder to be higher in the Area B case than in Area A. Again, therefore, it seems highly likely that layout is a contributory factor in the much lower burglary record in Area B.

We then went on to look at some modern developments around Bedford, where a major issue was the treatment of edges between the built develop-ment and open space that abuts it. Locations such as this are potentially vulnerable to crime in the sense that they present an opportunity for intruders, and so the treatment of these edges – both the boundaries themselves and how the adjacent property addresses them – is a matter of considerable importance. Figure 5.7 illustrates something of the range of approaches to this problem. We also saw a locality in Bedford where a footpath connecting two residential areas appears to be a major factor in explaining the high incidence of crime and antisocial behaviour experienced, because it brings people through a residential area when they have no specific purpose for being in that area. This illustrates a common problem in urban areas, where something that

5.7 Approaches to boundary treatment in a new development on the edges of Bedford. The figure consists of four examples of how the problem of boundary treatment has been tackled in recent developments on the edges of Bedford. The aim here is to achieve an appropriate treatment that limits the scope for intruder access yet is satisfactory in aesthetic terms. Readers are invited to assess for themselves the balance achieved in these four examples.

5.7 *continued*

is part of the general movement network and has been for some time can nevertheless make some adjacent locations very difficult as places to construct new housing because of the inherent vulnerability of such sites, not just to crimes such as burglary but also to general antisocial behaviour, such as youths moving through the area and misbehaving noisily in so doing. Some theorists would have us believe that this is a desirable process because it brings animation and eyes to the street, but this example seems to suggest that this picture can often be far from the lived reality experienced over prolonged periods of time by local residents.

Overall, then, Peter's experience is of development on a sizeable scale, of attempts to get planning for crime prevention given serious consideration as part of the process of managing that development, of the difficulties (including difficulties in working relationships between police and planners) which can arise in these circumstances, and of the attempts to find a way forward based upon agreed design principles and process protocols. It has some similarities with the story of Stephen Town's experiences in Bradford, perhaps in particular in terms of the difficulties of establishing stable working relationships with planners based around a shared understanding of what both parties are trying to achieve in the process of managing development, but it also has some important differences – notably the fact that Peter works with four district councils, which each display different characteristics as local planning authorities, whereas Stephen works with a single large metropolitan district council. But both experiences are stories of people who have stuck to their guns in the face of difficulties, have found what appear to be ways forward (although at the time of writing the Bedfordshire example is probably more precarious than the Bradford example), and at the same time in their different ways have contributed to national debates about planning for crime prevention. Some of this contribution has been around bolstering police support for the principles of Secured by Design in the face of pressures to compromise, and both Stephen and Peter would share our view that the recent process of diluting SBD to make it fit with the guidance on *Safer Places* has been a retrograde step. In this sense at least, they can both be seen as being among the small number of 'movers and shakers' in an ALO community where being outspoken does not seem to be a particularly common characteristic, and it may well be that this has also been an important element in each of their local stories as well.

Conclusions

As we said at the outset of this chapter, very little is actually known about the work of ALOs (at any rate in the sense of it being formally written down as part of the literature of the field), and so the primary purpose of this chapter has been to contribute to improving this situation by our focus on two case study officers. The significance of what ALOs actually do is clearly an important factor in understanding not merely whether SBD as a whole appears to be successful but also whether some elements of it are more effective than others, since it is ALOs who actually apply SBD to real-world cases (Cozens *et al.*,

2004). But we would also argue that understanding what ALOs do, how they do it, and in particular how they relate to planners is essential if the British government's intention that contributing to crime prevention should become an important objective for the planning process is to be translated into an effective operational reality (Morton and Kitchen, 2005). What we think our two cases have shown is two ALOs struggling with this agenda but also making some real progress with it, and thereby offering valuable lessons to their colleagues in similar situations up and down the country. As we said at the outset, we do not claim that these two cases are necessarily 'typical' (whatever that may mean in this particular situation), but what we do hope is that they are informative. Future work needs to add more in-depth study to this contribution, not just in terms of further British cases but also in looking at international comparisons. Is this an insight into a police contribution likely to be of growing significance across much of the world, or is this in large measure a particularly British initiative which does not necessarily offer much potential inspiration to practice elsewhere?

There are two particular elements of these cases that we wish to reflect on in this concluding section. The first is simply to do with the relative importance of the work of ALOs as this is perceived within the police service itself. How significant is this work, and how deserving is it of resources in competition with all the other elements of police work clamouring for attention from stretched police budgets? How important is it that ALO work is grounded in police operational experience? Is this simply a technical area best left to specialists of various kinds, or is it something that serving police officers should be encouraged to see as a field in which they can make a positive contribution drawn from their operational experience and can develop their careers accordingly? And what do these considerations have to tell us about the need to develop training initiatives, so that the officers who do become ALOs can do that job as effectively as possible? These seem to us to be important questions for the police service. Our cases suggest that the contributions that ALOs can make to the quality of life in their localities are significant, and as a consequence they suggest that the police service should approach the above questions from a positive standpoint. But the cases also suggest that the characters of the individuals themselves, and in particular how they have responded to the various difficulties that they have encountered, have been significant components of what has been achieved. So, this implies that in terms of the management of human resources the police service should look carefully not just at the numbers of people in the ALO service but at the capacities of those individuals to cope with the sorts of experiences we have detailed in this chapter.

Our other reflection is simply around what these experiences say to us about the development of ALO–planner working relationships. Clearly, this is still a work in progress. An important dimension of these relationships is around human interactions, in the sense not just of ALOs meeting planners but also of people with different backgrounds trying to work together and learning to respect and value each other's contributions – or not, as the case may be, since it seems likely that one dimension of the difficulties we have reported in our two cases is that some of the planners our ALOs have encountered have been much more willing to value their contribution than have others. There is a sense in which this will improve over time simply by virtue of becoming more commonplace, but it seems to us that the results of a strategy of sitting back and relying on improvements to happen are likely to be patchy (at best) and slow. The major challenge facing the system in England at present is the challenge of getting sensible crime prevention policies written into the new round of development plan making being embarked upon as a consequence of the provisions of the Planning and Compulsory Purchase Act 2004. We see this as a challenge to ALOs, because the evidence suggests that they find this harder to engage with than with the individual cases presented via the development control process. But we also see this as a challenge to planners, because they need to see ALOs as people whom they must bring into the process if their development plans are indeed to contribute properly to achieving the public safety dimension of sustainable communities (Office of the Deputy Prime Minister, 2005a). These two challenges can be put together and can be seen as an opportunity; and if this is grasped over the next few years, we could expect ALO–planner operational relationships to improve considerably. We hope that our two cases can and do contribute some inspiration and some useful lessons to these processes.

6

Crime prevention and urban regeneration

Developing practice in the United Kingdom

Introduction

The focus of this chapter is the urban regeneration process in the United Kingdom (what in other countries might be called urban renewal or urban revitalisation), and particularly how work in the field of crime prevention has moved from being a barely considered element in a process that was essentially about property development to being a central feature of a holistic process that aims to improve not just the quality of localities but also the quality of the lives that people lead within them. The British case is an interesting one in this context, because the regeneration effort is based upon two considerations in particular. The first is that the significance of major urban areas to the national economy is at last being recognised. As David Miliband, at that time the Minister of Communities and Local Government, put it at the formal launch of the new Sheffield City Strategy on 31 October 2005: Britain has over 50 large urban areas with populations in excess of 100,000, and so if they are doing well then we can be fairly sure that Britain as a whole is doing well (see also Office of the Deputy Prime Minister, 2006). The second is that the need for regeneration is recognised as being very widespread, which is not surprising in a country where most urban areas are relatively old and have been through several economic cycles, and thus urban regeneration practice has both a strong national policy dimension to it and a considerable amount of local variety. These characteristics make the British case of interest elsewhere, and the story of how crime prevention has moved from the periphery to the centre of this process is of itself part of that interest.

To this end, the first part of the chapter looks at the development of urban regeneration policy in the United Kingdom and at how the role of crime prevention within that process has itself evolved. After this, the chapter looks at two case studies in some depth. The first is what might be seen as a 'process' case, which is the role of Sheffield's Crime and Disorder Reduction Strategy within the overall approach to regeneration in the city. The second, by contrast, is what might be seen as a 'product' case, which is the award-winning

Blackthorn CASPAR project in Northampton, where crime prevention measures played a major part in the regeneration of a housing estate. It should be noted that these case studies have been chosen not because they are in some senses 'representative' of British urban regeneration practice (although an argument of this nature could be developed), but because each in an important sense constitutes practice at the best end of the spectrum. Sheffield City Council won the award of Council of the Year, 2005 at the Local Government Chronicle Awards on 14 March 2005, in part because of its work on the regeneration of the city in partnership with others. The Blackthorn CASPAR project was the inaugural winner in 2002 of what became the Deputy Prime Minister's Award for Sustainable Communities; and for present purposes it is helpful that it is also a project which has been extensively evaluated, which cannot be said to be the case with all such projects. So, these are two cases where quality of achievement has been publicly acknowledged, and they have been chosen for presentation in this chapter primarily for this reason. The chapter concludes with a reflective commentary on the ground that has been covered and on some of the lessons it might offer.

The development of urban regeneration policy in the United Kingdom

A much-used definition of urban regeneration in the British context is as follows:

> comprehensive and integrated vision and action which leads to the resolution of urban problems and which seeks to bring about a lasting improvement in the economic, physical, social and environmental condition of an area that has been subject to change.
>
> (Roberts and Sykes, 2000, p. 17)

It could be argued that, by this definition, much of the major urban improvement work of the nineteenth century, which was usually led by local government, was urban regeneration (see, for example, Briggs, 1982). The emphasis, though, was very much on physical work, using the growing powers of local authorities to do physical things which improved urban living conditions (for example, the construction of sewers, the acquisition of clean running water, and the ability to build houses). Local authorities did not generally acquire the power to undertake more socially oriented activities (for example, many aspects of education, social services and planning) until the twentieth century, and even then it can be argued that the ability to take the kind of comprehensive view argued for in the above definition was largely absent for much of the early part of that century. As a result, conventionally the process of urban regeneration in Britain is seen as starting with the slum clearance phase, which in most British cities ran from around the mid-1950s to around the mid-1970s and in many ways was about finding a response to urban living conditions which had remained relatively unchanged often for a century or more (see, for example, Roberts and Sykes, 2000, chapter 2).

The scale of this activity in some cities was enormous. In Manchester, for example, by 1955 some 70,000 dwellings had been declared unfit for human habitation (Manchester City Council, 1995, pp. 23 and 24), and the process of slum clearance and the construction of new housing – including about 23,500 houses built outside the city's boundaries because the density of the new housing overall was much lower than that of the housing it had replaced (ibid.) – dominated the next two decades. Demolishing and rebuilding on this scale is the equivalent of both knocking down and building a sizeable town or small city over a period of twenty years. Some of the new housing stock that was constructed in this period has not stood the test of time well; for example, most of the estates studied by Alice Coleman in London were built during this period as part of the process of slum clearance, and her work chronicles the experience of crime and antisocial behaviour which she argues was inherent in the design approaches adopted to the creation of that housing stock (Coleman, 1990). One particular type of problem encountered during this period was the attempt to create a new type of housebuilding industry in Britain, through the large-scale use of prefabricated elements assembled on site. The well-known Hulme Crescents in Manchester were an example of this approach, and the desire to replace them with something better that did not exhibit many of the same problems (including those of crime and antisocial behaviour) was what gave rise to the approach to the redevelopment of Hulme from the early 1990s utilising the principles of new urbanism (Hulme Regeneration, 1994; Schneider and Kitchen, 2002, pp. 241–256).

The slum clearance phase came to an end in the mid-1970s, and with it came a recognition of the need for more holistic approaches to the inner areas of Britain's major cities, which were in decline; indeed, it could be argued that the process of slum clearance had actually contributed to this spiral of decline (see, for example, Department of the Environment, 1977). Crime and antisocial behaviour featured relatively little in this analysis (although there was a recognition in the study of Lambeth in inner London that this was one of the problem areas voiced by local people; ibid., p. 40), and hardly at all in what were seen as the contents of more holistic approaches to these areas. In any event, these approaches, which were carried forward into statute via the Inner Urban Areas Act 1978, did not survive for long because the 1979 general election brought in a Conservative government headed by Margaret Thatcher and a different philosophical approach to the process of regeneration.

In essence, the approach of the incoming Conservative government was to see the local authorities' responsibility for inner-city areas as part of the problem, and therefore as needing to be bypassed. It was also to see market disciplines as the solution to the economic problems of those areas and their people, and thus the 1980s was characterised by regeneration led by new organisations which were creatures of the central state and by an emphasis on the achievement of property development (Imrie and Thomas, 1999). Although many aspects of this approach continued throughout the Conservative administration led by John Major in the early 1990s, that also brought a recognition of some of the limitations of the approach of the preceding decade. Among the most important of these were the following:

- local authorities were such important players in regeneration areas anyway that they simply could not be excluded from the urban regeneration process;
- successful regeneration needed to involve local communities much more effectively than had often been the case in the past, so that it became not simply something 'done to' local communities but aspired to be 'done with' them and therefore to address the matters which were of major concern to those communities;
- property development was capable of achieving certain things, but an approach that focused mainly on this dimension of activity underemphasised many other elements which were important in improving the life circumstances and opportunities of local residents;
- the key players in the regeneration process needed to be encouraged to work together through partnership mechanisms if there was to be any realistic prospect that more holistic approaches to regeneration could be turned into effective action.

The importance of these points was underlined by a study of what had actually been achieved during the previous two decades of policy towards inner urban areas, which looked at the experiences of Greater Manchester, Merseyside, and Tyne and Wear and came to the conclusion that their relative economic and social circumstances had changed relatively little despite all this policy attention (Robson *et al.*, 1994). But what that study also did was to capture the views of the intended beneficiaries of all this activity – the residents of the areas benefiting from the application of urban policy – about the things that mattered in their perception of the quality of life in those areas (ibid., p. 340). The results of this exercise are reproduced as Table 6.1. This shows violent crime in first position, non-violent crime in fourth position, and 'what the area looks like' (heavily influenced by antisocial behaviour factors such as vandalism and graffiti) in seventh position among the top ten factors in this list. Put another way, many of the factors on which property-based approaches to urban regeneration had not particularly focused, such as crime and health, were shown to be at the top of the lists of residents' concerns, suggesting very strongly that the basis of urban regeneration activity needed to be broadened if it were indeed to address the issues that concerned local residents about the quality of life in some of the most deprived localities in British cities.

It is instructive to compare the list in Table 6.1 with the list reproduced earlier, in Box 4.1, which was asking a very similar question of people across a wider geographical spread of localities a decade later. In both cases, crime issues stand at number one in the list and the quality of health services stands at number two; in other words, the same issues top both lists. These are not the concerns of the 'traditional' property-based approaches to urban regeneration, but are very much the concerns of more recent and more holistic approaches to regeneration. The distance by which crime comes top of the list has actually grown by the time of the later study, although this may be explained by the fact that the Robson study separated out violent and non-violent crime whereas the more recent ODPM study summarised in Box 4.1

Table 6.1 Factors rated by local residents as 'very important' to the quality of life in areas benefiting from urban policy initiatives up to the early 1990s

Rank order	Factor	Percentage of residents rating this as 'very important'
1	Violent crime	79.3
2	Quality of health care	73.7
3	Cost of living	71.9
4	Non-violent crime	67.2
5	Quality of housing	64.2
6	Quality of welfare services	61.7
7	What the area looks like	61.3
8	Employment prospects	59.2
9	Pollution	58.2
10	Unemployment levels	58.0

Source: Robson *et al.* (1994, p. 340).

The survey base is 1,299 residents in parts of Greater Manchester, Merseyside and Tyne and Wear.

did not. The message of these two studies, undertaken a decade apart, is very clear: measures to combat crime (and to reduce people's fear of crime, although this is a more contentious proposition) need to be at the heart of urban regeneration initiatives which seek to improve the quality of life in deprived areas, even though until relatively recently they have not been.

The component of regeneration activity where most attention had been paid to crime-related issues was housing (Goodchild, 1997, pp. 49–57 and 189–195). Edgar and Taylor, reflecting in the late 1990s on what had been achieved and what had been learned up to that point, summarise the position as follows:

> Crime presents problems and generates anxiety across all housing tenures and throughout the country. It is particularly severe on some social housing estates where the vulnerable and the disaffected come together. Noise, harassment, vandalism, theft and drugs are often cited as disincentives to urban living, although the relatively affluent and more rural areas are not immune.
>
> Clearly, the causes of crime must be tackled through social and educational programmes, but the effects must also be addressed to create greater feelings of security. Most of the crime which is most troublesome takes place in the vicinity of the home. Schemes to combat anti-social behaviour, such as neighbourhood watch schemes and community safety strategies, have a part to play, while improved physical security and improved surveillance act as deterrents. In terms of physical regeneration, the extra cost of Secured by Design measures is very modest in new residential areas and refurbished

estates and this can reduce very considerably the opportunities for crime. Overall, improved housing management and meaningful community involvement are often the key to tackling crime.

(2000, pp. 159–160)

The incoming Labour government in 1997 was well aware of the need for regeneration to be looked at in much more holistic ways, for new mechanisms to be put in place to help with its delivery, and for the scale of regeneration to be substantially increased if it were to be more commensurate with the scale of the problem. The Social Exclusion Unit put the position as follows:

Over the last generation, this has become a more divided country. While most areas have benefited from rising living standards, the poorest neighbourhoods have tended to become more rundown, more prone to crime, and more cut off from the labour market. The national picture conceals pockets of intense deprivation where the problems of unemployment and crime are acute and hopelessly tangled up with poor health, housing and education. They have become no go areas for some and no exit zones for others. In England as a whole, the evidence we have suggests that there are several thousand neighbourhoods and estates whose condition is critical, or soon could be.

(1998, p. 9)

When looking at the contribution that crime patterns and experiences make to this situation, the Social Exclusion Unit noted four facts about the situation in England as a whole which demonstrated very clearly why the need to tackle this problem had to become a much more significant element of the regeneration effort than it had been to date:

- 40% of crime occurs in just 10% of areas;
- 10% of residents in inner city areas are burgled once or more in a year – double the rate elsewhere;
- half the people who were victims of crime were repeat victims, accounting for 81% of reported crime;
- 25% of ethnic minority residents in low income multi-ethnic areas say racially motivated attacks are a very or fairly big problem for them.

(ibid., p. 28)

Thinking about the strategic position in regeneration as a consequence of facts such as this led to the establishment of a new vision for neighbourhood regeneration:

within ten or twenty years, no-one should be seriously disadvantaged by where they live. People on low incomes should not have to suffer conditions and services that are failing and so different from what the rest of the population receives.

(Social Exclusion Unit, 2001, p. 8)

As a consequence, two long-term goals have been established:

- In all the poorest neighbourhoods, to have common goals of lower workless-ness and crime, and better health, skills, housing and physical environment.
- To narrow the gap on these measures between the most deprived neighbourhoods and the rest of the country.

(ibid.)

This is a hugely challenging vision and goal statement, and the processes of achieving it were seen as requiring new or improved activities under three broad headings:

- new policies, funding and targets;
- better local coordination and community empowerment;
- improved national and regional support.

The primary characteristics of the urban regeneration system put in place by these initiatives can best be summarised as follows:

- *The biggest central government financial commitment ever was made to the urban regeneration process* (ibid., Chapter 4), including taking a longer-term view of some types of initiatives than had been the case before. In many ways, large-scale and sustained funding is the *sine qua non* of regeneration if it is indeed to tackle deep-seated problems in the localities that have experienced the multiplicity of problems set out in the diagnoses of the Social Exclusion Unit quoted above. The geographical spread of the problem that has been identified requires a congruent response, which is why 88 local authority areas (approaching 25 per cent of the local authorities in England, and including all of its major urban areas) are the beneficiaries of Neighbourhood Renewal funding. In addition, the need to broaden out the regeneration agenda so that it addresses all the key issues that impact upon the quality of life in a deprived locality, and does not just concentrate on achieving some property development, represents another significant funding challenge. When the problems are looked at like this, it is not too difficult to see why the financial commitment to regeneration needed to be the biggest it has ever been.
- *New structures were needed both at the level of whole local authorities and for areas the subject of neighbourhood regeneration initiatives.* 'Local Strategic Partnerships' were required to be established in the 88 local authority areas that were the beneficiaries of Neighbourhood Renewal funding, and in practice most other local authorities also chose to establish mechanisms of this nature to bring together the key players locally in the provision of services and in the process of shaping the economic future of localities. At the neighbourhood level, many new local structures were established depending upon the initiatives being undertaken, all around applying the principles of partnership and of more effective community involvement to this process of local recovery.

- *The greatest range and amount of national policy advice and guidance about the process of regeneration at various spatial scales that has ever been seen was assembled*, spearheaded by a new arm of government (the Neighbourhood Renewal Unit). This was done in part as an attempt to improve coordination between government departments, which have traditionally been weak at focusing on small localities and integrating their activities so as to produce a coherent response to the concept of area-based priorities. This contains what might be seen as a paradox, because regeneration at its heart is about discovering what works on the ground in a particular locality and working with local communities rather than about top-down approaches guided by views from afar. It also contains a risk, in the sense that it can suggest an inappropriate one-size-fits-all approach reinforced by the funding and monitoring mechanisms in place. Nevertheless, what is being attempted here is the most comprehensive attempt to date to tackle what had been seen as one of the major problem areas of previous regeneration activity. This is that central government policy and practice do inevitably impact on individual localities but have been delivered in such a fragmented and uncoordinated manner that they have not contributed very effectively to successful regeneration.

In this new approach, tackling crime as part of the urban regeneration process has moved in a period of little over a decade from the periphery to the centre of government thinking. In recognition of this, the Social Exclusion Unit describes the 'root problems' that neighbourhood regeneration initiatives need to address as being unemployment, crime and poor services (2001, p. 24). In this context, we will now examine in some depth two cases that illustrate aspects of how crime prevention is being tackled as an integral element of urban regeneration. The first is the strategic process of tackling crime as a component of urban regeneration at the scale of a whole city, through the work of Sheffield First for Safety, which is an arm of the Local Strategic Partnership for Sheffield; so this is a *process* case study. The second is the Blackthorn CASPAR project in Northampton, which is an estate regeneration programme in which crime prevention was a very significant element; so this is a *product* case study.

The work of Sheffield First for Safety/Sheffield First Safer Communities Partnership

Sheffield First for Safety/Sheffield First Safer Communities Partnership is a component element of the Sheffield First Partnership, which is the local strategic partnership for the city of Sheffield. Sheffield is a city of just over 500,000 people located in South Yorkshire, and grew in large measure because of the iron and steel industry; the brand 'Made in Sheffield' was seen the world over as a guarantee that its products were of good quality. In recent times traditional industries have declined considerably, and the city has had to reinvent itself to make its way in the contemporary world. The process of regeneration can be seen as a contributor to this activity of managing change.

The structure of the Sheffield First Partnership changed during 2005, and so Figure 6.1 shows the structure as it was up to 2005 and Figure 6.2 shows the structure from 2005 onwards, when Sheffield First for Safety became the Sheffield First Safer Communities Partnership. The reason for the change in structure was to align the organisation of the local strategic partnership more precisely with its analysis of what are seen as the component elements of a successful city, which is the basis for the City Strategy (see below). What is clear from Figures 6.1 and 6.2, however, is the central role that action to prevent crime plays in this process, with in essence the Sheffield First for Safety Partnership (Figure 6.1) and the Safer Communities Partnership (Figure 6.2) being the same organisation with a different name. In the terms of Figure 6.2, then, the Safer Communities Partnership is seen as a delivery body; it is about ensuring that things get done, as distinct from championing activities to others.

The local strategic partnership (Sheffield First) takes the lead in the regeneration process in the sense that it is responsible for the overall city strategy. So, the city's Crime and Disorder Reduction Strategy (Sheffield First for Safety, 2002) sits within the framework provided by the City Strategy (Sheffield First Partnership, 2005). The lead on the former document is taken by Sheffield First for Safety/the Safer Communities Partnership, which started out its life as the free-standing statutory partnership under the 1998 Crime and Disorder Act but was subsequently incorporated into the local strategic partnership.

The driving force behind the Sheffield City Strategy is a set of 12 propositions said to be the features of a successful city (ibid., p. 7). These are derived from a piece of research undertaken on competitive European cities (Parkinson *et al.*, 2004), as modified as a result of a consultation process carried out in Sheffield. They are reproduced as Box 6.1.

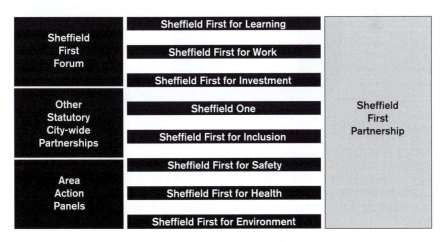

6.1 Structure of the Sheffield First family of partnerships up to 2005.

Source: Sheffield First Partnership

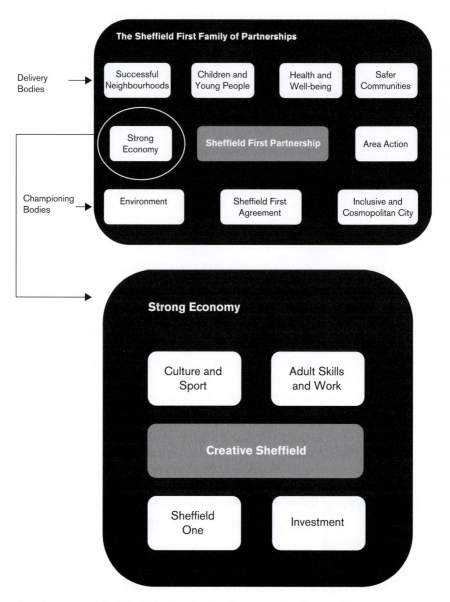

6.2 Structure of the Sheffield First family of partnerships from 2005.

Source: Sheffield First Partnership.

For present purposes, two points in particular stand out from the list in Box 6.1. The first is that, hardly surprisingly, low crime is identified in its own right as one of the features of a successful city. The second point is that low rates of crime, and public expectations that localities will be safe places, must also be component elements of some of the other features on this list. Three examples will serve to make this point. The first is that it is inconceivable that

---

Box 6.1 The twelve key features of a successful city, according to the Sheffield City Strategy

- Strong economy
- Vibrant city centre
- Well connected
- High employment and high skills in a learning city
- An exceptional cultural and sporting city
- Attractive, successful neighbourhoods
- Great place to grow up in
- Good health and well-being for all communities
- Low crime
- Environmental excellence
- Inclusive and cosmopolitan city
- Well run and well regarded.

Source: Sheffield First Partnership (2005, pp. 7).

---

a city centre could be regarded as being 'vibrant' if at the same time high levels of street crime were being experienced and people were afraid of using city centre spaces at certain times of the day or night because they felt unsafe there. The second is that a neighbourhood is most unlikely to be regarded as attractive and successful if high levels of vandalism and graffiti are being experienced and if levels of burglary and car crime are high. The third example is that environmental excellence must surely be not only about how a locality looks but also about how it functions, and an area where the design and layout provide numerous opportunities for crimes to be committed could not be regarded from this perspective as being an excellent environment. It can thus be seen that the need to address problems of crime is deeply embedded in the City Strategy, and that how successfully this is achieved will make a major difference to the extent to which Sheffield actually exhibits several of the features in Box 6.1.

The stated aim in the City Strategy in respect of crime is as follows: 'Our aim is to create a city where residents and visitors can go about their business and leisure activities safely without crime, anti-social behaviour or concern for personal safety being significant barriers' (Sheffield First Partnership, 2005, p. 24). Specifically, the approach is to tackle crime, fear of crime and antisocial behaviour where these issues are worst and also where they have the most damaging effects on the regeneration and renewal of the city (ibid., p. 25).

The starting point in the City Strategy for looking at how this aim might be achieved is a recognition of the fact that, in comparison with the other major cities of England, recorded crime statistics show Sheffield to be relatively safe. The trajectory of overall recorded crime in 2004/05 was downwards, with notable reductions in domestic burglaries, theft from vehicles, theft of vehicles and robberies. Violent crime was on the rise, however, as was generally the case nationally, and while some of this appears to be attributable to relatively recent changes in national standards for crime recording by police forces, it was accepted that this was a real concern and a key priority (ibid.; for a general discussion of the issues surrounding police recorded crime, see Schneider and Kitchen, 2002, pp. 29–36).

The fact that recorded crime in Sheffield was moving in the right direction could itself be seen as evidence that thinking strategically about crime through the process of partnership was proving to be successful. Cause and effect are always very difficult to establish in this field, especially since there is almost certainly a multiplicity of factors that influence an outcome such as this, but it is a plausible proposition that the process of partnership was a contributory element in Sheffield's improving performance in relation to crime statistics over this period.

The City Strategy then identifies five challenges in the field of crime, which are summarised in Box 6.2. Clearly, the action involved in responding to these key challenges is about much more than environmental works and policies, but it is interesting to note the extent to which this response needs to include environmental considerations. For example, much of the so-called high-volume crime, such as burglary and car crime, is often inherently capable of an

---

Box 6.2 The five key challenges in the field of crime, Sheffield City Strategy, 2005–2010

- To do better at preventing antisocial behaviour occurring and recurring, and to ensure responses, when incidents do occur, are as swift and effective as possible.
- To ensure that 'high-volume' crime or 'acquisitive' crime such as burglary, vehicle crime, criminal damage and common assault are tackled alongside crime that is much less frequent: robbery, serious assaults, gun crime.
- To tackle the issue of substance abuse, notably the misuse of Class A drugs and the effect this can have on individuals' propensity to offend and reoffend; the effect of alcohol misuse on the incidence of violence, particularly in the 'night-time' economy; and the effects of drugs markets and drug dealing in the city's communities.
- To target the city's most prolific offenders and develop intensive multi-agency work to ensure these people are effectively sanctioned and helped to change their behaviour.
- To ensure that young people at risk of offending are given every possible opportunity to make better choices, and to support other vulnerable groups such as those working in the sex industry, witnesses suffering intimidation, and those experiencing domestic abuse or racist incidents.

Source: Sheffield First Partnership (2005, p. 24).

environmental response, and there is also an environmental dimension to the problems associated with alcohol misuse and violence in relation to the night-time economy. The place of environmentally related action in the overall strategy towards crime in the city becomes even clearer when the next step down the strategic planning chain is considered, which is the identification of priorities for action. What the City Strategy has to say about priorities is extracted as Box 6.3. The particularly striking element of this statement for present purposes is the emphasis it puts on place, both in the introductory material and in the third of its five priorities for action. Place-based crime prevention activity is clearly seen here as an important contributor to the overall approach, sitting alongside other aspects of crime prevention work.

Box 6.3 The priorities for action in the field of crime, Sheffield City Strategy, 2005–2010

We will achieve a safer city through work that prevents people becoming victims of crime, that helps prevent offending or re-offending and that makes locations or places less prone to criminal or antisocial behaviour.

The approach is to tackle crime, fear of crime and antisocial behaviour where these issues are worst and where these issues have the most damaging effect on regeneration and renewal.

The Safer Communities Strategy for 2005–2008 has been agreed and describes the priorities for action. These are anti-social behaviour, burglary, substance misuse, vehicle crime, and violent crime. We will do this by:

- Making a particular effort to protect young people from persistent criminal behaviour through support for effective parenting, ensuring schools and colleges provide clear messages about personal responsibility, providing good opportunities for work and leisure;
- Focusing efforts on those already engaged in illegal activity. We need to ensure that the worst offenders – in terms of criminal activity and those persistently causing antisocial behaviour – are targeted and prevented from causing harm to individuals and communities.
- Ensuring that our neighbourhoods, car parks, streets, green spaces and venues effectively deter criminal activity and do not provide a haven for drug and alcohol abuse or robberies.
- Ensuring that victims and witnesses of crime have confidence in the Criminal Justice system, to come forward and give evidence and are supported to prevent re-victimisation. This is particularly important for victims of 'hate crime' such as domestic abuse and racist incidents.

> • Ensuring that offenders who are misusing drugs are iden-
> tified and, alongside any sentence imposed, that they are
> supported to access effective treatment to help reduce their
> offending.
>
> Source: Sheffield First Partnership (2005, p. 25).

As Box 6.3 indicates, it is then the job of the more detailed strategy for crime
and disorder reduction to develop and to operationalise this broad strategic
framework. Sheffield's crime and disorder reduction strategy (Sheffield First
for Safety, 2002; Sheffield First Safer Communities Partnership, 2005)
undertakes this task, and it is rolled forward every three years. Part of the
process of preparing the strategy for the 2002–2005 period involved extensive
public consultation about priorities, and Table 6.2 shows the results of a
household survey about this issue. The issues that emerged from this process
of public consultation as top priorities were carried forward into the strategy
as the main priorities, with the exception of the problem of drugs, which was
seen as one of four cross-cutting issues (the other three were young people
as offenders, prolific adult offenders and the use of CCTV) because people's
drug abuse habits and the need to find money in order to satisfy them were
seen as the causes of many of the 'acquisitive' crimes (Sheffield First for
Safety, 2002, pp. 27 and 28). More detailed strategies were then prepared in
respect of each of these priorities, and we will look in more detail at the strategy
for tackling burglary, partly because it emerged from public consultation as the
top priority and partly because of these priorities, it is probably the one that is
most amenable to environmental action, as we have noted in Chapters
2 and 3.

*Table 6.2 Public views about priorities for Sheffield's crime and disorder
reduction strategy, 2002–2005*

Priority	Percentage in favour
Burglary	76%
Drugs	62%
Violent crime	61%
Vehicle crime	42%
Antisocial behaviour	38%
Domestic violence	10%
Racial or religious abuse	9%
Victimisation due to sexuality	3%

Source: Sheffield First for Safety (2002)

Note: The study involved a postal survey of 12,000 households which achieved a 45%
response rate and so the above percentages reflect the views of 5,400 households in
Sheffield.

One of the key factors in the process of assembling the detailed strategy to combat burglary was the recognition from the household survey that 8 per cent of respondents said that they had suffered a burglary in the previous year (ibid., p. 12). Another factor was the recognition that burglary rates varied hugely across the city, with the rate in the ward with the worst problem being well over six times that of the rate in the ward with the smallest-scale problem; and with many of the wards showing the highest rates of burglary being among Sheffield's most economically and socially deprived wards. The responses to this issue in terms of actions to be undertaken were grouped into three clusters: continuing the 'target-hardening' measures in the areas with the highest incident rates, continuing the measures that tackle burglary offenders, and ensuring adequate support for victims (ibid., p. 13). These measures are summarised in Box 6.4, and in essence the strategy for 2005–2008 sought to roll these forward through prioritising domestic burglary, prolific burglary offenders and areas with high levels of burglary, especially those with high repeat incidences (Sheffield First Safer Communities Partnership, 2005, p. 15).

For present purposes, perhaps the most interesting point to note in respect of the list of actions in Box 6.4 is the high proportion of them that could be described as being environmental or community-based in their nature. People in some other countries (i.e. other than Britain) will also note with interest the intention to make more effective use of CCTV in residential areas, which in some parts of the world would be seen as a very controversial issue because of its intrusion into privacy and its threat to personal liberty. There is no doubt that it is possible to make homes much more difficult to break into through the careful choice of things such as locks and bolts, as well as larger items such as doors and windows (see, for example, Crouch et al., 1999, chapter 5). Similarly, action to improve street lighting, to trim shrubbery so that it does not offer hiding places, and to ensure through environmental clean-ups that a locality looks as if it is cared for can all contribute to reducing the perception of a burglary opportunity (ibid., chapters 3 and 6). What may have the potential to add further value to physical actions of this nature is the involvement of the local community through schemes such as Neighbourhood Watch and neighbourhood wardens (Colquhoun, 2004, pp. 293 and 294), although it should be noted that an authoritative US review (Sherman et al., 1997) concluded that, at best, community-based activities of this nature could be regarded as 'promising'. What may prove to work best of all, however, is all of these elements working together as part of a coordinated approach which is driven by a clear and widely supported strategy.

There is some evidence suggesting that packages of this nature have had a positive effect in Sheffield. The burglary rate per 1,000 households in the ward with the worst problem in the city in 1997/98 (just before the first round of crime and disorder reduction strategies) was 87, and by 2000/01 this had become just under 50 in that ward and 63 in the ward that by then had the worst record (Sheffield First for Safety, 2002, p. 12). As noted earlier, this broad trend appeared to have continued during the life of the 2002–2005 strategy (Sheffield First Safer Communities Partnership, 2005, p. 9), and the 2005–2008 strategy set a further target of reducing the incidence of domestic

Box 6.4 Measures to tackle burglary in the Sheffield crime reduction strategy

1 *Continuing the 'target hardening' measures in the areas with the highest incident rates*

- Packages that improve individual properties, such as locks, bolts, spy-holes and intruder alarms, and alley-gating, plus specific work with the most vulnerable residents such as elderly people.
- Improved street lighting.*
- Environmental improvements, such as cutting back shrubbery and regular clean-ups.*
- Introduction of neighbourhood warden schemes.*
- Use of neighbourhood watch schemes;*
- Effective use of CCTV.*

2 *Continuing the measures that tackle burglary offenders*

- Intensive supervision and surveillance programmes by the police and the probation service, including the provision of support services to change behaviour and attitudes.
- Specific policing operations in defined communities.
- Measures to make property less attractive to a burglar, such as property-marking.

3 *Ensuring adequate support for victims*

- The provision of crime prevention advice.
- Identifying those households subject to repeat offences and offering additional support.

* In some parts of the world these elements would not be regarded as target hardening. So, this is a wider usage of this concept than would be found elsewhere.

Source: Sheffield First for Safety, 2002 (p. 13).

burglary by the end of this period by 30 per cent as compared with the 2003/04 figure (ibid., p. 15). Of course, many factors contribute to results of this nature, and it is most unlikely that strategic work of the kind reviewed here would by itself be responsible for large-scale changes of this nature. But strategic work of this nature is important to establish what needs to be done and to provide a framework and a focus for doing it. So, it is reasonable to conclude this review by suggesting that the experience of the process of undertaking crime and disorder reduction strategies in Sheffield has been a positive one, and offers lessons for elsewhere about the value of work of this nature.

The Blackthorn CASPAR Project, Northampton

The Blackthorn CASPAR project (CASPAR = Crime and Anti-Social Behaviour Partnership) was the inaugural winner of the Office of the Deputy Prime Minister's Award for Urban Renaissance in 2002. Essentially it was a project to tackle the wide-ranging problems of an estate of around 2,200 houses mainly built by the Northampton Development Corporation in the 1970s. Northampton is a county town in the south-eastern part of the English Midlands, just over an hour north of London by road or by rail. Its population, at around 200,000, has grown significantly since the 1970s as a result of a decision to graft what was in effect a new town onto the existing town; this is why it had a development corporation overseeing the building of houses such as those on the Blackthorn Estate, which is on the northern outskirts of the town. Thus, the Blackthorn CASPAR project involved an element of retrofitting an estate that was little more than two decades old. The photographs in Figure 6.3 provide some images of the estate, from which readers should be able to see the kind of place it is. Essentially, it consists of a series of accesses off a perimeter road, many of which take the form of culs-de-sac; and many of the ways through the estate consist of pedestrian footpaths, some of which certainly feel quite intimidating to walk along. Although it would not be regarded as a 'Radburn' layout (Kostof, 1991, pp. 79 and 80) in all its aspects, it has many of the characteristics of this type, especially the extensive segregation of pedestrians and vehicles; and certainly some of its contemporary problems can be said to derive from this layout. In a phrase, it was a creature of its time, and it is an interesting case to look at in part because it is similar to quite a lot of development from that period.

6.3 The Blackthorn Estate, Northampton.

a *Typical example of the housing layout on the Blackthorn Estate, with access to front doors via a footpath system and with the housing grouped around a landscaped area.*

6.3 The Blackthorn Estate, Northampton (continued)

b *A children's play space on the estate, which benefits from a prominent and well-overlooked location. The photograph was taken during school hours, which is why there are no children using the facility.*

c *A very typical problem on the Blackthorn Estate, which is that many of the footpath systems are at the rears of dwellings. It is not easy to make such systems attractive to use, especially when rear fencing is reasonably stout in order to make intrusion more difficult.*

6.3 The Blackthorn Estate, Northampton (continued)

d *Example of an access that has been blocked off, so as to make it harder for those with no business in the locality to threaten the nearby housing. It could be argued that this has been relatively crudely done, but it did appear on-site that it had been effective.*

e *Example of gating introduced into the footpath system by the CASPAR project, in particular to slow down speeding motorbikes.*

6.3 The Blackthorn Estate, Northampton (continued)

f One resident's approach to the need to deter intruders. This action illustrates the existence of a problem.

g Typical example close-up of the relationship between the fronts of houses and the footpath system on the Blackthorn Estate.

6.3 The Blackthorn Estate, Northampton (continued)

h Communal car parking areas both in a free-standing block and next to lock-up garages. The key questions here are around how safe these are, and how safe residents perceive them to be.

The Blackthorn CASPAR project had four main aims:

- to make the estate a safer place;
- to reduce crime and antisocial behaviour without displacing it to surrounding areas;
- to coordinate more effective joint working by all agencies;
- to involve the community fully (British Urban Regeneration Association, 2002, p. 6).[1]

The need for the project can be readily understood from three headline points (ibid.):

- Recorded burglary rates in the CASPAR area just before the project began showed that the Blackthorn estate was experiencing about six times the rate for Northampton as a whole; and the rate for Northampton was itself about 20 per cent above the national average. So, this was a high-crime locality in a town where overall crime levels were significantly higher than national averages.
- Around 12 per cent of all the crimes in Northamptonshire occurred on this single estate. So, the crime figures for the Blackthorn estate had a significant adverse effect on the crime figures for the town of Northampton and for the county of Northamptonshire.

- As a consequence, the estate experienced many void properties, a large turnover of tenants and much antisocial behaviour from young people, and drugs were widely in use.

The main elements of the Blackthorn CASPAR strategy fall into nine broad groups, as follows (Pitts *et al.*, 2002, pp. 40 and 41):

1 structural/administrative/legal initiatives;
2 information gathering;
3 information sharing;
4 information giving;
5 environmental/situational crime prevention;
6 environmental improvements;
7 social/youth crime prevention;
8 policing/enforcement;
9 pre-existing/parallel provision or initiatives.

The range of actions undertaken in these nine groups are summarised in Box 6.5.

Box 6.5 The Blackthorn CASPAR project: key initiatives

1 *Structural/administrative/legal initiatives*

A multi-agency Action Team was established as the basis for monitoring issues and identifying projects, with a primary focus on 'issues around the housing, education and diversion of young people committing crime and antisocial behaviour'. The most significant elements of this work were undertaken at the front end of the process since this involved the manning of future actions, but the Team's membership expanded as the process unfolded. A critical initiative stemming from this seems to have been the relocation of the CASPAR Coordinator and Community Beat Officers to the Briar Hill Centre in the area.

2 *Information gathering*

A survey of residents was undertaken which achieved a 42 per cent response rate and which identified some key priorities. This was followed by two public meetings, which agreed to delegate the responsibility for developing these priorities to smaller groups.

3 *Information sharing*

The production and distribution of a newsletter was undertaken by the Residents Association and the Tenants Participation Manager.

---

4 *Information giving*

A 'good news' strategy was developed, which resulted in 12 press articles and 2 media interviews in the first phase of the project.

5 *Environmental/situational crime prevention*

Key projects included the erection of anti-motorcycle barriers (because motorcycle nuisance had been identified as a top priority issue in the residents survey), the introduction of CCTV surveillance of shops at an entrance to the estate where young people gathered in groups, better street lighting, the blocking off of some pathways, and the introduction of improved fencing, turning a road of sheltered housing into a cul-de-sac, and the relocation of two repeatedly victimised households identified as a result of studies of juvenile nuisance.

6 *Environmental improvements*

The main projects here were a litter pick on the estate involving young people, and the targeted clearance of rubbish by the local authority Cleansing Department.

7 *Social/youth crime prevention*

Key projects have included the establishment of a youth club for 11- to 17-year-olds by the Community Beat Officer, the involvement of young people in community arts projects, the refurbishment of and further construction works on a multi-sports complex, the creation of MEGABYTES (a computer-based community access centre) by refurbishing a vacant shop, and the creation of more local recreation facilities in parks.

8 *Policing/enforcement*

A series of campaigns targeted suspected offenders, focused on particular types of crime (especially thefts from vehicles but also juvenile nuisance) and raised police profile/presence in the area. In addition, a Crime and Disorder Unit was formed to tackle antisocial behaviour across the Borough of Northampton.

9 *Pre-existing/parallel provision or initiatives*

Essentially, this was about encouraging the existing residents association and the (not very active) Neighbourhood Watch schemes in the area, the formation of a new residents group, and the creation of 'social action' projects designed to engage young people in worthwhile community-based action.

Source: Summarised from Pitts *et al.* (2002, pp. 42 and 43).

So, this initiative involved a major collaboration between the police, the local authorities and the local community, and represented a comprehensive attempt to tackle identified problems not just by spending money on physical changes but also by changing some existing administrative practices. Thus, community engagement, environmental action, information flows, extensive and coordinated police and other agency action, and the provision of alternatives which deflected young people away from crime and antisocial behaviour were all key elements of the strategy here, taking as the starting point both the views of local residents as assembled via a survey and the accumulated knowledge and experience of agencies who had worked in the area. It is likely that this across-the-board approach made a big difference to the success of the initiative, because it is questionable whether each of these elements if undertaken in isolation would have been successful.

The success of the project is exemplified by the fact that it was the inaugural winner of the Office of the Deputy Prime Minister's Award for Urban Renaissance. But much more important in judging the success of this project than the fact that it won a national award is its effectiveness in tackling the local problems that it was established to address. The views of the judging panel for the national award about this are reproduced in Box 6.6.

The last comment in the extract in Box 6.6 is of particular significance, because it is important to note how context-specific the Blackthorn CASPAR approach was. The general principles of the project may well be capable of being applied in other situations, but to be as effective as in this instance, they would have to be tailored to both the specific circumstances on the ground and the particular people and organisations working on the project. This is not a one-size-fits-all approach, but a tailored project. It is also a project that spent a relatively small amount of money (in comparison with the cost of many urban regeneration projects), with the physical works budget put at £400,000 at the time the project won its award, with a further £150,000 in the pipeline (British Urban Regeneration Association, 2002, p. 2). This does not, of course, include 'softer' costs such as the time of participants from the various agencies, which undoubtedly would add significantly to these figures, but nonetheless this shows that a project of this nature can be carried out without it being necessary to throw very large sums of money at it.

One of the other advantages of this project is that it has been extensively evaluated, including by independent assessors (Pitts *et al.*, 2002). Perhaps one of the most significant elements this evaluation recorded was that, as well as the public welcome for the significant reduction in the volume of crime taking place on the estate, residents perceived several other changes to have taken place as a result of the project which they regarded as being significant. These are summarised in Box 6.7.

Some of the elements recorded in Box 6.7 would be quite difficult to put numbers against, but that does not make them any the less important. What that set of views shows more than anything else is that this project contributed significantly to a real and worthwhile improvement in the quality of life on an estate which had previously been troubled, and the value of this to the residents themselves was clearly very real. The researchers also felt that there

Box 6.6 The Blackthorn CASPAR project: what did it achieve?

Statistics covering the total number of recorded crimes in the Blackthorn estate area appear to confirm the success of the project in these terms, since an overall number of 832 in 1998 had fallen by nearly two-thirds to 292 in 2001. Just as important, the residents feel greater ownership of the estate and facilities have been developed to provide community growth. There is a general feeling that things are much better, and that residents are fully involved in the decision-making process. Communication between the Borough Council, County Council, Police and community is excellent and is vital to sustain momentum. Problems are debated along with the Good Neighbours Project, Youth provision, Mums and Tots Group Play Schemes and Holiday Provision, Lifelong Learning Service, Neighbourhood Warden and Elderly Residents Groups. Council housing now has a waiting list, and the value of private housing has increased.

One of the strengths of the project is the sharing of information with all relevant organisations and agencies. This has led to a greater degree of partnership working which in turn has involved the implementation of longer-term strategies to overcome the problems. Targeting known drug criminals (especially dealers) resulted in arrests, and when they were eventually released from custody they were made to feel unwelcome and many moved away. Consequently, the next generation of dealers has not materialised.

The main benefit of the project lies in the residents reclaiming their streets and feeling that they are living in a safer environment. The project has dealt with a very complex problem, adopting an integrated approach, based on thorough research and the formulation of an effective strategy. All members of the community have been involved and nobody has been excluded. The project has addressed the causes and not just the manifestation of the problems and has been very targeted to a particular set of circumstances – as a result it may not be easily replicable in other cities.

Source: British Urban Regeneration Association (2002, p. 7).

Box 6.7 Resident perceptions of the benefits of the Blackthorn CASPAR project over and above the reduction in recorded crime

- Enhanced community spirit: for example, greater participation in community events, and children playing out on (previously dangerous) streets.
- Greater confidence within the community – both in their own capacity to effect change and in the willingness and ability of the local authorities and the police to respond to their needs and demands.
- Higher levels of engagement in community activities, such as meetings and events.
- People were starting to choose to move into the area, resulting in house prices going up and the number of void council-owned properties diminishing
- The changed physical environment, such as better street lighting, fewer trees and overgrown hedges and shrubs, and safer streets (because of barriers and traffic calming).
- New and improved facilities: a new children's play area and a new multi-purpose sports facility.
- Greater take-up of community-based training courses.
- More provision for children and young people in the form of clubs and activities.

Source: Summarised from Pitts *et al.* (2002, p. 12).

---

were five 'implicit theories of change' that the available evidence strongly suggested had been supported in practice:

1 Increasing the level of interaction between residents and between CASPAR personnel and residents around the development of community facilities (such as pre-school play provision and youth clubs) raised the morale of residents, improved their relationship with the CASPAR worker and the collaborating agencies, and developed a sense of commonality between residents and an enhanced willingness to act together with professionals against crime and disorder.

2 Inter-agency information sharing by a variety of means (such as joint project management, the development of information-sharing protocols between agencies, and the creation of a forum for informal discussion and support) contributed significantly to the effective delivery of several elements of the Blackthorn CASPAR package.

3 Neighbourhood wardens, through the provision of various types of counselling, advice and assistance, helped to reduce the opportunity for

and to deter burglars, to reduce the fear of crime and criminals among residents, and to increase the willingness to supply information and to give evidence against targeted criminals;

4 The placing of 'good news' stories in the local press raised the morale of local residents and gave them a greater stake in the neighbourhood; helped to attract more bona fide tenants to the area and thereby to fill voids and to displace squatters, and to increase the attractiveness of owner-occupation on the estate (which not only raised property prices but also increased further the numbers of local residents with a financial stake in the area); and contributed to collective efficacy;

5 Improvements to landscaping and to lighting deterred opportunist crime, deterred motorcycle nuisance and danger, deterred car dumping, deterred illicit car selling and deterred fly-tipping.

(Pitts *et al.*, 2002, pp. 14–20)

Taken together, the results of these evaluation processes are impressive, and they suggest that this was a successful project with lessons to offer about how environmental works, when taken together with the other elements of the Blackthorn CASPAR package and in particular with close working with the community and effective partner–agency cooperation, can contribute to a significant reduction in the experience of crime on a problem estate. This makes this an important project, because situations like that experienced on the Blackthorn estate before the start of this project are not uncommon either in Britain or in much of the rest of the world. It could be argued that what was done here was not very dramatic or even very high-profile (at any rate, until it won a national award), but what it does appear to have been is successful at any rate in its own terms. And this, more than anything else, is what makes this a project from which valuable lessons can be learned.

At the same time, it is important to keep these conclusions in perspective. Barry Poyner, in revisiting his carefully collected data about the experience of crime in relation to localities in Northampton and Harrow, paid particular attention to the Blackthorn Estate, in part because of the award-winning status of the CASPAR project (Poyner, 2006, pp. 68–83), and this is very helpful because it offers a rather different perspective on this particular case study. His stance is essentially that the problems experienced on this estate which gave rise to the need for the project derive at least in part from significant design faults, which have tended to get worse over time (ibid., p. 80). Thus, the Blackthorn CASPAR project is about trying to find ways of coping with an inherently flawed situation and of improving the experience of living on the estate for its citizens as much as possible, but it does not eliminate the original design characteristics that have contributed significantly to the estate's experience of crime in the intervening years. Poyner supports this stance by looking at the detailed evidence in relation to three types of crimes, comparing in each case data from 1987 and 2000: burglary, theft of cars, and thefts from inside cars. It should be noted in fairness, therefore, that the more modern data relate to the position during the life of the Blackthorn CASPAR project rather than at its end. What this showed was that there had been a reduction in both car theft and theft from inside cars[2] over the period in question, but that the rate of burglary had stayed at much the same high level (ibid.).

The principal design feature of the Blackthorn Estate that Poyner sees as encouraging burglary is easy entry from back paths to back gardens. For theft from inside cars, the principal design weaknesses are seen as the many footpath connections and general maturity of foliage in front gardens, which may reduce surveillance of the street from the houses. In this latter instance, Poyner believes that the CASPAR project has had a positive impact on theft from inside cars because of the removal of overgrown landscape material (especially around communal parking areas), because of increased police activity, and because of adaptive behaviour by residents in finding other ways of parking cars rather than using the designated communal parking spaces (ibid.). We can certainly relate to this last point, because one of the elements that was very noticeable during our visit to the Blackthorn Estate was the large number of cars parked away from formal spaces on locations such as grass verges on access roads.

Poyner's overall conclusion is as follows:

> In both crimes (burglary and theft from inside cars) there is an emergent principle that if the layout and design is essentially secure to start with, then it will remain safe or improve. This may include designs with the opportunity for improvements to be made by residents. If the design and layout is basically flawed with weaknesses such as insecure back gardens easily entered from back paths, communal parking and extensive networks of footpaths then the problems of crime will often continue to grow. The secondary development of social problems such as the establishment of illegal drug markets seems to emerge in already established crime hot spots. No doubt the selling of drugs and the high crime levels feed off each other.
>
> (ibid.)

So, what are we to make of this? Is this essentially a contradictory view to that of the formal evaluation of the Blackthorn CASPAR project? We would suggest that it is an important marker that should make us stop and think carefully about situations such as this. The Blackthorn Estate experienced high levels of crime, we would suggest, in part because of its design. In this respect, it is like a large number of other housing estates from a similar period up and down the country. The Blackthorn CASPAR project shows that it is possible to intervene in situations such as this and do things which make the position better for residents. This is both a worthy and a desirable outcome, because it is simply not a practical possibility to go round demolishing every housing estate where the individual houses still have a considerable proportion of their planned life remaining but where the layout of the estate contains crime-encouraging characteristics such as easy entry to back gardens, insecure communal parking areas and an extensive network of footpaths providing ready access and escape routes. So, physical works and community-related developments that improve this situation for local residents are desirable; and the Blackthorn CASPAR project shows that this can be a positive process. But it has not eliminated all the crime-producing design characteristics, as our photographs in Figure 6.3 show, and it is difficult to see how it could have done. So, this remains an inherently unsafe layout. The real lesson of Blackthorn CASPAR, therefore, may be that while something can be done to make this situation better, it is surely preferable not to construct housing layouts like this in the first place, since doing so almost certainly designs-in crime problems throughout the life of the estate, which subsequent intervention may limit but will not remove.

Conclusions

What we have discussed in this chapter essentially is three propositions. The first is that as the urban regeneration process in Britain has become more highly structured, has expanded both the scale and the span of the activities carried out in its name, and has seen an ever-greater broad policy drive by central government alongside its increase in funding for urban regeneration, so issues of concern about crime have moved to centre stage. The days when urban regeneration was mainly about property development, and when issues to do with crime scarcely got a look in, have long since gone – although it should be noted in this context that the heyday of the focus on property development (around the mid-1980s) also preceded the period when the relationship between planning processes and crime prevention discussed in Chapter 4 started to be explored in government policy documentation. Today, urban regeneration, especially at the neighbourhood scale, is about improving the quality of people's lives in deprived localities, and concerns about crime prevention are a central feature of work of this nature, just as they tend to be in resident feedback about their experiences of living in such localities.

The second area that this chapter has explored is the process of thinking strategically about crime prevention in an urban regeneration context, using the structures and processes visible in Sheffield as a case study. One of the primary characteristics of these particular arrangements is that two previously separate sets of processes – the requirement to establish crime and disorder reduction partnerships under the Crime and Disorder Act 1998, and the structure of regeneration partnerships operating under the aegis of the local strategic partnership – have been merged, thereby giving formal expression to the role of crime prevention in urban regeneration. The Sheffield case illustrates the strategic process in action, and shows how concerns about crime prevention are embedded in views about what needs to be done to improve the city and the lives of its citizens. It would, of course, be possible to tackle issues such as action in the built environment to reduce the opportunity to commit crime without such a strategic framework being in place, and in many parts of the world this is indeed what happens. It would also be possible for the structures that were put in place to be less formal and less top-down than they are in the British case; and it is important to acknowledge in this context that there is concern both about the time and effort involved in this kind of partnership working and about whether in effect it adds commensurate value or merely complexity (Urban Task Force, 2005). But the British model offers the opportunity to study both the pluses and the minuses that derive from such a highly structured process, and for the purposes of this book that is a useful thing to be able to do.

The third focus of this chapter has been on an example of the kind of multi-purpose and multi-agency approach to problems of crime and antisocial behaviour in a problem estate where the recent intervention has been fostered by the urban regeneration process, and in particular by its emphasis on regeneration at the neighbourhood scale. The Blackthorn CASPAR project was an award-winning project because of the clear evidence that it had been able to make a difference to the quality of people's lives, and ultimately that is the primary purpose of this kind of action. There is probably nothing particularly remarkable about the individual elements of the Blackthorn CASPAR project, and there is no doubt that most of them could be found replicated elsewhere in one form or another. But what marks it out from the norm is that these elements were undertaken in an integrated manner as part and parcel of working closely with the local community, and also with the intention of getting public agencies delivering services to the estate to work together more effectively. This holistic approach appears to have been the hallmark of the success of the project, and it may well be that the most important lessons that it offers are around taking initiatives in mutually reinforcing ways in close conjunction with the local community rather than around the contents of the individual initiatives themselves. Nevertheless, the project has not eliminated all of the elements in an inherently unsafe layout that cause it to be described as such, and it is often the case that, for very practical reasons, retrofitting activities of this nature are only able to bring about a certain amount of improvement. So, the project demonstrates that activities of this nature are worthwhile if they can make things better for residents, but it also surely suggests to us that it would have been better to have avoided these kinds of issues arising in the first place by the adoption of a less crime-inducing layout.

Taken together, these elements demonstrate how crime prevention has become a central element in the process of urban regeneration in Britain, and how environmental actions sit alongside other kinds of actions in strategically driven approaches to the task of crime prevention. Whether the British model is something that other countries would wish to replicate depends upon many factors, including how readily such approaches would sit within their cultures of governance, but there are surely lessons to be learned from the British experience irrespective of the views taken about whether to copy it. Looking at examples of good practice, as this chapter has done, is one way of seeking to learn from experience, and as well as offering lessons for elsewhere, one of the characteristics of the cases looked at here is the role that evaluation plays in contributing to improving the processes being studied themselves. Perhaps the most important lesson here from both of these perspectives is the value of seeing crime prevention in an urban regeneration context, because it is not merely a desirable thing in itself but also a major contributor to improving the quality of life in a locality. There are many possible ways of doing this, but whatever ways are chosen, the connection between crime prevention and all the other actions taken in the name of urban regeneration (or whatever it may be called in other parts of the world) is of critical importance.

7

The development of place-based anti-terrorism strategies in the United States

Introduction

This chapter describes the incorporation of place-based crime prevention theory and practice into emerging anti-terrorist planning and design strategies in the United States. While many nations have experienced terrorism, we concentrate on the United States by virtue of worldwide repercussions resulting from the cataclysmic attacks of 9/11, and the sheer immensity of response, which touches in one way or another virtually every discipline, profession and public policy across the globe (Eisinger, 2004). In so doing, the chapter addresses the problems of defining terrorism and delineates differences between anti-terrorism and counter-terrorism, spelling out elements of each. The long history of terrorism is briefly discussed, with a special emphasis on place-based terrorist attacks. Four major planning- and urban design-related anti-terrorist theories and orientations are described, involving 'target shrinking', 'scatter-gun', 'Let Cities be Cities' and 'target hardening' approaches, and each theory is critiqued relative to fundamental urban quality of life and security design issues. Commonalities and conflicts between place-based crime prevention and anti-terrorist planning and design are explored, as well as suggestions as to whether or not the differences can be reconciled.

The chapter then discusses two examples illustrating the adoption of place-based crime prevention approaches as the bases for anti-terrorist interventions. The first example is derived from a major recent study of 113 major transit operators in the United States, and the second comes from the design and implementation of an anti-terrorist site plan for a major anti-drug smuggling facility in Key West, Florida, to protect it against narco-terrorist attacks.

The chapter concludes with an assessment of the relationship between place-based crime prevention strategies and anti-terrorist planning and design practice, including lessons learned.

Definitions

Terrorism

In the context of horrific events such as 9/11 and the Madrid and London transit system attacks, it is reasonable to think that the definition of terrorism is clear-cut and unambiguous. In fact, defining terrorism has been a contentious international issue since it emerged formally onto the world stage in the mid-1930s, following a series of assassinations and related violent incidents. In 1937 the League of Nations' Convention for the Prevention and Punishment of Terrorism attempted a definition as '[a]ll criminal acts directed against a State and intended or calculated to create a state of terror in the minds of particular persons or a group of persons or the general public' (League of Nations, 1937).

Though remarkably durable and having an influence on subsequent attempts to define terrorism, this characterisation never achieved widespread acceptance. Indeed, the League and its successor, the United Nations, have struggled mightily with the task of achieving a unified definition of terrorism inasmuch as none is accepted by all UN member states (Saul, 2006). This problem, according to the UN Office on Drugs and Crime, which defines terrorism as 'the peacetime equivalent of a war crime', presents one of the most formidable barriers to the development of effective *counter-measures* to terrorism (see http://www.unodc.org/unodc/terrorism_definitions.html). The classic response is to say that what some states call a terrorist, others call a freedom fighter. But this evasion provides subjective justification of virtually all terrorist acts and begs the question as to whether there are not universal standards of human conduct and decency that set baselines for fundamental behaviour, no matter what the cause or country. It further obscures the fact that terrorism persists because, as some argue, it tends to provide rewards to perpetrators, irrespective of the purity or malice of their motivations (see Dershowitz, 2002).[1]

In the United States, terrorism has been defined variously by different federal agencies and offices. One widely used definition has been '[t]he unlawful use of force and violence against persons and property to intimidate or coerce a government, the civilian population, or any segment thereof, in furtherance of political or social objectives' (Code of Federal Regulation, Title 28, Section 0.85). The National Counterterrorism Center (NCTC), an agency established by presidential order in 2004, counts terrorist incidents as those that are 'premeditated; perpetrated by a subnational or clandestine agent; politically motivated, potentially including religious, philosophical, or culturally symbolic motivations; violent; and perpetrated against a noncombatant target' (National Counterterrorism Center, 2005, p. vii). The definition excludes 'ordinary criminal activity, genocidal events, and tribal violence', as well as 'hate crimes to the extent that they [can] be distinguished from terrorist attacks' (p. vii).

Although there is no common definition, the *functional* aspects of terrorism tend to be common. They include the infliction of harm – often unspeakable acts – including damage to structures as well as personal and psychological damage to individuals and to the public by *politically powerless* groups (this latter part is subject to much debate). Terrorist acts are often accompanied by publicity in which the acts are justified on the grounds that they serve a higher good. The end goals sought usually involve a fundamental change in public policy and behaviours which may have social, political and ideological (including religious) implications.

As we know from daily news reports, terrorism is manifested in many ways, including bio-terrorism; attacks on civil transport, including aviation and seafaring vessels; assaults against buildings, bridges, ports and other structures; cyberterrorism; and sabotage of industrial and agricultural products and processes, and critical infrastructure, such as dams, water supplies and power plants.[2] A primary strategy, of course, is assaults against people directly, especially people in massed groups. The list has grown considerably over the past 40 years as terrorists have taken advantage of the evolution of technology and mass media coverage and have expanded the range of targets and the relative sophistication of attacks. This is so even though most terrorist attacks are variations on a few basic themes, usually involving explosive devices of one sort or another and common delivery modes, such as vehicular transport. Certainly, other means and modes are possible, such as the mailing of biological pathogens, as in the autumn 2001 anthrax attacks in the United States (Heyman, 2002).

We distinguish between *place-based* terrorism (and anti-terrorism measures) as compared to that which, by target focus, is not tied to an environmental feature or element and is not likely to be influenced by design or planning strategies. For example, cyberterrorism, biological terrorist attack, and industrial or agricultural sabotage are not generally place based, although they may incidentally involve place elements. In most other forms of terrorism, places are integral to the act either directly or indirectly, and therefore may be subject to design or planning intervention techniques. The 9/11 attacks were place-based attacks, though the mode of transport used makes mitigation and counter-terrorism (discussed below) the main planning and design responses, as distinct from anti-terrorist defence. Only a relatively small proportion of common crimes, such as burglary and vandalism, have strong place-based elements, although these may certainly play a role in other offences, such as shoplifting and assaults.

Another fundamental element that distinguishes terrorism from common crime is incidence and repetition. The NCTC tracks terrorist incidents around the world and reports a total of 13 incidents in the United States between February 2004 and May 2005 (National Counterterrorism Center, 2006). Compared to that, the Federal Bureau of Investigation (2004) identifies 10.3 million property crimes and nearly 1.4 million violent crimes in 2004. This disparity greatly influences threat and risk assessments and response at all levels of government and in the private sector, and has significant impacts on indemnification policies and practice (Federal Emergency Management Agency, 2003a, b, 2005; American Academy of Actuaries, 2004).

At the international level, recent data released by the NCTC suggest that the number of terrorist attacks, including kidnappings, exceeded 10,000 worldwide in 2005 (National Counterterrorism Center, 2006). Most of the increase in incidents stems from attacks in Iraq, although comparing data from year to year is complicated by changing government definitions of terrorism, which, as noted above, explicitly include attacks against civilians.

Anti-terrorism

We concentrate in this chapter on *anti-terrorist* measures as distinct from *counter-terrorist* measures. Anti-terrorism refers primarily to *defensive* measures that can be taken to protect people and property from terrorist acts, whereas *counter-terrorism* refers primarily to *offensive* measures to combat terrorism (Federal Emergency Management Agency, 2003a). The latter category of activity is rightfully the province of military and law enforcement agencies such as, in the United States, the Department of Defense, the FBI and the CIA. The former category can involve a wide array of activities and actors, including civil defence and emergency management authorities, and state, regional and city planning agencies. Each can have a say in local-level urban design and place management activities. There are, as well, a host of place-based anti-terrorist planning, design and management responses made by private individuals to defend against terrorist attack.

Following 9/11, significant federal resources – hundreds of millions of dollars – have been directed to states and to local police agencies for them to develop databases that support existing anti-terrorist intelligence-gathering efforts, or to create new ones. The theory behind this investment is that 'local cops are America's front line defence against terrorism' (Kaplan, 2006, p. 42), and that 9/11 proved that national law enforcement and intelligence agencies have not done a very good job of sharing information with local police. The view is that, like politics, 'all terrorism is local' (International Association of Chiefs of Police, 2005). The results of this federal largesse have been a local technology and data-gathering boom that has been credited with reducing crime rates, but has also been criticised because of the lack of binding guidelines to constrain civil rights violations by untrained and overzealous police (Kaplan, 2006). In this context, local police investigations have been accused of blurring the already fuzzy line between anti-terrorism and counter-terrorism.

Within the general category of anti-terrorist – defensive – planning there are two general types of action and a third that crosses both categories. The first is *preventive* measures and the second is *responsive* measures. The third type of action, *mitigation*, applies to both prevention and response.

Preventive strategy, in relation to place-based anti-terrorist land use and urban design, is epitomised in the United States by the National Capital Planning Commission's *National Capital Urban Design and Security Plan* (2002b, 2004, 2005) for Washington, DC, which includes a focus on the city's 'monumental core' area, an area that contains a large number of potential terrorist targets. This plan suggests a range of zoning, transportation and street-level design changes aimed at melding security with aesthetics. London's 'ring of steel', a defensive cordon around the city comprising surveillance, guardianship, access control and target hardening applications, provoked by a series of Irish Republican Army (IRA) attacks in the 1990s is another example of place-based anti-terrorist planning and design that incorporates defensive and preventive strategies. The London approach is being considered by New York City as a means of better protecting lower Manhattan from terrorist attack and as a strategy to fight crime as well (Mollenkamp and Haughney, 2006).

Responsive measures include, but are not limited to, policy planning that minimises the *effects* (especially the long-term ones) of terrorist attack on the rebuilding of property and the reintegration of affected or damaged areas into the fabric of the existing community. Examples here are the planning and regeneration policies adopted in Manchester in response to the 1996 IRA bomb attack, which devastated the city's centre (Kitchen, 2001), and the extraordinary efforts surrounding the repair and revitalisation of Ground Zero in New York City. In the latter case, some have argued that the magnitude of the disaster and the public stakes involved overwhelmed planning and political processes that sought to expedite redevelopment efforts and help restore public confidence (Hajer, 2005).

It is clear that responsive measures to terrorism can be crafted by private parties as well as by public agencies. One example is the recommendation of the Rand Report, commissioned by the Building Owners and Managers Association of Greater Los Angeles (BOMA), which suggested policy and programme changes by government *and* the private sector to deter or mitigate the effects of a terrorist attack on the 18 high-rise buildings (those over 500 feet, or *c.* 150 metres) in the city's central business district (Archibald *et al.*, 2002). The importance of private-sector participation in anti-terrorism planning and design is emphasised by the fact that approximately 85 per cent of the nation's infrastructure, including that which is considered 'critical', is owned and operated by private enterprise (White House, 2003).

Mitigation strategies seek to reduce the impacts of terrorist attack by minimising damage to targets or by displacing them to others that are less vulnerable but also less desirable (from the perpetrator's point of view). There is a growing body of crime prevention literature on displacement, some of which has undoubtedly influenced anti-terrorist planning and design (Schneider, 2003; Schneider and Kitchen, 2002). Examples of anti-terrorist strategies that combine prevention and mitigation can be seen in the execution of new design, target hardening, guardianship and public educational elements in the New York, Paris, Madrid, Tokyo and London transit systems following long-term 'low-level' attacks (for example, from the IRA in Britain and the Basque nationalists in Spain) and after recent spectacular attacks such as those perpetrated in Madrid and London (Taylor *et al.*, 2005). We will discuss these applications in more detail below.

A brief history of terrorism

It is ironic that while most definitions of terrorism crafted by states seek to avoid terms that implicate government action itself, the term is derived from horrors inflicted by the ruling Jacobins during the French Revolution (1789–1799). The French word *terrorisme* (from the Latin for 'to frighten') originated in the course of the 'Reign of Terror' initiated under the direction of Maximilien Robespierre following the death of Louis XVI in 1793. Robespierre (1794) said:

> If the spring of popular government in time of peace is virtue, the springs of popular government in revolution are at once virtue and terror: virtue, without which terror is fatal; terror, without which virtue is powerless. Terror is nothing other than justice, prompt, severe, inflexible; it is therefore an emanation of virtue; it is not so much a special principle as it is a consequence of the general principle of democracy applied to our country's most urgent needs.
>
> (Quoted by Halsall, 1997)

Also, atrocities committed by the Nazi, Soviet and Khmer Rouge regimes lend incontrovertible credence to the notion that terrorism is not the sole province of the politically powerless or non-state groups. Nevertheless, common modern parlance associates the terrorist label with groups or individuals out of power rather than those in power.

Aside from the mass murders of the twentieth century committed or sanctioned by the regimes above, the long history of terrorism – extending back far beyond the Jacobins – is marked instead by small-scale individual acts such as assaults and assassinations on individual citizens and public officials. Indeed, many modern terms associated with such deeds – zealotry, assassin, thug – are rooted in the predations of ancient religious sects and cults on individuals.[3] Modern mass terrorism is largely a function of the available technology, including weapons and communication media, and especially television and the Internet. Before explosives and automatic weapons, terrorist attacks generally could only be perpetrated on a small-scale basis or, with a little imagination, extended through the use of fire. Indeed, the first 'modern' terrorist is an arsonist, John Akin, nicknamed 'John the Painter'. A Scot by birth, Akin also earned the reputation as the first international terrorist after he tried to burn down English dockyards and associated buildings (Bristol and Portsmouth) in support of the American Revolution. For his efforts he was hanged in 1777 in front of 20,000 spectators from the mast of a ship in Portsmouth harbour (Warner, 2004).

Burgess (2003, pp. 2–7) categorises the evolution of terrorism from the 1790s onward into four periods: (1) 'nationalists and anarchists', including Italian revolutionary Carlo Pisacane and Russian anti-Tsarists in the 1870s; (2) 'terrorism and the state', including covert Serbian support for the assassination of Archduke Franz Ferdinand, which helped precipitate World War I; (3) 'terrorism since World War II', characterised by the emergence of nationalist and anti-colonial terrorism across the world, particularly in Algeria, Cyprus, Ireland, Kenya and Palestine; and (4) 'contemporary terrorism', which surfaced full-blown in the United States following Oklahoma City and the two attacks on the World Trade Center, and especially 9/11.

But well before Oklahoma City and 9/11, terrorism began to emerge widely as a factor in US public perception and then in policy after the first American commercial airliners were hijacked in the late 1960s. Killen (2005) reports that over 150 US aircraft had been taken, mostly to Cuba, by the end of 1972. Most of these crimes were perpetrated by mentally unbalanced persons and by 'escaped convicts, fugitives and the occasional Black Panther' (ibid., p. 22). Virtually all were acts of loners, and relatively few of them had serious political (as opposed to personal) objectives. Nevertheless, these events came to presage the age of mass terrorism, and they pressed the federal government under the Nixon administration to begin to implement anti-hijacking measures.

Although there had been other small-scale terrorist attacks that stirred the public and authorities in the United States, notably the long-running New York City 'Mad Bomber'[4] case in the 1940s and 1950s, and the two-decade-long saga of the 'Unabomber'[5] case, nothing captured the attention of the public and policy makers more than the first bombing of the World Trade Center in New York City in 1993 and the subsequent devastation of the Murrah Building in Oklahoma City two years later. These two attacks opened the door to the modern era of terrorism in the United States, and the events of 9/11 pulled the nation – along with the rest of the world – inextricably across the threshold. There is a vast and growing literature on the events leading up to and surrounding 11 September, which we shall not attempt to recount here.[6] Moreover, there are seemingly endless reports and analyses that flow from the events of that day, and these too are beyond the scope of our present discussion. Rather, we turn to a discussion of some fundamental anti-terrorist theories that have influenced the initiation of *place-based* anti-terrorist measures in the United States undertaken by federal and state and, in some cases, by private institutions.

Some anti-terrorist theories and orientations

Although there are undoubtedly others, we identify four provocative theories that have implications relating to place-based anti-terrorist planning and design interventions. There is no doubt that other views will emerge as academic and professional study of this area matures and as both terrorism and anti-terrorist technology continue to evolve.

The first of these is what we term the *target shrinking* theory. It is opined by planning professor John Friedmann (2002), who suggests that the potential for terrorist attack in the United States can best be reduced through a shift in fundamental consumption philosophy and in the resulting planning, design and development practice. He argues that 'green' design and sustainable building practices would reduce Americans' consumption of a disproportionate share of the world's resources, especially compared to that of citizens of developing nations, and would effectively limit the 'footprint' of American cities making them less likely targets. There are, of course, many reasons other than their impact on terrorism for considering arguments of this nature, but for present purposes we focus on this particular proposition.

Friedmann rejects the notion that we can escape terrorism by hiding behind walls or by making the nation's cities fortresses, as implied by the 'ring of steel' conceptions for New York City and London. His argument is to change the essential nature of targets so as to reduce their real *and* symbolic value to terrorists. In so doing, his proposal represents a fundamental shift of values and lifestyles that in his view would lessen the attractiveness of US cities as targets. It opens the question as to whether public policy can be redirected to effectuate such prescriptions without extraordinary market pressures brought on by high fuel prices, without advances in technology that would obviate demand for petroleum and related products, or without the push of cataclysmic events such as other 9/11s. Furthermore, it only indirectly addresses issues in the terrorists' own nations and cultures and, uncomfortably, turns the terrorism equation on its head by asking, 'Who really are the victims and victimisers?' Friedmann's views are echoed by others who suggest that terrorism is the product of a lack of social justice and equity relative to harvesting the fruits of the free market system, leaving those on the outside 'embittered and hateful' (Vernon Jordan, paraphrased in Ziegler, 2005, p. 143).

A second viewpoint, which we call the *scatter-gun theory*, has also been called 'defensive dispersal' (Ziegler, 2005, p. 100). Its history stretches back to the early Cold War period when urban planners took the lead in urging the government to adopt policies that would deconcentrate US cities as a means of protecting them against nuclear attacks and making them more resilient to their after-effects. Among those espousing the view at the time was a president of the American Institute of Planners (AIP), Tracy B. Augur, who argued that a 'dispersed pattern of small, efficient cities' would make the nation's cities more durable following an attack (Augur, 1948, p. 29). The call was heeded by academics, by practitioners and by a variety of federal agencies, and was subsequently incorporated into fundamental federal housing legislation enacted by Congress.[7] Ziegler (2005) and Dudley (2001) document the spread of this concept and argue convincingly that it was a major impetus behind the construction of the nation's interstate highway system, the primary catalyst of urban sprawl and suburban development in the United States.

This old strategy for nuclear survival has been carried forward by some, such as historian Stephen Ambrose, into the new age of anti-terrorism planning. Ambrose suggests that, as a result of technological advances, 'it is no longer necessary to pack so many people and office [*sic*] into such small space in lower Manhattan [or other large cities]. They can be scattered in neighboring regions and states, where they can work just as effectively and in far more security' (2002, p. A24). Resource equity issues aside, Ambrose argues for the diffusion of targets as a *strategic* response to terrorist attack. Others, such as planner Joe Feinberg, echo Augur in suggesting that the answer lies, in large part, in regional decentralisation that will reduce the vulnerabilities of densely packed central cities.

He argues that this is the logical extension of a trend that is already under way for businesses, and specifically large corporations, in the United States (Feinberg, 2002). This thesis is supported by census and housing construction data showing that Americans generally continue to move from large cities to suburbs and 'exurbs' (Ziegler, 2005), a pattern of sprawl representing a tendency that has been under way in the United States for almost a century. Feinberg suggests that it is possible to reduce the daytime concentration of population and vehicles in the United States' central cities, which makes traffic congestion a terrible problem and disaster evacuation a nightmare. He links this argument with one that would put emphasis on reinvigorating the American railway system, which would help reduce the terrorist vulnerability of air travel since, he says, we are far too reliant on airline transportation. (One could argue, however, that this would simply lead to displacement to other targets, as the London and Madrid railway bombings illustrate.) Feinberg's view reiterates the Cold War's nuclear survival strategy as it focuses on moving the target rather than transforming it, although the rapid decentralisation of cities would no doubt have that effect nevertheless.

A third viewpoint is expressed by the 'let cities be cities' theory, named after comments by Sam Casella, past president of the American Institute of Certified Planners (Casella, 2003). This thinking stands in contrast to the views already discussed and is echoed by many planning, urban design, growth management and anti-terrorist academics and practitioners across the United States. Casella argues that the decentralising of development does not necessarily offer increased security since terrorism is a 'dynamic threat, not limited to tall buildings' or to dense settlements (ibid.). To illustrate that point he notes that 'We could scatter Manhattan's population to the winds and still offer the juicy target of a college football stadium packed with 100,000 people on a Saturday afternoon. The answer to terrorism is eradication of terrorism, not eradication of targets' (ibid.). Casella suggests that population and industrial sprawl are the wrong answers to terrorism since they promote too much reliance on pollution-emitting vehicles, on the spread of road networks, on inefficient land use systems and on policies that ultimately degrade needed human connectivity. Moreover, he points out that dense urban areas are the crucibles of civilisation and that dispersing them would give terrorists a great victory yet would not make us any safer (ibid.). Much the same argument is made by Langdon and other new urbanists (see Chapter 3), who suggest that 'the war against terrorism threatens to become a war against the liveability of American cities' (2004, p. 1).

A fourth viewpoint is voiced in the context of the *target hardening theory*. It focuses less on moving targets or dispersing them and more on making them more resistant to attack through physical reinforcement or alterations. It is generally associated with types of *access control*, a fundamental place-based crime prevention principle found in defensible space and CPTED (discussed in Chapter 2) and included in situational crime prevention theory as a means of reducing opportunity and increasing risk to offenders (again, see Chapter 2). Elements of this approach are perhaps best expressed in the previously mentioned *National Capital Urban Design and Security Plan*, which proposes to secure the nation's monumental core area better by developing a coordinated array of integrated and aesthetically pleasing 'reinforced street benches, trash cans, lampposts, and other street side elements to serve as kerbside vehicle barriers' (National Capital Planning Commission, 2004, p. A2).

These are intended to be alternatives to the overused bollards and planters that are found throughout Washington and other major US cities. The ultimate aim is to provide effective access control against terrorist threats yet minimise the visual and physical intrusion of the mechanisms into public spaces. In the conception of the Federal Emergency Management Agency (2003a, 2005), such approaches create environments that are more troublesome to attack and more resilient to the consequences of attack, and that provide more protection to citizens in the event of an attack.

Though a time-honoured and effective approach to crime prevention, target hardening has been criticised when applied to cities as a defence against terrorist attacks. Some have linked increased reliance on target hardening to a growing 'militarisation' of urban civil society, accelerated by recent terrorist attacks but growing out of other causes as well (Graham, 2005). One of the most notable critiques comes from Oscar Newman, father of defensible space. Newman suggests that 'the vast majority of anti terrorist efforts should go into *counter-terrorism* efforts', such as 'eliminating terrorists', since that is 'far more cost effective than target hardening and it will keep us from imprisoning ourselves and closing down that very aspect of our society that is the envy of every impoverished and authoritarian nation in the world: its openness' (Newman, 2001). Newman reasons that access control efforts are likely to be ineffective against terrorists, who would merely find ways around the barriers. Indeed, terrorists, like ordinary criminals, are infinitely adaptable. In recognition of this, architects, planners and designers who specialise in crime prevention applications are beginning to create designs that at least keep up with or, optimally, are a step ahead of criminals, including terrorists. This is consistent with Ekblom's notion that designers should think through the potential *misuse* of their end products as much as they consider their designed, 'proper' uses (1997b).

There is undeniable validity to Newman's arguments. Despite that, and despite the fact that target hardening can be ineffective and have counter-intuitive consequences, such as fear-inducing 'fortressing' (Blakely and Snyder, 1997; Schneider and Kitchen, 2002; Gamman and Pascoe, 2004), there is empirical evidence suggesting its effectiveness in crime prevention (Pascoe and Topping, 2000) and anti-terrorism, although in the latter case, this is mixed. Israel's El Al airline, probably one of the most prized terrorist targets, and the security perimeter that is currently under construction along Israel's borders with Palestinian lands are examples of effective target hardening applications.

El Al has not had any hijackings since 1968, before its current security system was put into place. That system combines layered physical security including hardened targets, guardianship and extraordinary management policies, including extensive passenger interrogations. So effective is El Al's perceived security that its ticket sales actually soared following 9/11, unlike those of most other airlines. Passengers too frightened to fly with other carriers opted for El Al instead, presumably because of its reputation for effective security (Walt, 2001). At a different scale, the controversial Israeli security perimeter system has dramatically reduced suicide bombings in Israel. Indeed, this access control device has been perceived as so successful in decreasing attacks that it has been endorsed overwhelmingly by an otherwise fragmented Israeli public as the prime means of protecting the nation from attack by Islamic suicide bombers (Yaar and Hermann, 2004).

Against this view, critics point out that such physical means of combating terrorism ignore long-term political and economic solutions, while providing only a temporary and largely imperfect fix. Moreover, there is evidence that target hardening applications do not always work, such as that documented by Lum *et al.* (2006) relative to fortifying embassies against terrorist attack. As of this writing, similar questions are being raised in the United States in relation to a proposal to construct a layered security fence across the Mexican–US border aimed at controlling the flow of illegal migrants as well as potential terrorists (Lo Scalzo, 2006).

As the foregoing arguments illustrate, there are a number of philosophies about planning- and design-related responses marshalled against terrorist threats. Threaded throughout these arguments are fundamental notions about the evolution and functions of cities, about human behaviour in relation to environmental design, and about strategic and day-to-day anti-terrorist responses. Some of these ideas are seemingly opposed to each other, while others are compatible within limited frameworks. Among the menu of possibilities discussed is a range of place-based anti-terrorist measures that have grown primarily out of the stream of thinking associated with CPTED and, to a lesser extent, situational crime prevention, both of which are linked, at least in part, to target hardening approaches. We turn now to the connections between CPTED, situational crime prevention and anti-terrorist planning and design, and consider what these approaches have in common and how they are at odds. Following that, we provide some illustrative examples of such measures in practice in the United States.

Place-based crime prevention strategies and anti-terrorist planning and design

In searching for reasonable, cost-effective strategies to combat terrorism, the importance of place-based crime prevention strategies, and especially CPTED, in anti-terrorist planning and design has grown significantly since 9/11. Evidence of this comes from public-sector agencies such as the Department of Homeland Security (DHS), which now incorporates a range of 'CPTED anti-terrorism' guidelines into *The Office for Domestic Security Preparedness Guidelines for Homeland Security* (Department of Homeland Security, 2003, pp 15–18), and FEMA (now an agency within DHS), which suggests that CPTED principles be implemented in site planning and landscape design to mitigate terrorism and technological hazards (Federal Emergency Management Agency, 2003a–d, 2005). These inclusions are in sharp contrast to omissions in the 1995 hearings of the US House of Representatives' Subcommittee on Buildings and Economic Development, which conducted extensive investigations of the security of federal buildings soon after the bombing of the Murrah Building in Oklahoma City. Not a single reference to CPTED or to any of the other place-based crime prevention strategies is made in the voluminous testimony (Committee on Transportation and Infrastructure, 1996). In less than seven years, CPTED has become a prime design and planning tool of federal agencies in the war against terrorism in the United States.

Private professional groups such as the American Institute of Architects also now embrace CPTED principles in relation to anti-terrorism building and site design (Demkin, 2003), and transit officials who oversee rail and bus and ferry systems report a substantial jump in their reliance on CPTED. For example, when asked whether there were linkages between anti-terrorism and the crime prevention strategies embodied in CPTED, most of the respondents to a large-scale survey of operators of major rail systems in the United States believed that they overlapped or were directly connected, as noted in Table 7.1.

It is doubtful whether the identification of anti-terrorism with crime prevention planning strategies as suggested by Table 7.1 would have taken place before recent terrorist events. Indeed, research in other areas, such as school security, suggests that many otherwise knowledgeable respondents (school facility managers, principals, school resource officers) had little knowledge about place-based crime prevention strategies generally prior to 9/11, much less about their linkage to anti-terrorism (Florida Department of Education, 2003).

Some differences and conflicts between anti-terrorism and place-based crime prevention

Now, connections between place-based crime prevention strategies and anti-terrorist planning are made by consultants who suggest, for example, that CPTED and anti-terrorism strategies are extremely compatible, differing only in relation to the level and types of threats (Atlas, 1999). Despite the perceived congruence of CPTED and anti-terrorism strategies, however, there are some significant differences between them, stemming largely from distinctions between the nature of most common crime and most terrorism. For instance, most crime in the United States is aimed at acquiring property. For those committing larceny-theft and motor vehicle theft (which comprise the largest of the 'Part 1' crime categories as defined by the FBI[8]), there is generally no intent to destroy or damage the target; quite the contrary. In these circumstances, stealth and concealment from observation are desirable, so that increased natural surveillance has a valuable part to play in deterrence.

However, most significant terrorist attacks are not acquisitive in nature but rather involve violence against persons and property. Terrorists bent on such attacks, and especially those on suicide missions, are not likely to care whether they are observed in the consummation of the act, and indeed this may be a sought-after goal (or reward), as we have seen from Internet videos of roadside bombings posted by Iraqi insurgents. Increased surveillance – a primary strategy of place-based crime prevention approaches (see Chapters 2 and 3) – is therefore *variably* effective, depending upon *where* and *how* it is focused in the continuum of the act. In this context, other CPTED and place-based strategies, such as those related to access control, may be much more

Table 7.1 Perceived connections between anti-terrorist and anti-crime strategies by transit agency respondents

Agency opinion	All systems		Systems with rail		Systems with multimodal transfer or enclosed station		Systems with neither	
	No. of systems	Percenage of systems	No. of systems	Percenage of systems	No. of systems	Percenage of systems	No. of systems	Percentage of systems
Completely separate from one another	8	7%	1	4%	6	12%	1	3%
Partly overlap one another	44	41%	13	46%	20	41%	11	35%
Considered hand in hand	50	46%	13	46%	19	39%	18	58%
Don't know	6	6%	1	4%	4	8%	1	3%
Total systems	108	100%	28	100%	49	100%	31	99%

Source: Adapted from Taylor et al. (2005).

effective than others in deterring terrorist attack, as we have noted in relation to the Israeli security perimeter installation. Consistent with suggestions made by Clarke (1997) concerning the use of situational crime prevention, and in terms of what we know about the importance of local context in designing effective crime prevention generally (Schneider and Kitchen, 2002), interventions must be *customised* to the specific circumstance, whether these entail terrorist acts or common crimes.

In some cases, CPTED and anti-terrorist design and planning prescriptions provide directly conflicting advice. The classic example is 'stand-off' distance, or the 'distance between an asset and a threat' in the parlance of the National Capital Planning Commission (2005, p. 9). In practice this generally translates as the separation of vehicular traffic from building façades. Conventional anti-terrorist planning, such as that embodied in the *National Capital Urban Design and Security Plan*, seeks to maximise the distance between traffic and buildings, with the suggested minimum setback from the kerb being 20 feet (about 6 metres) (National Capital Planning Commission, 2002b, 2005). Figure 7.1 illustrates the six areas suggested by the plan to zone the spaces between structures and the street traffic in contemplation of design interventions that buffer buildings and their occupants from vehicular-related bombings. Beyond the building's interior and perimeter (Zones 1 and 2), the external (public) areas comprising Zones 3–5 are the most important in which to effect physical changes, since they are closest to the structural façade. Doing so is likely to be costly and problematic in most cities because of existing infrastructure. Moreover, changes here can have significant implications for pedestrians, parking design and traffic circulation. One relatively cost-efficient approach is to insert layers of 'hardened' street furniture within these zones, which is a strategy proposed by the *National Capital Urban Design and Security Plan*, and discussed in more detail in Chapter 8.

As Figure 7.2 suggests, the general anti-terrorist advice is to distance or insulate, wherever possible, public buildings such as courthouses and agency headquarters from traffic. These recommendations embodied in the DC plan are touchstones for other public jurisdictions across the United States, and for other nations as well. For example, Australia's *Urban Design Guidelines for Perimeter Security in the National Capital* draw heavily on the DC plan's specifications (National Capital Authority, 2003). Conflicts with place-based crime prevention planning and design strategies occur inasmuch as the recommendations they provide emphasise connections with the street (including pedestrian traffic) to maximise surveillance. This is an outgrowth, in part, of Jane Jacobs's 'eyes on the street' philosophy (Jacobs, 1961), but is also one that tracks much older design principles meant to dissuade predators generally (Schneider and Kitchen, 2002). A primary way of doing this, of course, is through window placement and façade design that maximise glass (glazing) coverage. But, aside from the blast wave itself, glass (even 'safety glass') becomes shrapnel in bomb attacks and is a primary instrument of injury and death (Norman, 2004). Thus, more exposed glass front (with the possible exception of hardened or blast-resistant glass) closer to the street tends to equal more risk.

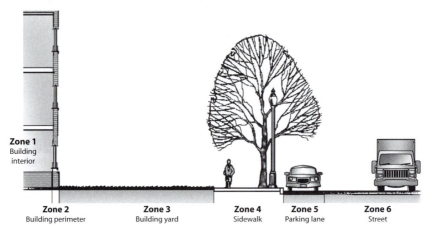

7.1 *Building zones.*

Source: Courtesy of National Capital Planning Commission

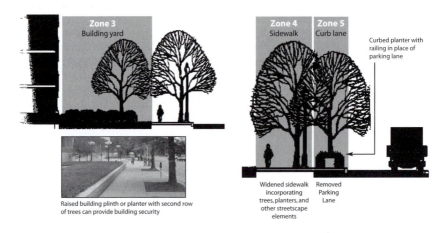

7.2 *Changes to building zones.*

Source: Courtesy of National Capital Planning Commission

An additional and related conflict occurs between anti-terrorist design and CPTED preferences for the inclusion of ground-floor retail or business uses so as to diminish the presence of 'dead zones' at the building street level. For example, Zelinka and Brennan, new urbanist designers who incorporate CPTED principles in their work, suggest that street-level, open storefront design tends to promote 'reciprocal natural surveillance' which increases the 'positive relationships between the public and private realms' (2001, p. 169). This is good crime prevention advice (and probably good business advice as well), but it is not necessarily compatible with anti-terrorism planning and design. For example, while not prohibited under new federal security regulations, ground-floor retail uses are reportedly frowned upon by the DHS Federal Protective Services in the design of federal office buildings (Langdon, 2004), presumably because they attract a variety of shoppers, something that is inherently desirable from an urban vitality standpoint but a factor that increases risk from an anti-terrorist perspective.

This is but one example of a larger argument to the effect that new anti-terrorist design for public structures in the United States may be undoing many of the advances that American city centres have made in recent decades in forging connections with pedestrians and invigorating urban life generally. In this context, some anti-terrorist design is seen to be not only antithetical to crime prevention advice but also anti-urban by virtue of its potential to isolate civic structures from civic life. Moreover, there is a dearth of empirical evidence showing that at least some forms of anti-terrorist interventions actually work, and, given that uncertainty, there is a real question as to whether the costs required in order to implement them, in quality of life, civil liberties and actual fiscal outlay (increased from $9 billion a year in 2000 to over $32 billion in 2005), are worth the price (Lum *et al.*, 2006). Answering these fundamental questions and reconciling the few but important conflicts between anti-terrorist and anti-crime design prescriptions is challenging. To do so will certainly involve careful consideration of detailed design issues as they relate to human behaviour at local scales, while balancing quality of life considerations with real and perceived security needs.

Despite differences noted above, place-based crime prevention advice and anti-terrorist advice are generally congruent and overlap considerably. This is demonstrated by respondents to the transit survey noted earlier and is discussed below in more detail. This congruence is also evident in the application of place-based anti-terrorist strategies for the Joint Interagency Task Force East (JIATFE) anti-drug facility plan, based largely on CPTED and environmental criminology theories, also discussed below.

Two examples of place-based anti-terrorism applications

Rail transit planning and design

The first example comes from a recent study of transit system security completed for the Mineta Transportation Institute (Taylor *et al.*, 2005). It provides one of the most comprehensive public assessments of current place-based security (including anti-terrorist) applications ever attempted. Using a multi-faceted methodology that involved extensive review of archival materials, survey research among respondents who operate both rail and non-rail facilities (such as ferries and bus terminals) and in-depth interviews to produce case studies, the work presents benchmark research on US and international transit security. While completed just prior to the London Underground and bus bombing of 2005, it nevertheless includes pertinent research from Britain conducted before those attacks.

The authors pay particular attention to system security issues, including physical design, a focus that had been neglected by previous transit studies. Transit systems, and especially railways, are especially vulnerable to terrorist attack because they attract large numbers of people who are in constant movement, and thereby provide attractive targets as well as the opportunity for terrorists to remain anonymous. Moreover, they are 'very open and accessible, with fixed, predictable routes and access points' (p. 19). Far greater numbers of passengers flow through large transit systems more rapidly than through airline terminals, which are consequently easier to secure.

In surveying 113 of the major transit operators in more than a hundred American cities, the work assessed five issues,[9] among them how much 'relative importance they [transit system operators] place on different security strategies such as CPTED, public education and user outreach, policing, and security hardware and technology' (p. 4).

Among other things, the report found that a significant majority of respondents were knowledgeable about CPTED and, since 9/11, confidence in CPTED to prevent transit terrorism had dramatically increased. Figure 7.3 depicts a comparison of the surveyed transit system views on the importance of CPTED strategies before and after 9/11.

Before 9/11, the study notes that transit security officials were less knowledgeable about CPTED and concentrated far more effort on personal and property crimes than on terrorism (p. 78). When compared to other anti-terrorist approaches such as policing, the use of security hardware and technology, and public education and outreach, respondents rated the effectiveness of various security strategies highly, as depicted in Table 7.2. Though

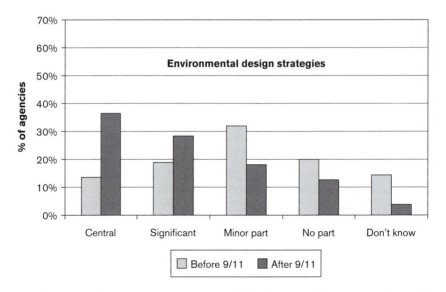

7.3 Perceived importance of environmental design strategies as part of security planning by transit agency respondents.

Source: Taylor *et al.* (2005)

Table 7.2 Perceived relative effectiveness of four types of security planning strategies by transit agency respondents

Strategy	Agency type	Very effective	Somewhat effective	Not effective	Don't know	n
Policing	Rail	40%	53%	7%	0%	27
	No rail	24%	57%	9%	10%	79
	TOTAL	28%	56%	8%	8%	106
Security hardware/ technology	Rail	27%	62%	4%	7%	26
	No rail	26%	53%	13%	9%	80
	TOTAL	26%	55%	10%	8%	106
CPTED	Rail	32%	50%	9%	9%	21
	No rail	19%	62%	11%	8%	37
	TOTAL	24%	58%	10%	9%	58
Public education/ user outreach	Rail	22%	49%	18%	11%	27
	No rail	11%	43%	20%	26%	80
	TOTAL	14%	44%	19%	22%	107

Source: Taylor *et al.* (2005)

not the top-ranked strategy, CPTED was assessed as 'very or somewhat effective' by more than 80 per cent of rail and non-rail operator respondents.

The study also asked where those transit operators who use CPTED strategies actually employ them in facility design. Figure 7.4 depicts the responses.

It is clear that most of the strategies are related to access control concerns and focus on entry, exit and gates where screening systems can intercept problems and choke them off as necessary. Attention to such areas tracks fundamental place-based crime prevention recommendations in CPTED and situational crime prevention relative to opportunity reduction and increasing the risk and efforts to reach targets (see Chapter 2). Parking facilities and vehicles also are obvious concerns, because of the possibility of the transport and concealment of explosive devices. There is significant evidence from the crime prevention literature that car parks are problematic spaces generally, owing to the low density of people and high density of vehicle targets (Smith, 1996; FDOE, 2003). Similarly, vending machines are targets of common crime inasmuch as they contain cash and goods, and they are of anti-terrorist concern since, if not properly designed and sited, they can provide niches in which to secrete explosive devices.

Circulation areas, such as pathways, are places where surveillance and control of individuals are problematic for both anti-terrorism and common crime prevention, and the environmental criminology literature has long singled out these routes as concerns, especially when pathways connect to trouble spots such as bars or deserted parking lots (Rondeau *et al.*, 2005). Hidden

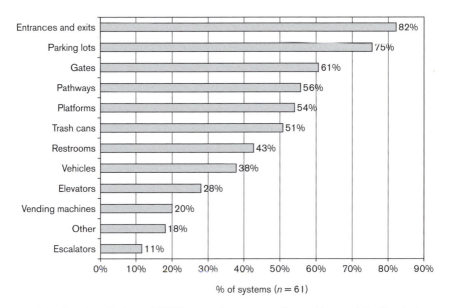

7.4 Identification of where CPTED strategies are actually used in transit facility design by transit agency respondents.

Source: Taylor *et al.* (2005)

areas such as rest rooms and elevators are similarly important subjects in both literatures, and the former figure especially in school facility design.[10] Furthermore, Newman (1973) singled out the placement and design of elevators as a fundamental problem in the design of Pruitt-Igoe.

The one system component area where crime prevention and anti-terrorism differ is the control of litter bins. There is little in the crime prevention literature that speaks to these as problems or concerns, with the exception of the role that they play in helping maintain clean, cared-for environments and thereby minimising 'broken windows' cues. However, the removal or hardening of litter bins has long been a feature of anti-terrorist planning, going back to the 1991 IRA bombings of London railway stations and before (Jenkins and Gerston, 2001).

Table 7.3 depicts specific CPTED strategies relating to the system components identified above. Security cameras, lighting and visibility are the most frequently implemented tactics in relation to each component. Guardianship ('monitoring by staff/security') is next most likely to be implemented, followed by locational strategies concerning gates and vending machines.

It is clear from the results of this survey that specific CPTED and related place-based crime prevention strategies are increasingly being adopted in the design and planning of transit systems in the United States. This is so despite the fact that only a minority of survey respondents (22 per cent) report that comprehensive CPTED guidelines have been developed, with most of those being the products of in-house security teams (Taylor *et al.*, 2005, p. 90). This leads one to the conclusion that most of the strategies shown in Table 7.3

Table 7.3 Matching of CPTED strategies with transit facility components as identified by transit agency respondents

CPTED strategy	Systems component										
	Platforms	Entrances and exits	Gates	Elevators	Escalators	Restrooms	Pathways	Parking lots	Trash cans	Vending machines	Vehicles
Lighting	✓	✓		✓	✓	✓	✓				
Visibility (clear lines of sight)	✓	✓		✓	✓	✓	✓				
Use of glass and natural light	✓	✓		✓			✓				
Keep clear of obstacles	✓										
No hidden corners/dead areas	✓	✓					✓				
Limit access paths/points		✓	✓					✓			
Electronic access control		✓	✓	✓							
Security cameras	✓	✓	✓	✓		✓	✓	✓			
Emergency telephones						✓	✓	✓		✓	✓
Emergency alarms						✓					
Monitoring by staff/security			✓		✓			✓		✓	✓
Curved entrance wall without doors											
Explosive resistant									✓		
See-through containers									✓		
Location[a]			✓						✓	✓	
Minimal/low landscaping							✓	✓			
Fencing								✓			
Public information signage			✓								✓
Large windows											✓
Secure parking											✓
Vandal- and graffiti-proof											✓

Source: Taylor et al. (2005)

a Configure location of gates to be able to close off sections of station. Locate vending machines.

were adapted ad hoc, grafted onto existing security systems in the most pragmatic ways possible. This conclusion is supported by the findings that other means of protection were more likely to have been quickly implemented following 9/11, such as changes in policing, inasmuch as some CPTED strategies that involve physical design alterations are more difficult to implement quickly. These include securing seats in railway cars (to prevent the hiding of objects beneath them), removing recessed telephones, filling in building voids, and installing access controls on all doors and gates (ibid., p. 109). There is no doubt, however, that comprehensive anti-terrorist security strategies, based largely on place-based crime prevention approaches, are on the agendas for transit authorities across the United States.

New York's new World Trade Center Terminal is a model for this, inasmuch as it incorporates security by design throughout its construction. Given the city's pre-eminent role in public transit in the United States, and its prominence as a result of the 9/11 attacks, there is every reason to believe that this approach will become the prototype for retrofit as well as new transit planning and construction around the country.

Messages from this research on transit systems are that 9/11 has significantly spurred the adoption of anti-terrorist design and planning strategies, and that these strategies incorporate many of the classical place-based crime prevention approaches. In this context, these theories, and especially CPTED and situational crime prevention, provide a connected framework that links environment, management, human behaviour and intervention strategies in a way that did not previously exist. The fact that such strategies have increasingly been subject to empirical scrutiny and research (Sherman *et al.*, 1997; Schneider and Kitchen, 2002) has supported their adoption in transit and other uses. This trend can only be bolstered by the vast increase of computer power being directed at homeland security issues at national and, since 9/11, state and local levels. This entails national crime (and other) databases that are connected to local and state intelligence 'fusion' centres, whose establishment is 'among the hottest trends in law enforcement' (Kaplan, 2006, p. 44). Besides the obvious possibilities for civil liberties abuses, this development also provides an extraordinary opportunity to devise research designs based upon the new data available and to test crime prevention theory and intervention strategies in comparative settings, which has not been feasible until now. We shall discuss this opportunity further in Chapter 8.

Joint Interagency Task Force East (JIATFE) anti-terrorism design and planning

The second example of the application of place-based crime prevention theory to anti-terrorism is the retrofit and redesign of a US Department of Defense facility in 1997–1998. The work was completed for the Joint Interagency Task Force East, which is located within the Key West Naval Air Facility (NAF) in Key West, Florida. JIATFE is a multifaceted agency that combines the Department of Defense, Department of Transportation (US Coast Guard) and Department of the Treasury (US Customs Service). It also includes representation from the Drug Enforcement Administration, the Federal Bureau of Investigation, the Defense Intelligence Agency, the Naval Criminal Investigative Service and the National Security Agency. Besides those from the United States, JIATFE consists of liaison officers from Great Britain, France, the Netherlands, Argentina, Brazil, Colombia, Ecuador, Peru and Venezuela. It is one of the United States' chief anti-narcotics smuggling agencies and, following the Oklahoma City bombing in 1995, was one of the first federal agencies that took action to protect its facilities from the threat of terrorist attack.

The objective of the JIATFE project – undertaken by a team of university planning and design faculty and students – was to devise a plan that would increase 'force protection'[11] for the facility using defensible space and CPTED principles and techniques. JIATFE's facilities and site had not been significantly changed since their original design and construction in the 1950s, and were jeopardised by vulnerabilities in access control, by changing narco-terrorist tactics, by the future sale of adjoining base property to the City of Key West through the Base Realignment and Closure (BRAC) programme[12] and by Key West NAF's then open base policy. Some of these issues were exacerbated by the fact that the facility is located close to the centre of Key West, a major tourist city. JIATFE's mission of collecting and disseminating narcotics intelligence to counter-drug centres, law enforcement agencies and international counter-drug partners made it a target, according to a threat assessment conducted by the US Atlantic Command's Anti-Terrorism and Force Protection (AT/FP) Assessment Team.

Figure 7.5 depicts most of the original site layout for the JIATFE complex, which consisted of four two-storey linear buildings (in the upper left foreground) linked together by walkways. Together they comprised approximately 150,000 square feet (14,000 square metres) of office and equipment space, with security ratings ranging from secret to top secret.

As Figure 7.5 illustrates, vehicles could closely approach the facility from several sides, and parking was permitted adjacent to the front entry of the building. Also included (see the redesigned site in Figure 7.7 later in the chapter) is a 'tower farm' at the rear of the last building, located adjacent to one of the southernmost beach fronts in the United States. The farm is an array of radar antennas and electronic eavesdropping devices that point towards Cuba and which electronically sweep the major Caribbean and eastern Pacific drug transit routes from South America.

The main security concern of JIATFE staff was attack by a vehicular bomb transported at the behest of a 'lone wolf' narco-terrorist[13] intent on disrupting surveillance long enough to move a major drug shipment across the US border. JIATFE officials wanted a plan that would be cost-effective and more aesthetically pleasing than traditional, *ad hoc* military security designs which are usually added piece by piece and concentrate on target hardening or 'bunkering'. Indeed, original plans to protect the complex envisioned a series of concrete barricades of a type used in traffic control ('Jersey barriers'; see Figure 7.6) to be dropped in place around the building's perimeter. This was rejected by the agency's commanders as being antithetical to the goals of providing a humane and aesthetically pleasing working environment for the

7.5 Original Joint Interagency Task Force East (JIATFE) site.

Source: US Navy

200 or so military and civilian personnel who staffed the facility. Indeed, much the same logic generated the planning and design suggestions included in the *National Capital Urban Design and Security Plan*, which were conceived as a response to the extemporised and 'hastily erected jersey barriers, concrete planters, and guard huts that ring our buildings and line our streets' (National Capital Planning Commission, 2002b, p. 1), and which were created in reaction to Oklahoma City and to the World Trade Center attacks. Prior to and just after these events, systematic environmental design security planning was rare in both military and civilian applications in the United States.

The problem of developing a comprehensive site plan that took into account both security and aesthetic concerns dovetailed with the academic and professional practice objectives of the multidisciplinary consultant team. Of particular interest was the challenge of combining a sustainable natural design approach that exploited existing indigenous materials with the use of high-tech electronic surveillance and access control systems. As a background to the project, the consultant team reviewed the existing academic literature on place-based crime prevention and examined case studies focusing on major terrorist attacks on US targets to date, including Oklahoma City, the attack on the Khobar Towers barracks at Dhahran Air Base in Saudi Arabia, and the 1983 attack on the US Marine barracks in Beirut, Lebanon. The consultants also reviewed context documents, including existing city and county comprehensive plans as well as available traffic circulation data, and examined blast pattern data generated by military engineers and consultants on the basis of the Oklahoma City explosion (Hinman, 1995).

7.6 Jersey barriers surrounding the entrance to the Philadelphia Mint.

Internal vulnerability studies had long identified critical issues: uncontrolled access to the base itself and parking within 30 feet (9 metres) of JIATFE buildings. While the overall base policy could not be changed at that time, access to the JIATFE site itself could be altered to achieve an acceptable stand-off distance. The challenge was also to permit reasonable VIP and visitor access, as the facility is visited by congressional delegations and dignitaries from other nations. Other planning and design challenges – undefined building entrances and overall lack of territoriality, incomplete and inadequate facility fencing, inadequate lighting that was not completely coordinated with CCTV coverage, poor building connections and internal blind spots, impacts on adjacent land uses and neighbourhoods, as well as cost and aesthetic considerations – were linked either directly or indirectly to the fundamental access problem.

Additional issues included an unprotected loading dock (which needed to service 18-wheeled delivery trucks), unrestricted access to the facility's dumpsters, and the lack of a viable system for screening mail and small packages. Finally, an open athletic field used by base personnel adjacent to JIATFE permitted virtually unimpeded straight-shot vehicular access to the buildings through an open field adjacent to the complex.

Planning and design process and solutions

The planning process addressed many of the concerns expressed by JIATFE above as well as others discovered during site research. All designs were informed by place-based theory, particularly CPTED, and environmental criminology, and by the pertinent empirical literature related to environmental crime prevention available at that time, which in 1996–1997 was limited.

Some design solutions concentrated on target hardening approaches, such as the introduction of new access control elements disguised as decorative features ('transparent' security design) that could also serve other functions, such as a visual focal point or as space signatures. An example of this was the recommendation of a cemented array of flagpoles placed near the front of the entry building which would restrict vehicular access but also became a feature of the VIP and ceremonial entrance to the complex. Other designs focused on attempts to attract 'legitimate users' (military personnel and their families) onto the site to improve surveillance. One such attempt was the design of a jogging path around the open athletic field directly north-east of the site and the addition of picnic tables adjacent to a proposed new, and secured, loading dock area. Another design solution incorporated a pedestrian boardwalk along the south-west perimeter of the site, bordering the ocean and the tower farm. Many of the ideas were not reasonable from a cost standpoint, or simply were not practical. For example, one design included a 'moat' around the main complex, a result of ideas gleaned from historical research, but completely impractical because of local environmental considerations as well as economics.

Final recommendations took into account the Navy's blast analysis, which identified the footprint and estimated severity of structural damage at varying stand-off distances from the complex. Final plans included a redesigned main entry to the core building and electronic access control at the entrance to the car park (card swipe and proximity card readers). Traffic circulation pattern recommendations included the addition of a curved entry road to reduce the possibility of cars being able to accelerate on a straight path and crash through the gate arms. This was a lesson learned from review of a case study of the bombing of the Marine barracks in Beirut in 1983, where suicide attackers used a straight-shot approach to the facility after gathering momentum and crashing through gates and fences and into the facility (Beck, 1983). All the designs either eliminated roads or controlled entry to the ones immediately adjacent to the core buildings. A fundamental planning decision was to divide the complex into priority-based security zones.

A non-exhaustive list of planning and design suggestions derived from place-based crime prevention theory and practice is depicted in Table 7.4. As in the Mineta transit study, most of these changes concentrate on access control strategies. However, surveillance, territorial reinforcement, boundary marking and the generation of legitimate, protective activities close to the facility also figure in the mix. Figure 7.7 illustrates the redesigned site after most of the recommendations noted were implemented. Approximately $2 million was allocated for CPTED-based security upgrades and the process

Table 7.4 Joint Interagency Task Force East place-based anti-terrorist strategies derived from place-based crime prevention theory and practice

Anti-terrorist planning/design recommendation	Primary place-based crime prevention strategy and theory
Redesign the main entrance of core buildings; including a ceremonial, circular drive for VIP visits and redesigned walks and planters in front of the entry building, including hardened flagpoles siting.	Territoriality and access control (CPTED)
Control access to all parking areas inside the most critical blast zone and control access on the roads inside that zone.	Access control (CPTED)
Redesign the adjacent athletics field and include spaces for recreation such as football and other sports activities and which incorporates a landscaped jogging path around its perimeter.	Activity generation and surveillance (CPTED, environmental criminology)
Realign main entrance road to a curvilinear orientation and install a series of roundabout drop-offs to reduce approach speeds into the complex. Design 'S' and 'Z' turns into the complex only.	Access control (CPTED, environmental criminology)
Wherever feasible, utilise natural, locally occurring materials such as palm trees and coral rock.	Boundary marking, access control (CPTED)
Integrate and coordinate lighting and CCTV around the core buildings. Upgrade both.	Surveillance (CPTED)
Design a secured, covered walkway for internal employee/document circulation within a secured fence line.	Access control, surveillance (CPTED, environmental criminology)
Segregate the main parking area from VIP parking. Control entrance to parking by electronic card access and by CCTV.	Access control, surveillance (CPTED)
Restrict and redirect delivery truck traffic to a secure, transhipment point, and close adjacent (on-base) streets to through traffic.	Access control (CPTED, environmental criminology)
Add lots for satellite parking requiring demolition of existing structures on those sites.	Access control (CPTED)
Add signage and way-finding assistance throughout the site.	Territorial reinforcement (CPTED, environmental criminology)
Utilise steel-fabricated, 'CPTED-compliant' vertical slat fencing to replace chain link around the entrance.	Access Control, Surveillance (CPTED)

7.7 Redesigned JIATFE site.

Source: Courtesy of Alan Mather

took several years to complete, although the security redesign process for the facility is still continuing as new threats and new technologies emerge (Mather, 2005).

As we have indicated, one of the key recommendations of the approach was the use of natural, local materials where feasible. Figures 7.8 and 7.10 illustrate the incorporation of coral rock and palm trees as both access control, boundary marking and territorial reinforcement strategies. These materials were relatively inexpensive, reasonably flexible, aesthetically appealing (especially when compared with alternatives) and used to supplement more costly and less sustainable electronic and mechanical access control entry features. Figures 7.9 and 7.10 depict differences between the original entry to the site and the redesigned entry, which now includes an array of new design features.

At the time this project was conceived and implemented, the adaptation of CPTED to anti-terrorism design was a new and somewhat daring concept. Nevertheless, it provided a reasonable and durable framework on which to base a systematic security design and plan for this facility. Taken together, the above design and planning recommendations created a layered system of natural and artificial defences that has succeeded in protecting the site, thus far, from narco-terrorist attack.

Messages from this project are that place-based crime prevention-based planning and design theory can connect a jumble of otherwise disjointed anti-terrorist designs and provide a systematic intervention strategy based on evidence and experience. Moreover, such strategies can combine sustainable environmental design features with facility management practices and produce

7.8 Use of coral rock and palms for border definition and vehicular access control, JIATFE.

Source: Courtesy of Alan Mather

7.9 Original JIATFE entry.

Source: Courtesy of Alan Mather

7.10 Redesigned JIATFE entry.

Source: Courtesy of Alan Mather

aesthetically appealing, reasonably humane environments for even the most sensitive targets. If this is possible here, then security design that respects the context and appearance of urban, civic space is certainly feasible.

Conclusions

Once the primary province of the police, there is evidence that planners, architects, urban designers and landscape architects are becoming more conversant in (and more comfortable with) CPTED and related place-based crime prevention theory and practice (Schneider and Kitchen, 2002; Demkin, 2003; American Society of Landscape Architects, 2005). Some may have been dragged kicking and screaming to this place, whereas others have eased into it. In whichever case, we argue that this is largely the result of the adoption of anti-terrorist legislation, guidelines, rules and strategies at all levels of the US government, but especially at the federal level following recent terrorist attacks. Such efforts have greatly accelerated knowledge about place-based crime prevention theory within government as well as within the private sector. This makes a great deal of sense, since these theories supply a logical frame-work in which to fit environmental security interventions. As is illustrated by the JIATFE case study, they provide the connective threads linking *ad hoc* anti-terrorist strategies in a fabric that otherwise would have taken much more effort and time to weave.

This synergistic connection between crime prevention and anti-terrorist practice will undoubtedly lead to new technological developments relating to crime prevention (which we discuss in Chapter 8), to new local practice variations of crime prevention efforts, to the evolution of *existing* theory of place-based crime prevention and to the development of *new* theory. Such changes will no doubt be related to the enormous quantity of data about human behaviour and the environment that are being generated as a result of the massive investments being made by the US government in anti-terrorism technology and training.

What is ironic, but not necessarily surprising, is that this investment has probably provided more tangible crime-prevention benefits than anything else. Indeed, there is a startling lack of evidence that either anti- or counter-terrorist efforts actually accomplish their intents. A recent study by Lum *et al.* (2006), which reviewed six intervention strategies (among them fortifying embassies and the use of metal screening devices) across 20,000 studies, found only seven studies that provided even 'moderately rigorous' evaluations of the effectiveness of anti-terrorist strategies, and some of these concluded that the interventions either did not work, or 'sometimes increased the likelihood of terrorism and terrorism related harm' (p. 3). Thus, the massive outlay of funds (along with disruption to the urban civic environment) may not be justified by obstructed terrorist attacks but may be justified by crime reduction results, which will be statistically easier to support. Empirical research is yet to support this conclusion, but anecdotal evidence points towards that hypothesis. The way forward in this regard is wide open.

8

The application of new technologies to place-based crime prevention

Introduction

In its broadest sense, technology is the application of tools to help solve practical problems. Crime prevention tools are, by definition, artificial devices that facilitate human defences against crime. In this chapter we describe crime prevention tools relative to environmental design and planning elements, with the acknowledgement that there are a multitude of crime prevention technologies and management innovations, such as those related to cybercrime, fraud and other 'white-collar' offences that are beyond our present discussion. Rather, we sample the stream of technological interventions devised over the ages to protect property and people from criminal predation, paying special attention to new technologies associated with place-based crime prevention. Even confining ourselves to this slice, we concede too that we cannot, in one chapter, identify all applicable tools and innovations, and that, given the pace of technological change, it is likely that at least some of the ones we discuss will be outdated relatively soon. What is salient, however, are the implications they have in relation to crime prevention theory and to resulting place-based crime prevention design processes and strategies. In the ultimate analysis, this seems to us to be among the most important considerations for the development of the field.

In particular, we are interested in questions concerning:

- the extent and ways in which technological change is associated with the evolution of security design, especially in terms of access control, target hardening strategies and the adaptive, co-evolutionary reactions of offenders;
- the growing use of technology to mark and surveil territories, two fundamental and intimately connected place-based strategies that embody trends towards the increasing reliance on added-on tools to prevent crime, as distinct from basic design approaches;
- the explosion in environmental tracking, modelling, data collection and data

mining technology, with extraordinary implications for crime and terrorism prevention as well as for the infringement of basic civil liberties;
• the development of new product designs based on nanotechnologies, ranging from apparel to street furniture, that have crime prevention applications but that are also freighted with issues relating to the evolution of distal warning and reaction systems, and the substitution of mechanical guardianship for human guardianship.

A fundamental, but largely unanswerable, question implied by these points is whether (and to what extent) technological change remains subservient to theory and to the security design process or whether it leads them. While it is likely that there is a pendulum swing, the velocity of change in the post-computer era is propelling the arc further in one direction, with implications for place-based crime prevention planning as a field as well as for society as a whole.

To organise this discussion, we group the tools into categories associated with classical place-based theory – access control, territoriality and boundary marking, surveillance – and create new typologies for warning, crime-analytic and modelling tools that do not fit neatly into any one place-based category. The chapter concludes with a discussion of emerging and envisioned tools for place-based crime prevention and explores their implications for their intended purposes as well as possibilities for counter-intuitive results.

Tools for access control

Tools need not be complex or high-tech to be important in crime prevention. Felson (2002) argues that simple inventions such as barbed wire and steering-wheel locks can have major impacts on opportunity and can dramatically affect crime rates. Access control is an opportunity-reducing principle and one of the earliest organising concepts leading to the creation of simple innovations to fend off criminal attacks. At the community level, the use of city walls and related systems, such as castles and fortified buildings, illustrates the impact that such basic technologies can have on civilisations. The use of walls reaches back into the origins of human history and is particularly associated with the rise of urban life (Mumford, 1961; Kostof, 1991, 1992; Schneider and Kitchen, 2002; McCrie, 2006). Besides protecting populations from attack, they served as containment vessels for growing cities, defined the edges separating rural and urban space, and marked the boundaries of tax and service responsibilities of governments. As such, they are fundamental territorial instruments as well as access control tools.

The composition, design, structure and placement of walls have been subjects of much interest over the centuries (Duffy, 1979). Their intimate connection to other technologies, such as those involving cannonry and ballistics, illustrates the long and systematic linkage that characterises crime prevention and crime facilitators. Although history repeatedly shows that they are conquerable by determined and adaptive foes, walls and related community-level barriers remain extremely popular crime prevention tools used by groups and individuals to the present day (Blakely and Snyder, 1997; Blandy *et al.*, 2003; McCrie, 2006). Indeed, as noted in relation to community gating in Chapter 3, their utilisation continues to grow in many places around the world.

While wall systems are macro-scale crime prevention tools designed to protect entire communities and, in some cases, civilisations, there are a vast array of smaller-scale access control technologies that have similar, albeit less grand, intents. These include those associated with the layout of streets themselves, street design elements, and micro-level features associated with buildings and structures.

Street-level design

In a biological analogy, streets comprise both the skeleton and the circulation systems of the city. Like bones, streets provide urban structure and form, and like arteries and veins, they carry goods, people, communication and crime, among the general flow of city life. In terms of land area, streets generally contain the largest amount of urban public space, and their influence on neighbourhood and city viability has been argued to be disproportionate to even this imbalance (Jacobs, 1961; Appleyard, 1980). The relationship of street layout to crime in terms of the 'permeability' argument has been discussed at some length throughout this book, although it is worth pointing out that the idea of deterring crime and other unwanted activities by restricting access through street layout is not new (Kostof, 1992). Gating and the placement of other impediments to public street access have been used as crime prevention tools for centuries, and are variably effective depending upon context and upon which set of premises and data one chooses to accept out of those available.

One notion, widely shared by police, is that controlled-access neighbourhoods using single entry and exit roads are best for crime prevention purposes.[1] Seen from the standpoint of situational crime prevention, such designs minimise escape opportunities and thereby increase efforts and risks to fleeing offenders. Some police also suggest that confusing neighbourhood street patterns also serve to deter crime inasmuch as offenders will be less willing or able to negotiate them, although the same argument holds for the police as well. Similar tactics have been used since medieval times, when herders embedded their livestock in the centre of rings of circular ditches cut into the land, making it more confusing and difficult for thieves to negotiate quick exits. Ekblom (1997a) suggests that strategies that perplex predators have analogies in nature relating to target (prey) selection, where large and confusing herds, schools and coveys make it challenging to single out individual victims. In this context, confusion is facilitated by physical design and abetted by the weight of numbers.

Street-level technology

Despite the real or potential effectiveness of these approaches, most planners and urban designers do not intentionally produce confounding street layouts, although these may result as a consequence of other developmental factors that change community street patterns over time (Kostof, 1991, 1992). Some of these may be the outcome of city growth or decline, or stem from environmental changes made to control traffic, increase pedestrianism or deter unwanted activities, including crime, among many possible reasons. Examples of such interventions come from small-scale 'passive' and 'active' street-level tools that are used by traffic engineers, planners and police as means to control access to neighbourhoods and urban districts. Passive tools are fixed in place and do not move in reaction to immediate environmental or remote stimuli. These include the use of geometric, physical devices such as pinch points, chicanes, medians, planters, speed humps, bumps and some bollards, although there are many other related engineering and design elements (Zelinka and Brennan, 2001). Active elements have mechanical or electronic components that respond to stimulus from external sources. Cities across the globe have become increasingly sophisticated in the use of these tools, as is evidenced by the evolution of the bollard from a passive to an active device.

Bollards and other barriers

Bollards are among the most fundamental access control devices and are used as decorative and landscaping elements and to channel pedestrians and traffic. They are also employed as a defence against ram raiding and to prevent vehicles from penetrating security zones around buildings and districts, while at the same time allowing pedestrians to circulate freely. They come in a bewildering array of styles and composition, and may incorporate lighting fixtures or electronic components. 'Passive' bollard systems designed to prevent criminal or terrorist attacks are fixed in place, usually embedded in concrete several feet deep into the ground. The bollard itself, often a steel cylinder filled with concrete, extends above the ground at least to vehicle bumper heights (Federal Emergency Management Agency, 2003b). While a primary feature of the bollard is that it is a barrier to entry, modern bollards may be flexible and yield to varying pressures, or they may be removable entirely. Crash-rated bollards are designed to withstand the impact of vehicles and remain operable afterwards. The US Department of State has developed bollard standards for use in embassies and related facilities across the world, requiring them to stop a vehicle dead in its tracks, not merely impede it (US Department of State, 2003). According to some vendors, these standards have become the *de facto* requirement for those selling anti-terrorism vehicular barriers generally.[2]

Some bollards are 'active' security features and are retractable, using electrically triggered, hydraulic or gas mechanisms allowing periodic access to vehicles depending on local commercial or security needs. In whatever form they come, bollards are a ubiquitous component of modern urban security design, so much so that they may blend into the landscape. Indeed, some are aesthetically designed to complement the streetscape, such as those depicted in Figures 8.1 and 8.2. Other bollards remain unadorned and brutally functional, not unlike the Jersey barriers depicted in Chapter 7, a fact that has undoubtedly contributed to the concerns expressed by urban designers and others about the 'bollardisation' of many major cities across the globe.

8.1 Design-sensitive access control.

Source: Courtesy of Wausau Tile Inc., Wausau, Wisconsin

8.2 Thematic bollards.

Source: Courtesy of Wausau Tile Inc., Wausau, Wisconsin

The effectiveness of bollards against ram raids has been pragmatically demonstrated at commercial and industrial sites throughout Britain, although we are not aware of empirical work on the subject other than that of Jacques's history of ram raiding (1998) and Donald and Wilson's study of the social psychology of ram-raiding groups (2000).

Bollards can be designed to blend into the streetscape, but a strikingly less subtle approach to street-level access control consists of active barriers that actually change the street grade in an effort to stop vehicles. These are meant to be seen as impediments and are more expensive than passive elements inasmuch as they generally incorporate mechanical and electronic devices that are costly to install and maintain. One widely used element is a type of road barrier that uses pneumatic or hydraulic pressure to lift a heavy metal barricade above the road surface as an obstruction to oncoming vehicles. These barricades are remotely operated and are often associated with hardened guard booths or checkpoints. Virtually impenetrable, they are used to protect high-risk government and private facilities, and comply with government crash standards. Figure 8.3 illustrates one such installation, a 'Delta barricade', named after the company that manufactures it.

Street furniture

Acting like bollards and barriers, hardened street furniture, such as that depicted in Washington, DC's *National Capital Urban Design and Security Plan* (see Chapter 7) is also used to protect against both criminal ram raiding and terrorist attacks (National Capital Planning Commission). These passive

8.3 A high security surface mounted Delta barricade.

Source: Courtesy of Delta Scientific Corporation

elements include light and utility posts, drinking fountains, kiosks, planters, tree enclosures (pits), bicycle racks, parking meters, seating, litter bins and artworks. The design, manufacture and testing of street hardened street furniture is a complex process, with standards only recently starting to emerge (General Services Administration, 2002; National Capital Planning Commission, 2002b; Federal Emergency Management Agency, 2005). Their subtle incorporation into dense urban environments illustrates the quest for 'transparent' security design, or security design that blends in seamlessly and aesthetically with the existing streetscape.

Figures 8.4 and 8.5 illustrate various types of hardened street furniture that have been suggested for insertion within the security zones between the street and the building façade (zones 3–5; see Figure 7.1) in Washington, DC.

How effective any of the street-level tools depicted here prove to be against criminal and terrorist attack is still speculative, inasmuch as there is no empirical evidence to support any conclusions. Oscar Newman is quoted by the *Boston Globe* as arguing that adaptive criminals and terrorists will easily find ways around such impediments. He reasons that they protect against perhaps 10 per cent of possible attacks, saying, 'They are effective in reducing the risk you've thought of, but not the one you haven't thought of' (Flint, 2002). Even if they do work, the question is whether relatively small reductions in crime and unknown deterrence in terrorism are worthwhile, given the enormous expenditures to be made. There is no doubt, however, that the use of such interventions makes us *feel* better even if we are not that much safer. Whether the illusion puts us more at risk than we would have been otherwise is an issue yet to be resolved. Further, such add-on interventions epitomise our willingness to harden targets in the public arena with the possible risk that if the targets they ostensibly protect are successfully attacked, such reliance will (rightly) be dashed. The hope is, of course, that even if bollards, barricades and street furniture fail to protect us against criminals and terrorists, at least some of them will not also be eyesores, which would indeed add insult to injury.

Micro-level access control technology

Locking devices

There is a wide range of access control technology at a smaller scale than street design technology such as bollards, barriers and street furniture. Much of this begins with locks and locking devices, perhaps humanity's earliest mechanical creations. McCrie (2006) reports a museum containing a 4,000-year-old Egyptian pin lock and notes that a multi-point locking chest is the oldest piece of furniture owned by the Bank of England. Locks of varying types are incorporated into most devices that control environmental entry, especially at the window, door and building scale, although they have been integral to community gates and often are components of wall and barrier access control strategies. In the latter case a variety of entry systems has evolved since medieval times, ranging from the use of mechanical keys to the use of bar code, swipe card and proximity card electronic entry. Ratte (1997) documents the

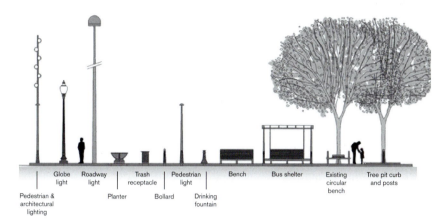

8.4 Examples of hardened street furniture.

Source: Courtesy of National Capital Planning Commission

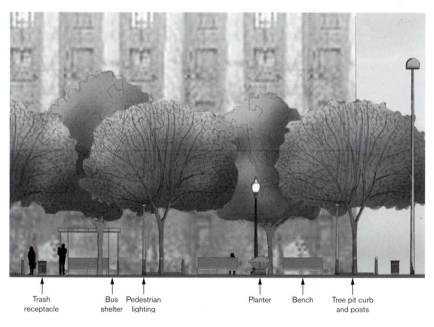

8.5 Streetscape incorporating hardened street furniture.

Source: Courtesy of National Capital Planning Commission

operation of locked city gates in Florence as early as 1323, and emphasises that the keeper of the keys and locks was a very important person in the community.

The improvement of locking devices, including vaults and safes, over time parallels the development of standards and rating systems to assure consumers that such products actually perform as advertised, especially in relation to burglary. Underwriters Laboratory (UL), the British Standards Institution (BSI) and Eurosafe are examples of groups that develop and maintain such standards. As noted above, such co-evolution also characterises the linkage of crime prevention technology to criminal enterprise, and can be found in examples of adaptive design by offenders to hardened targets.

One example is derived from larceny, where the use of a widely available implement has been adapted to steal bicycles. Some inventive (or perhaps just bored) individual found that the empty barrel of a common plastic ballpoint pen fitted perfectly into the chamber of a hardened and expensive U-lock and, with a bit of jiggling, could snap it open. News of this innovation spread quickly among offenders, aided by the Internet, which also fortunately alerted the bicycle community and the lock manufacturer, which has since changed the design to deter bike thieves (Polgreen, 2004).[3] This was a welcome reaction inasmuch as bicycle theft and the design of secure bicycle locations are large and growing concerns in many US and European cities (Gamman *et al.*, 2004). Indeed, this crime has significant environmental design and sustainability implications as gasoline prices continue to rise. Because of this, there is little doubt that thieves will develop newer and more inventive ways to filch bicycles.

Another, longer-term example of co-evolution comes from burglary, one of the most important environmentally based crimes. Ekblom (1997a) recounts the intertwined history of safe design and safe-cracking technology to illustrate similarities between biological evolution and crime prevention. From the mid-nineteenth century to shortly after World War II, safe builders and safe-cracking burglars were linked in a competitive struggle to see who could outpace the other. As metal sheathing for safes became more resistant, burglars adapted better drills and torches to open them. The struggle finally culminated with the design of a combination of target hardening and alarm systems that has virtually eliminated safecracking, a (rare) example of a technological victory over one form of crime.[4] Poyner (2006) reports similar, more limited success in which modern security systems that have been systematically designed into new vehicles (as distinct from add-ons) have been successful in significantly reducing both car thefts and thefts from cars. Although such success is by no means assured at the residential level, modern home door and window fittings are following in the same path, with reinforced framing systems augmented by electronic alarm systems that may be electronically linked to a central, often remote monitoring station or possibly directly to the police. There is evidence that such systems do indeed deter burglars, although Pascoe and Lawrence (1998) in Britain and Sampson (2003) in the United States argue that high false alarm rates can offset the positive effects of such technology in terms of policing costs. Moreover, it is ironic that integrated security design for existing homes, likely to be people's most valuable asset, arguably lags far behind other security applications, with add-ons such as burglar alarms being the most popular crime control feature.

Electronic and biometric access control

Nevertheless, electronic access control systems have proliferated in recent times and may be found in door entry systems that include, especially in non-residential applications, a range of options, including optical recognition turnstile systems and wireless video linkages. Even a cursory review of offerings on the Internet demonstrates the wide variety of electronic entry and perimeter access control systems now on the market. These include 'smart' fences that detect motion, vibration and pressure and that transmit information to central monitoring stations.[5] Some of the most common approaches for door and gate access control that replace mechanical keying include keypad entry, bar coding, swipe cards and proximity cards. Of these, proximity card systems using radio frequency identification (RFID) technology are currently the most popular, as they have become more economical to maintain than swipe card systems. They are also reasonably reliable, do not require physical contact between card (they may instead be tags or badges) and reading devices, and facilitate quick transactions, an important feature when a significant number of entries must be processed.

Other, newer access control devices include biometric systems that recognise unique physical characteristics such as hand geometries, iris patterns, voices, faces, fingerprints and blood vein patterns. These are projected by industry research groups to be in strong demand as their technical reliability increases and as their costs decline (Freedonia Group, 2003). Many of the latter systems include computer-linked information retrieval along with alarm functions, so that managers and police can be alerted to unauthorised entry and also keep track of authorised entries and exits. The market for these products is being pushed along by concerns about terrorism that have come to fill in the gaps left, at least in the United States, by falling crime rates. The Freedonia Group, which conducts international business research, estimates that the annual US market for electronic access control systems of all types will climb to more than $7 billion by 2007.

These, as well as other electronic access control systems, are retrofitted into existing architecture and are likely to be increasingly incorporated into new building structures and community gates. It is likely that biometric systems will be combined with nanotechnology (as discussed below) to create new generations of 'smart' buildings and streetscape. As we noted in Chapter 7, one of the fringe benefits of the proliferation of electronic access control and screening devices developed for the war on terrorism, and especially closed-circuit TV, is that they are catching criminals, probably more so than terrorists. One London police press officer said, 'The fact that we're getting ordinary people – burglars stealing cars – as a result of it is sort of a bonus' (quoted in Rosen, 2001, p. 42).

Tools to mark territory

In the context of place-based crime prevention, territoriality involves the marking of places such that they are perceived and interpreted as being controlled, owned and defended. Hence, territoriality is intimately connected to boundary marking, surveillance and access control. Territorial hierarchies that distinguish public from private space and that separate privacy zones are important concepts in the crime prevention literature (Newman, 1973; Altman, 1975; Brown and Altman, 1991) and are strategies employed both consciously and intuitively by residential and urban designers. The technology of territoriality includes physical changes in surface materials, texture, design, elevation, landscape and colour, employed either separately or in combination. Territories can also be marked by fencing, signage, sound, lighting, and by overall site design, which may blend all the foregoing. One of the most common tools to designate territory is the simple paving stone, which can be infinitely variable in pattern, colour and texture and which is employed across a range of urban settings. Pavers (also called segmented paving) have been used from Roman times to surface roads and as a means to demarcate changes between public and private property.

Newer tools incorporate electronics and computers to mark territory. Fences are one obvious application. They have been electrified for many years to keep people and pets constrained and intruders out, but it is only recently that other components such as alarms, lighting, CCTV and computerised processing have been bundled into perimeter fencing systems. If such elements are hidden, as they often are, they may not be germane to territoriality, since one of its defining characteristics is that territorial marking needs to be *perceivable* (if not actually perceived) by others. A trend in streetscape and building design is the creation of 'transparent' security, such that security features are all but hidden from users (Nadel, 2004). Recent evidence suggests that this may have counter-intuitive effects inasmuch as users in some settings, such as courthouses, tend to feel safer when they can actually see security features such as guard stations and CCTV (Sahoo, 2006). But perception may not only be visual. Some markers may not be visible at all but may nevertheless be acutely perceivable.

Music and sound

For example, relatively new approaches to marking territory include the use of music and sounds. Timberg (2005) documented 'elevator' music (sometimes used interchangeably and incorrectly with 'classical' music) as a means of driving out teenagers and potential offenders from parks, parking lots, railway stations and underground stops in the United States, Britain, Australia and Canada. He notes that crime incident reports support the contention that this music actually works in reducing crime, although there are no independent empirical studies that verify this conclusion. He reports one police official in Palm Beach, Florida, as saying that after police there closed a bar in an area infested with drug dealers and began blasting classical music from the roof, 'the officers were amazed when at 10 o'clock at night there was not a soul on the corner. We talked to people on the street, and they said, "We don't like that kind of music."' Subsequently, she says, her department received requests from other police officials to explain exactly what steps it had taken. Its musical selections were mostly Bach, Mozart and Beethoven.

(Timberg, 2005, no page number)

Cornish and Clarke (2003) identify 'soothing music and muted lights' as an intervention strategy to reduce provocations, including frustration and stress, among their 25 techniques of situational crime prevention. On a quite different end of the sound continuum, but analogous to the elevator music principle, is a tool that irritates the listener. Called the 'Mosquito', this device produces annoying high-frequency sonic waves that, according to its inventor, only those under about 20 years old can hear since the cells in their ears have not degenerated, unlike those of older persons (Burson, 2006). News reports note that the Mosquito has been used by the Staffordshire and Gwent police forces in the United Kingdom with positive results in terms of reducing antisocial behaviour at various hotspots, such as outside convenience stores where youths gather. Interest in the device apparently has been expressed by police agencies in the Netherlands, Belgium, Japan and the United States. Military applications of more powerful sonic devices to mark territory and disperse crowds also have been explored in Iraq and Israel (Jardin, 2005). Other auditory devices employed to identify territory and warn intruders include recordings of ferocious dog barking and recorded verbal warnings which are triggered by movement or vibration, and are sometimes used in school and community facilities after-hours.

Lighting

Lighting is the fundamental facilitator of surveillance, one of the prime place-based crime prevention strategies, but is also used as a territorial marker. Crimes are made more risky by better site and building lighting inasmuch as offenders are more likely to be observed and subsequently identified in court. There is significant evidence that good lighting reduces both the fear and the incidence of crime (Painter and Farrington, 1997; Farrington and Welsh, 2002; Illuminating Engineering Society of North America, 2003). Lighting also serves to identify protected or special territories. For example, retail store designers and managers have long used lighting to focus on sale items in 'store-within-store' territories, with the potential side benefit of reducing shoplifting in these areas (Moussatche *et al.*, 2004).

Samuels (2005) identifies good lighting as a key design strategy in the community appropriation – territorial ownership – of public spaces, so that after dark such places become animated, lively and safe. This notion has an ecological analogy whereby crime and crime prevention are locked in a

Darwinian-type struggle, each attempting to adapt to (and overcome) the other's interventions (Ekblom, 1997a; Felson, 2002). In this framework, night-time community space is the territorial 'niche' that is up for grabs by virtue of good or bad lighting design. Implementing such design generally involves striking a balance between technical and cost issues, within the context of differing illumination standards applied to neighbourhoods, parking lots and roadways. Key planning questions to be answered are which territories are to be lit – that of the street (cars) or the pavement (pedestrians) – and how best to accomplish these sometimes conflicting aims (Zelinka and Brennan, 2001). From a place-based crime prevention standpoint, good lighting changes crime opportunity by changing crime niches, making targets more risky to attack in particular settings.

Good lighting responses also blend science with art and must be tailored to the local social and physical contexts. Indeed, in applying lighting technology to site conditions, lighting design must take many factors into account, one of which is colour rendition, the ability to distinguish among different colours. This is vital in identifying suspects and vehicles, and recognising territories after dark. Colour rendition is a function of the lamp source (for example, some current choices include metal halide and high-pressure sodium), the height and spacing of poles, and the chosen wattage. These factors must be adjusted to the existing and anticipated lighting distribution pattern in the areas to be illuminated, to the climate and to existing community lighting codes, if any (Tijerina, 2001). In a perverse territorial application, lighting that exaggerates skin blemishes reportedly has been used to discourage teenagers from congregating in some Australian shopping malls and other commercial areas, an application similar in concept to the Mosquito noted above (Edwards, 1999). Both examples demonstrate a trend towards technology that exploits human physical attributes in an attempt to protect and otherwise territorialise space. In the ecological analogy, the assumption is that as the palatable territory (habitat) for teenagers decreases, so will their opportunity to cause problems for shopkeepers and merchants.

Tools to aid surveillance

Electronic surveillance systems abound in the modern built environment in Britain and the United States, with CCTV being far and away the most common element. It continues to top the list of desired crime prevention technology, even though there is evidence that it is not as effective as once hoped and that its effects decay over time (Wright and Decker, 1997; Welsh and Farrington, 2003). Employed initially by British transit agencies and police, CCTV use has mushroomed in public and private applications across Britain (McCahill and Norris, 2003). After the 9/11 attacks the use of CCTV became a more viable security trade-off vis-à-vis privacy issues among Americans.

Research has found that the overall effects of CCTV in reducing crime are positive but generally small (Welsh and Farrington, 2003), and there is no evidence as to its role in preventing terrorism, although it certainly has been used to document it, as seen in the London and Madrid attacks of 2004 and

2005. Because of this, some critics suggest that while cameras make people feel safer, they are not cost-effective and simply displace crime to other areas. Other critics contend that CCTV 'lets technology usurp the role of police management' inasmuch as police will be more likely to be sent to places where cameras are located and not to other places (Fountain, 2006), and still others decry its potential for privacy violations (Jenkins, 2005). Nevertheless, CCTV has been endorsed as a viable ingredient of British crime prevention planning 'when implemented as part of a wider package' of design, lighting and place management elements (Office of the Deputy Prime Minister and the Home Office, 2004, p. 29), and is increasingly being used in the United States for similar purposes and for anti-terrorism.

For example, as of this writing, hundreds of new surveillance cameras are being installed in New York City, while existing systems are being upgraded in other major US cities, including Chicago. The New York cameras will have the ability to 'pan, tilt and zoom and are networked to the internet so that video images can be viewed and stored centrally' (Fountain, 2006, p. 14). Chicago is experimenting with pattern recognition software in an attempt to identify suspicious behaviour from archived files so that 'real-time' criminal or terrorist activities can be spotted. Behavioural pattern recognition in the physical environment seeks to replicate the success of computer-based identifications of friendship and contact patterns (networks) by intelligence agencies to track terrorist cells (Keefe, 2006). Thus far, it has not been successful, and research in this area continues, spurred largely by terrorism concerns although the results are likely also to have crime prevention applications. Some researchers suggest that cameras can be used to document postures, which can provide important clues to understanding people's activities relative to crime and crime prevention (Boulay *et al.*, 2006).

Chicago police credit their network of 'pods', or remotely controlled cameras that provide video directly to laptop computers in squad cars, with helping dramatically reduce the city's 2004 murder rate (Fountain, 2006). Even newer technology combines cameras with sensing equipment that recognises the sound of gunfire, uses microphones to triangulate the location and aims the camera lens in the appropriate direction. Police are alerted and remotely control the camera to focus on the scene of the shooting. Los Angles, Chicago, Philadelphia, San Francisco and Tijuana, Mexico, are reportedly using or testing these systems (Associated Press, 2005). These 'smart cameras' match recorded sounds against a sound library stored in the computer database to distinguish gunshots from other noises.[6]

Cameras are also used for traffic control purposes and to identify vehicle licence plate numbers. In Britain, one plan is for 'automatic number plate recognition' (ANPR) cameras to be erected every 400 yards along the motorway, according to the head of roads policing at the Association of Chief Police Officers (ACPO) (Smith and Gadher, 2005). ANPR systems are currently in use in strategic places on every motorway in Britain, and some cities, such as Northampton and London, use them routinely to enforce congestion taxes and other ordinances. Plans for their adoption are under way in a number of other British cities.

Despite their drawbacks, cameras remain a major tool in place-based crime prevention design and planning. Criminal adaptations have been largely confined to displacement to other, non-surveilled targets, to simple sabotage, or, in the case of armed robbers, to the concealment of identity (Wright and Decker, 1997). In many cases, however, criminals simply ignore cameras.

As the technology improves (moving, for example, from analogue to digital imaging) and as surveillance cameras become even more disseminated, it is possible that they will have a greater impact on crime prevention (as distinct from crime prosecution) than has been realised so far. One argument, however, is that cameras symbolise an over-reliance on added-on technology to prevent crime, whereas the emphasis ought to be on more thoughtful design of crime settings, including sites, streets and structures, which is at the heart of place-based crime prevention theory. If such devices can be grafted onto places and buildings as band-aid solutions to crime and terrorism, what does this say about the role and importance of the design process, in which we invest hopes for long-term and sustainable solutions to at least some place-based crime? Another argument is that omnipresent cameras will cause us to take surveillance for granted in everyday public life, making potential invasions of civil liberties more likely. Each argument calls for more careful examination of public policy that supports the blanket adoption of camera surveillance as distinct from other approaches.

Other, non-visual surveillance systems include those that sense the presence of metals, chemicals and biological agents and that warn guardians. Systems that scan for guns are commonplace in government facilities and in some high-risk schools. Of course, airports now routinely screen passengers and their luggage for weapons and chemicals associated with explosives. 'Multi-sensor' systems that sniff the air for a range of biological and chemical threats are being tested for use in other transit systems, including subways (Federal Transit Administration, 2006). These applications blur the already fuzzy line between surveillance and alarm systems.

Alarms and warning tools

Alarms can augment camera surveillance and contribute also to access control and territorial strategies. As such, they provide the feedback loop from threat to responder and may also alert intruders that their presence has been identified. Ekblom (1997b) suggests that some alarm warnings serve the same function for humans as mimicry does in insects and other animals in relation to increasing predator avoidance behaviour, and hence provide obvious territorial protection. Besides people (who served as watchmen), the earliest alarm systems were dogs, whose use probably pre-dated walls as security systems and who remain vital crime prevention tools to the present day. Other creatures have also been employed as warning systems, including geese and other loud birds encouraged to flock around some military and prison facilities (McCrie, 2006).

The effectiveness of alarm systems is directly related to the speed and clarity of communication links, with the earliest connections being based on sound, smoke and light signals. Electricity and the rise of telegraph and tele-phone technology revolutionised the speed and precision of alarm systems in the nineteenth and early twentieth centuries, and the computer and the Internet continue to transform it. Modern computer-based alarm systems can be programmed to bundle connections to a structure's utility systems, to activate CCTV, to police, to the owner or manager and to neighbours, among other functions.

In relation to place-based crime prevention there is cross-national evidence that modern alarm systems are effective against burglary (Mayhew and van Dijk, 1997), although data from the US are less clear-cut, even though there is support for the notion that burglar alarms combined with other security devices, such as dogs and strong locks, do reduce residential burglaries (Weisel, 2005; Sampson, 2005). Burglars pay attention to environmental cues (Felson, 2002), among them the possibility that structures are alarmed, even though experienced burglars may choose to proceed anyway.

To Ekblom, the increasing sophistication of alarms provides additional evidence of the evolution of defensive systems. He suggests that they mark the development of 'distal' reactions to threats, which provide significantly more warning to organisms than 'proximal' or direct contact threats. He says:

> These distal stimuli help to predict the proximal ones, alerting the potential victim while there is plenty of time and space to take avoiding action, or otherwise to make ready its defences. (The significance of the advantage bestowed by distal perception is evidenced by the fact that the eye has independently evolved many times in differ-ent biological lineages.) Most alarms used in crime prevention are proximal, like pain detectors – activated only when damage has been done: the window broken, the car driven away, the jewellery snatched. Developing automated security systems which perceive distal threats rather than wait for the pain seem promising.
>
> (1997a, p. 35)

Whether distal or proximal, alarm systems are intended to diminish crime opportunities by increasing offenders' risk and effort (Clarke, 1997; Cornish and Clarke, 2003), key factors in situational crime prevention theory. The evolution of more distal systems will undoubtedly depend on the amalgamation of existing alarm technologies with those that facilitate crime tracking, analysis and modelling as well as system miniaturisation, as described later in the chapter.

Crime tracking, analytic and modelling systems

Geographic information (mapping) systems

Computer-based mapping, commonly referred to as geographic information systems (GIS), has revolutionised both planning and place-based crime prevention planning over the past two decades (Weisburd and McEwen, 1997). The importance of this technology is emphasised by the establishment of the Mapping and Analysis for Public Safety (MAPS) programme within the US Department of Justice, by a recent report sponsored by Britain's Home Office that documented 20 major GIS crime mapping systems now being used in England and Wales (Chainey and Smith, 2006), and by crime mapping conferences that routinely draw participants from across the world.[7] As of this writing, approximately 100 active crime mapping websites in the United States were identified by the National Institute of Justice.[8] Many major urban police agencies across the world either now use this technology or are considering its adoption (Margolis, 2006).

The long-time concept and value of plotting crimes at geographic locations were reinvigorated by Chicago School sociologists in the 1920s and 1930s (Phillips, 1972; Harries, 1999; Schneider and Kitchen, 2002) and by environmental criminologists beginning in the early 1990s (Rondeau *et al.*, 2005). Since then, and following the adaptation of computers to mapping, GIS crime mapping has become an internationally recognised component of crime analysis and pattern recognition, and demand for skilled practitioners has skyrocketed in developed nations, especially in the United States and the United Kingdom (Boba, 2005). A main reason is that computer-based maps facilitate both visual thinking and communication far more than do static pictures, and for that reason they have become fundamental new tools in exploring existing and new hypotheses about crime at all levels.

Computerisation provides the ability to aggregate vast quantities of data about crime type, location, forensic details and police resources and responses, and display and statistically manipulate those data almost instantly, so that computer-based maps have become interaction tools as distinct from being merely passive surfaces on which to display images. How well those raw data are transformed into information, and then subsequently into knowledge and finally into wisdom about crime, is another matter that we shall discuss later in terms of future applications.

Figures 8.6 and 8.7 demonstrate the power of GIS to transform data into images that resonate in the brain. They show the same data in two formats, first tabular and then mapped. Figure 8.6 provides a partial listing of crimes reported to a police agency between 14 June and 14 September 2006. These incidents are identified by case number, by state criminal code violation number ('Statute Number'), by general type of crime ('Classification'), by date reported, by named premise, by sheriff's patrol zone in which the crime occurred, by address of the incident, by how they are classified relative to the US Uniform Crime Reports (UCR) code ('Part 1 and UCR Type'). While useful in this format, the data become spatially meaningful when they are represented as points on a GIS map, as in Figure 8.7. In that Figure we see that otherwise random criminal events cluster in certain spaces – crime hotspots. This perception of patterns marks a transition of data into knowledge, here as a ratcheting up of the understanding of relationships of criminal acts to physical features of the land.

As Figure 8.7 demonstrates, even untrained observers will immediately recognise that crimes such as burglaries are clustered around certain nodes in some neighbourhoods and along certain pathways (such as motor vehicle

http://192.168.3.24 - Query/Selection Results - Microsoft Internet Explorer

SORT METHOD: ⊙ Ascending ○ Descending
RESULTS: Layer= 'crime_core' ‖ Search area: Alachua County

Rec	CASE	STATUTE NUMBER	CLASSIFICATION	DATE REPORTED	PREMISE	PATROL ZONE	ADDRESS	PART 1 CRIME	UCR TYPE
1	06007350	810.02	BURGLARY RESIDENCE OCCUPIED	Wed, 14 Jun 2006 00:00:00	GARDEN APARTMENTS	08	75 SW 75TH ST	Burglary	5
2	06007353	810.02	BURGLARY CONVEYANCE	Wed, 14 Jun 2006 00:00:00	SUMMER CREEK SUBDIVISION	01	6005 NW 43RD AV	Larceny Theft	6
3	06007360	810.02	BURGLARY CONVEYANCE	Wed, 14 Jun 2006 00:00:00	EASTWOOD MEADOWS	03	925 SE 43RD ST	Larceny Theft	6
4	06007366	812.014	THEFT/AUTO/BUS/TRUCK	Wed, 14 Jun 2006 00:00:00		01	21221 NW 238TH AV	Motor Vehicle	7
5	06007372	810.02	BURGLARY RESIDENCE	Wed, 14 Jun 2006 00:00:00		02	19617 NE 132ND AV	Burglary	5
6	06007377	812.015	THEFT RETAIL	Wed, 14 Jun 2006 00:00:00	BEST BUY	09	3570 SW ARCHER RD	Larceny Theft	6
7	06007388	810.02	BURGLARY RESIDENCE	Thu, 15 Jun 2006 00:00:00	HOLLY HEIGHTS	08	8813 SW 4TH PL	Burglary	5
8	06007387	810.02	BURGLARY CONVEYANCE	Thu, 15 Jun 2006 00:00:00	KIMBERLY WOODS SUBDIVISION	08	4607 NW 35TH LN	Larceny Theft	6
9	06007398	810.02	BURGLARY CONVEYANCE	Thu, 15 Jun 2006 00:00:00	MAJESTIC OAKS	08	5800 SW 20TH AV	Larceny Theft	6
10	06007400	812.015	THEFT RETAIL	Thu, 15 Jun 2006 00:00:00	WALMART	09	3570 SW ARCHER RD	Larceny Theft	6
11	06007399	810.02	BURGLARY CONVEYANCE	Thu, 15 Jun 2006 00:00:00	GREENLEAF	10	7022 SW 46TH AV	Larceny Theft	6
12	06007402	810.02	BURGLARY CONVEYANCE	Thu, 15 Jun 2006 00:00:00	SOUTHWEST VILLA	09	3643 SW 20TH AV	Larceny Theft	6
13	06007401	810.02	BURGLARY BUSINESS	Thu, 15 Jun 2006 00:00:00	HOPEWELL BAPTIST CHURCH	05	4303 SW WACAHOOTA RD	Burglary	5
14	06007408	812.014	THEFT	Thu, 15 Jun 2006 00:00:00	ALACHUA CO CRIM JUSTICE CTR	03	220 S MAIN ST	Larceny Theft	6
15	06007416	812.015	THEFT RETAIL	Thu, 15 Jun 2006 00:00:00	WALMART	09	3570 SW ARCHER RD	Larceny Theft	6
16	06007426	810.02	BURGLARY CONVEYANCE	Thu, 15 Jun 2006 00:00:00	MEADOWS OF KANAPAHA	10	7830 SW 90TH LN	Burglary	5
17	06007429	812.014	THEFT	Thu, 15 Jun 2006 00:00:00	PARKER PLACE	08	13323 SW 31ST AV	Larceny Theft	6
18	06007446	812.014	THEFT	Fri, 16 Jun 2006 00:00:00		01	7510 NW 218TH ST	Larceny Theft	6
19	06007454	810.02	BURGLARY BUSINESS	Fri, 16 Jun 2006 00:00:00	MILLER ELECTRIC	03	21820 SE HAWTHORNE RD	Burglary	5
20	06007450	812.014	THEFT	Fri, 16 Jun 2006 00:00:00	SHELL STATION	10	7220 SW ARCHER RD	Larceny Theft	6
21	06007455	812.015	THEFT RETAIL	Fri, 16 Jun 2006 00:00:00	WALMART	09	3570 SW ARCHER RD	Larceny Theft	6
22	06007460	812.014	THEFT	Fri, 16 Jun 2006 00:00:00	WLUS/PAMAL BROADCASTING	03	3135 SE 27TH ST	Larceny Theft	6

Start | 3 Microsoft Offi... | Gatorlink VPN Dia... | 2 Solitaire Gam... | 2 Microsoft Offi... | All ACSO | 2 Internet Ex... | 12:29 PM

8.6 Tabular depiction of various crimes from a GIS database.
Source: Courtesy of Alachua County, Florida sheriff's office

theft along street corridors). This information is embedded in the tabular report in Figure 8.6, but is difficult to extract. The use of GIS mapping to identify crime patterns graphically acknowledges Gamman and Pascoe's important point that 'there is simply not enough visual imagery in the discourse about crime prevention' (2004, p. 9). In this context it is interesting to note that arguably the single most influential work on place-based crime prevention intervention is Newman's 1973 text *Defensible Space*, which for years also was arguably the best-illustrated work in the field. Zelinka and Brennan's lavishly illustrated book *SafeScape* (2001) follows this example.

GIS allows users easily to add electronic data layers ('themes') to base maps, including artificial or natural environmental features that contribute to better understanding of criminal events and responses. For example, the association of crimes with certain land uses – bars, fast food restaurants, parking lots – can instruct zoning decisions (in the United States) and planning permission (in the United Kingdom) and police agencies relative to resource allocations. Moreover, such linkages allow crime analysts to ascertain crime patterns better and to be able to predict likely events, say residential burglaries in a certain neighbourhood, on the basis, for instance, of a series of previous burglaries in adjacent neighbourhoods. While such patterns could also be portrayed on 'pin' maps (where crimes are identified on a map using actual pins), these are static compared to the GIS versions. Figure 8.8 illustrates the use of GIS mapping in a public presentation, where serious crime incidents

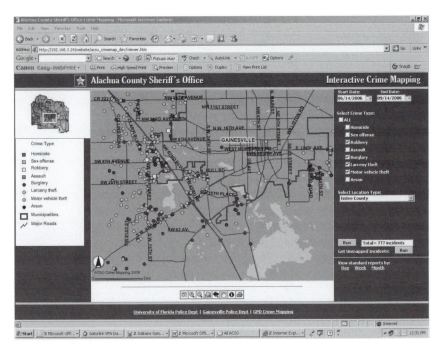

8.7 *Interactive GIS crime map, depicting crime clusters.*

Source: Alachua County, Florida sheriff's office

8.8 *Jacksonville, Florida sheriff's office: GIS crime analysts discuss crime patterns in a public presentation.*

are plotted in relation to land and highway features in the City of Jacksonville, Florida. The relative sizes of points on the map indicate the number of incidents at any one address.

Themes can be quickly changed and statistical associations can rapidly assess relationships through queries to the underlying databases. Users can then plot the results, which may take the form of a map showing, for example, the number of robberies where guns are used within a certain period of time and that occur within half a mile of all nightclubs in a city. Moreover, users can also access underlying databases and ascertain, for example, whether pawnshop records indicate increased gun transactions in these areas, or count how many parolees live in the half-mile 'buffer zone' around the nightclubs (assuming these databases are available).

Extensive resources have been devoted to GIS crime mapping in the United States and the United Kingdom, and the technology has been credited (along with many other things to be sure) with helping to bring down the US crime rate over the past decade. Much of this has been traced back to the New York City Police Department's adoption of computer-based analysis and accountability systems beginning in 1994 ('CompStat'), which subsequently became the model for the rest of the nation, and other parts of the world. To what extent the significant decreases in crime rates in New York, or in other parts of the United States that subsequently adopted New York-style systems, are due directly to GIS utilisation is arguable. The same issue has been raised in Britain recently, where a review of GIS systems (that have been 'embedded' in community safety partnerships) criticises local crime and disorder reduction partnerships (CDRPs) for not providing sufficient 'documented evidence' that they have in fact reduced crime, disorder and drug use, even though there is some verification based on reports from Birmingham, Oldham, the East Midlands and south Wales (Chainey and Smith, 2006, p. 6). It is likely that such evidence will emerge.

In the meantime there is no debate that GIS crime mapping helps police and planners better visualise gross crime patterns and plan accordingly, and it has become an important tool in communicating with the public.[9] Other technology, such as global positioning systems (GPS) tools, further enhances the utility of GIS mapping in terms of permitting more precise crime incident locations and, as a consequence, the opportunity for better analysis and more informed crime prevention interventions.

Global positioning systems

Global positioning systems (GPS) is a relatively new technology that was first developed by the US military in the 1960s and then quickly adapted to civilian use. Very simply described, it is based on digital satellite signals broadcast to the earth that electronic receivers use to plot relatively exact locations on the ground (National Academy of Sciences, 2003). The ability of GPS to identify actual physical locations of incidents (through latitude and longitude or x and y coordinates) is important to place-based crime prevention since it mitigates many practical problems associated with address-based crime mapping.

While GIS is a great leap in the ability to map crime incidents dynamically and plot them against the landscape, most GIS crime mapping applications depend upon the use of addresses that come from police reports. Problems inherent in police reports aside, addresses only generally identify the location of crimes, and that presents problems for crime analysis, since crime occurrence is a localised phenomenon. For example, consider the scenario where a large number of vehicular burglaries have taken place in a city's downtown car parks. Using a GIS system, their locations are identified by addresses in police reports, which are then 'geocoded', or entered onto a GIS base map. But urban car parks are often large places and it is important to understand where, as precisely as possible, the burglaries actually took place. Addresses alone generally will not provide this micro-level information, which is crucial to understanding the crime 'setting' (Clarke, 1997; Felson, 2002) and central to on-the-ground law enforcement.

Do the burglaries cluster along street fronts or within interiors of the sites? Are they adjacent to commercial sites? Do they aggregate near bus stops or train depots that are close to the lots? Along with other information in the GIS database, this may tell analysts whether the incidents were associated with transit schedules, whether crime settings were overlooked by adjacent structures, whether there was ambient lighting, or whether there were landscaping features that offenders used to camouflage their activities. While this information may be available in the police reports describing each burglary, it is a laborious process to extract such details (although this too will most likely change soon, as we shall discuss below), and addresses alone provide only limited assistance.

However, GPS points to a reasonably precise location on the site (as plotted by the investigators) and thus can direct crime analysts to spotting patterns that would not be evident through addresses. This is especially valuable where crimes take place in open fields or along highways, where street addresses can be virtually useless. Santa Monica, California, police have used GPS-enabled cameras that are linked to GIS base maps to photograph, pinpoint and eradicate graffiti on bridges, rights of way and culverts (Egilmez, 2004), and North Carolina has begun to use GPS to track truck crashes and vehicle enforcement systems (Hughes and Stanard, 2004). In the United Kingdom, police GPS applications have been focused primarily on transportation issues, such as a recent pilot programme among the Highways Agency and the Warwickshire and Surrey police aimed at expediting investigations at crash sites (Public Technology Net, 2006), although other applications are forthcoming.

Present GPS problems include technical difficulties of connecting to existing crime databases and the fact that GPS receivers generally do not work *within* structures or in places where reception of satellite signals is blocked. Other issues have been raised in relation to privacy issues, which will become even more relevant as GPS microchips are actually built into new cell phones and when local public safety agencies have the equipment to process call locations.[10] This is a double-edged sword inasmuch as GPS-enabled cell phones allow police and emergency rescue to identify callers' locations, an especially important consideration in those jurisdictions where cell phones are replacing wired phone systems. Despite these issues, it is arguable that GIS and GPS are analytic tools that move us further along the path towards the development of distal crime prevention systems as described by Ekblom – those that anticipate and respond to criminal predators before harm is actually done.

Three-dimensional modelling and photography

While GIS and GPS are valuable visualisation and locational tools, new virtual reality technology promises to enhance further the ability to recreate criminal incidents for crime prevention analytical purposes. Computer-based three-dimensional (3D) modelling technology allows users to change physical environments in ways impossible in the real world. Users can then explore the effects of the changes and ask 'what if' questions, such as what possible effects varying street-facing window coverage might have on car burglaries, or explore the potential impacts that types of residential entryways have on robberies. Three-dimensional computer models of these scenarios can be created using architectural and engineering (computer-aided design, CAD) plans, or static images such as photographs and sketches, or they can be scanned into computers using photogrammetry, a process that extrapolates two-dimensional photographic images into measurements which are subsequently drawn by the computer in 3D. Whichever process is used, the resulting images are generally easier for people (especially lay audiences) to understand than flat, 2D images since they are closer to real-world experience.

Figure 8.9 is a photograph of a building on a university campus and Figure 8.10 is one frame of a 3D image animation of the same site, used to evaluate possible additions to and modifications of the same building. The 3D image was created from architectural drawings of the proposed structure and depicts the façade that is to be retrofitted, along with some aspects of the surrounding environment. The 3D frames were animated, so that viewers could get a 'fly-through' inspection of the structure that would not be possible using 2D drawings or photographs. Building elements and landscaping details were changed in the animations to allow viewers to evaluate differing designs. The intent was to allow building managers and the university's police the opportunity to identify issues before the facility was constructed so as both to prevent crimes and to avoid the costs of additional retrofits. Lighting, entrapment spaces and surveillance issues were pinpointed as major concerns.

Three-dimensional urban simulation models allow users to interact with the images created and to compare hypothesised outcomes based on changes that they select. While computer-based graphic simulations of criminal events have been used for years in courtrooms in the United States, only relatively recently have these techniques been applied to crime prevention planning in broader contexts, such as 3D models, largely as a result of advances in software and computing power (Lodha and Verma, 1999; Brantingham and Brantingham, 2004).

8.9 Existing campus building.

8.10 Three-dimensional model of new building. Comparison of the photograph of the campus building site shown in Figure 8.9 and one frame from a 3D animation of the same site, shown here, is used to evaluate additions and modifications.

Using new software, 3D models have been used by police primarily for crash investigations but increasingly for crime scene work as well (Spraggs, 2004). GIS databases can form the basis for simplified 3D models, and CAD and GIS systems can be combined in hybrid models, which provide more complex project models. As noted, 3D models are particularly useful in communicating complex spatial relationships to public audiences. One of the most popular current applications in this regard is Google Earth, which allows users to view cities across the globe, some of which have been modelled using interactive 3D technology. This program permits one to move around the city, to 'drill down' (zoom) to relatively small-scale elements, and to tilt images. Among other things, this provides contextual information, such as the general massing of buildings and their relationships to nearby streets, plazas and parks. In the present version of Google Earth only simple, prismatic buildings are depicted, and without any scale-giving elements, such as windows or façade features. Nevertheless, because such representations are much easier to interpret than flat, overhead plan views, they are attractive for law enforcement and emergency response purposes.

A different type of image that is also easier to understand than plan views or 'flat' maps is depicted in Figure 8.11. This is one example from a series of oblique-angle aerial photographs of a cul-de-sac neighborhood. Here, specific building features such as windows and dormers as well as ground elements are clearly visible. The application provides a series of detailed photographs

8.11 Neighbourhood viewed using oblique-angle aerial photography.

Source: Courtesy of Pictometry International

that are taken from a number of angles. While one cannot interactively move around or walk through these images in the same way that viewers can with the 3D models described above, one can get a better understanding of the texture of the urban fabric than from simple building masses. There are, therefore, trade-offs between these two approaches that depend upon the needs (and resources) of the user.

Oblique-angle photocopy can be 'geo-referenced' such that ground locations can be determined relative to a base map, and these can be linked to GIS applications. In addition, multiple views of structures or environmental features can be shown and objects in the images, such as buildings, can be measured in terms of heights, elevations and area, and their distance from other objects can be calculated. Such details are useful in crime analysis and crime prevention planning, and can be essential in hostage situations and in emergency rescue responses. One company's website reports police describing the search for a shooting suspect in a residential neighbourhood, saying that their system

> gave us a lay of the land that we did not have before. We were able to see the actual structure and where garages were located near the apartment [the suspect] was in. These were not indicated on the apartment drawing provided by the complex. Having [this] system allowed us to see an accurate location of trees, contours of the land and other buildings we could use for cover.
>
> (Pictometry International, 2005)

The evolution of modelling is inevitably towards the merger of GPS, GIS, interactive 3D and photographic depictions such that viewers will have the ability to 'walk through' extraordinarily lifelike, albeit simulated, environments that are precisely mapped. Development of such programs depends on the availability of data and on increased computing power and speed, all of which seem likely to occur, given the current pace of technological progress and the burgeoning investment in crime prevention and, especially, anti-terrorist applications by governments and private enterprise.

Data mining: a new form of surveillance

The identification, analytic and modelling technology described above – GIS, GPS, 3D modelling and oblique-angle photography – are, at their root, evolved surveillance strategies that facilitate the ability to perceive, track and model objects in the physical world. Data mining is a different type of surveillance strategy, and one that will undoubtedly influence the course of place-based crime prevention. An emerging technology, it employs software programs that sift through vast quantities of data in an effort to discern patterns, sometimes applicable to the problem at hand or sometimes unfocused. In concept, data mining is related to the analysis of behavioural patterns to identify criminal activities, as described earlier, and is a means to filter and organise the detritus created in the course of addressing other issues. For example, police field interrogations and, especially, arrests generate a voluminous amount of information, including raw data about the arrestee, the circumstances of the offence, the crime target and the actions of the arresting officer. There is often valuable information hidden in these records – embedded patterns concerning offender behaviours, crime locations, targets and police knowledge[11] – that will be lost unless extracted and analysed. While this information may be stored in the head of the experienced crime analyst, it is ephemeral at best in terms of the organisational life cycle. Data mining programs help exploit the trove, organising and memorialising it in the process.

Data mining was first developed for business applications, and this remains its principal use today (Pyle, 2003), but its techniques and approach are being increasingly adapted to other uses, including anti-terrorism and place-based crime prevention. In this context, recently developed programs have the capacity to search and identify focused contents of structured databases, such as those underlying GIS crime maps and in police records management systems, as well as in unstructured sources, such as information contained in emails, white papers, presentations and extraneous documents. This information can then be networked to a variety of municipal agencies, a crucial aid in putting together the pieces that ultimately comprise the crime setting puzzle.

For example, while information about an assault in a park might be stored in various places in a law enforcement agency's computers, its design and planning implications affect the parks department whose landscape crew allowed hedges to grow too high, the public works department whose maintenance crew allowed burned-out lights to remain unfixed, and the planning department which permitted adjacent buildings to turn inwards, with windows facing away from public space. The collaborative implications of this capacity are obvious, and are especially important as public agencies are typically uncoordinated even while drowning in information overload. Data mining approaches are especially intriguing for place-based crime prevention planning purposes, since issues in this field generally involve a spider web of connected problems whose breadth and horizon transcend policing.

Data mining also has implications beyond individual jurisdictions, implications relating to both anti-terrorist and crime prevention applications. As was noted in Chapter 7, federally funded regional intelligence units are being established across the United States under the command of state and local law enforcement agencies. These 'fusion centers' (Kaplan, 2006) pool data from a variety of sources in an effort to overcome the lack of communication and information sharing that was found to characterise pre-9/11 US law enforcement (Bureau of Justice Assistance, 2005). While some of these centres (at present established in 31 states) concentrate on anti-terrorism, others cast a wider net and 'track all manner of criminal activity' (Kaplan, 2006, p. 44). By distributing databases across several jurisdictions, fusion centres have attempted to avoid the unfavourable publicity associated with the centralised Multistate Antiterrorism Information Exchange ('Matrix') system, which was discredited and shut down in 2005.[12] Nevertheless, the end result is basically the same inasmuch as computer queries can now access multiple, distributed databases almost as quickly as one central database. The essence of this data mining application is to integrate information and make it quickly available to law enforcement users in many jurisdictions. While the 'Big Brother' potential for abuse rightly disturbs civil liberties advocates, it is nevertheless a benchmark in the development of 'intelligence-led' policing, or that driven by information sharing, technology and training (International Association of Chiefs of Police, 2002). But the evolution of binding rules to control police applications of this technology has, unfortunately, lagged far behind.

Future technologies

Integrated systems and smart design

Predicting the future in relation to technology is an interesting exercise, since reality will obliterate speculation in short order. Nevertheless, present trends give us some insight into future developments. Naturally, they point to the continued application of computers to place-based crime prevention in crime tracking and modelling systems. Crime analysis, a burgeoning profession, will be hard-pressed to keep up with the explosion of new offence-related information available, irrespective of new programs designed to organise and integrate the data (Boba, 2005). There is no question too that present CCTV, GIS, GPS, 3D modelling and data mining systems will become more integrated and user-friendly as regards their fundamental surveillance and analytic functions.

Moreover, it is likely that these integrated intelligence functions will drive basic mechanical systems such as bollards, gates and fences as well as new lighting and sonic devices associated with territorial and access control at the building, site and street level. The development of 'smart' structures, streets and even districts is therefore not an unreasonable prospect, and one that further supports the evolution of distal security systems, those that Ekblom (1997b) has characterised as anticipating threats rather than simply reacting to them. Thus, computerised places will 'recognise' behavioural patterns consistent with terrorist or criminal activity, along with biometric features or other unique attributes, and instantaneously compare these with computerised security libraries. Alarms will alert access control, policing and other, related crime prevention functions long before actual attacks take place, and (in an ideal world, at least) responses will be shaped in accord with the threat.

Bionic security systems

Possibilities also exist for the merger of biological and electronic systems, with the chilling prospects of the incorporation of computer chips or other electronic devices into humans for security purposes. The use of embedded identity chips has gained headway as a result of the widespread adoption of GPS-enabled cell phones for emergency purposes, and the required use by students, in some school districts in the United States, of proximity badges for access control and activity monitoring, and as anti-kidnapping protection (Richtel, 2004). While the suggestion that tracking chips actually be implanted in people (children) has been attacked by civil libertarians and biological ethicists as outrageous fantasy, so were early speculations about the wide-spread uses of CCTV, especially in the United States. Terrorist events have largely obviated those concerns. A small number of people have already elected to have RFID and GPS chips implanted for health monitoring and security purposes, and it is relatively routine and non-controversial to implant RFID chips in pets and livestock. Sidener (2006) reports one application in which 100 employees of Mexico's Attorney General's Office's organised crime unit had implants permitting them access to high-security areas. Other spec-ulated applications foresee tracking of vulnerable individuals in high-crime areas. We conclude that such 'bionic' mergers are all but inevitable, especially in an increasingly fearful world.

Protection within very small-scale territories

The expanded use of high technology for bionic identification and tracking is only one aspect of the future of crime prevention planning. At a localised level it is likely that new designs in clothing and furniture will bring place-based security down to a much more personal scale. This trend is epitomised by extraordinary work being done at Central Saint Martins College of Art and Design in London, where students and faculty in its Centre for Design Against Crime collaborate with the Design Council, industry groups, law enforcement and crime researchers in pushing the boundaries of security design. Examples of their work include a line of 'Karrysafe' handbags and accessories that are advertised as both attractive and functional in terms of deterring theft and pilferage. The items include technological innovations in alarms and fabric designed to resist 'dipping, grabbing, lifting and slashing', reportedly the most typical means of bag theft.[13] The alarmed bags 'scream' when snatched. Figure 8.12 illustrates a bag being stolen, presumably accompanied by human *and* mechanical sounds.

The centre's faculty and students have already designed a range of anti-theft furniture, including the 'Stop Thief Chair' pictured in Figure 2.2. The chairs were initially designed to prevent the theft of purses and book bags in cybercafés, places where people are distracted from their belongings. Some of these creations have been featured in art galleries around the world, including a 2005 exhibition at the Museum of Modern Art in New York (Taraska, 2005). Both clothing and furniture seem very likely places to incorporate new developments in nanotechnology whereby tiny sensors, alarms and surveillance devices can be built into fabrics and materials at the manufacturing stage.

8.12 Karrysafe bag.

Source: Courtesy of and created by the Design Against Crime Research Centre, Central Saint Martins College of Art and Design, University of the Arts, London and Fonehouse/Vexed Generation. Image copyright Andrew Hobbs for DAC Research Centre.

Nanotechnology

Nanotechnology is defined as 'the creation of materials, devices and systems through the control of matter on the nanometer scale. A nanometer is one-billionth of a meter, roughly 10,000 times smaller than the width of a human hair' (Ames Research Center, 2003). Nanotechnology was envisioned by Nobel laureate Richard Feynman in 1959 as a new frontier in physics such that information and machinery could be miniaturised to atomic scales (Feynman, 1960). The implications of this are extraordinary for crime prevention and anti-terrorism planning and design, with neither field taking much advantage of it as yet. A 2003 conference sponsored by the United Kingdom's Institute of Nanotechnology highlighted this problem and included speakers on topics ranging from anti-graffiti paint coating to the incorporation of nanotechnology in the design of buildings against intrusion and terrorism (Institute of Nanotechnology, 2003). Nanotechnology raises the possibility of getting an evolutionary jump on offenders inasmuch as the manufacturing process may obviate quick, cheap and easy ways to defeat embedded security systems, at least in the short run.

The range of opportunities to use nanotechnology in crime prevention planning and design truly boggles the imagination, with possibilities extending across the classical and emerging place-based crime prevention strategies, from defensible space to space syntax and new urbanism. It brings up questions as to whether we will need to wonder about 'eyes *on* the street' as much as 'eyes *in* the street', or what type of civil liberties issues will surface when doors, windows and gates repel intruders long before they have even touched them. Will the pathways from pub to taxi keep us safe from assault even as litter bins and lamp-posts along the way admonish us to pick up our rubbish and not to walk on the grass?[14] Or, like the RoboCop of cinema fame, will networked robots patrol our streets – as suggested by the South Korean government – searching for lawbreakers and forwarding the information to police headquarters when they find them (Onishi, 2006). The future in these regards is both terrifying and fascinating: its realisation in either sense will certainly depend upon supporting political and social institutions, hopefully guided – in part at least – by new crime prevention theory.

Conclusions

We return now to the four considerations stated at the outset of the chapter. They focused on (1) the linkage of technological change to the evolution of security design in relation to access control, target hardening and the adaptive strategies of offenders; (2) the use of technology to mark and surveil territory, and the trend towards the adoption of add-on crime prevention techniques as opposed to designed approaches; (3) the implications of the growth in environmental tracking, modelling, data collection and data mining technologies for crime and terrorism prevention and for civil liberties; and (4) the relationship of new nanotechnology for the evolution of distal warning systems and the substitution of mechanical guardianship for human guardianship. We shall consider them in turn.

First, there is no question that technology and security design are inextricably linked throughout human history. Earliest settlements to present ones demonstrate this connection, and even though applications have become more sophisticated through the use of active barriers, electronics and computerisation, the basic principles of access control and target hardening have not changed much. Both approaches remain mainstays of place-based crime prevention inasmuch as they are undoubtedly effective in deterring certain types of crime under certain circumstances, even though both pose risks to the urban fabric, as noted in Chapter 7 in relation to anti-terrorist applications and to the fundamental notion of civic commerce in open democratic nations. As we noted in Chapter 2, C. Ray Jeffrey, CPTED's first proponent, dismissed later incarnations of it as little more than a series of target hardening prescriptions – perhaps too harsh an assessment in the light of its subsequent focus on more than mere bricks and mortar issues. One question is whether evolutionary victories in access control and target hardening, such as those evidenced by the virtual elimination of safe-cracking and reductions in some car thefts, can be matched in other areas such as home security design, where criminal predation is more personal and, arguably, more important. Striking the balance between reasonable opportunity reduction as suggested by situational crime prevention and fortressing, the worst-case scenario of target hardening, is a more difficult challenge now that we have new reasons by virtue of fear of terrorism and better technological means to do the latter.

Second, new technologies have provided us with innovative ways to watch, mark and protect our territories, warning off intruders in the process. Cameras, alarms and related smart electronic devices are the sentinels of the age, providing much sought-after remedies to security designs that were either badly thought out in the first place or not considered at all. The fact that some of the solutions, such as CCTV, are not nearly as effective as hoped, and that they tend to divert attention away from more fundamental social and economic issues, is a less considered side of the equation. That many of these systems will fail in the long run as their impacts inevitably decay does not diminish their short-term appeal, especially in the face of political pressures to act. Whether faith in naturally designed solutions to crime prevention in the built environment can survive the interim period is an open question, although there is evidence that the general wave of new support for all place-based crime prevention occasioned by the war on terrorism in the United States will continue to lift all the boats. Nevertheless, it is worth reminding ourselves that over-reliance on technology to watch and warn us against crime is an open invitation to disappointment. Perhaps some of the most unsettling messages relate to the development of technologies that target some population groups, such as teenagers, in attempts to drive them away from protected territories. No matter how much one may sympathise with store managers or homeowners, one cannot but wonder which other groups to disperse will be next in line and what new laws will be needed to regulate such actions.

Third, we have a unique opportunity to move place-based crime prevention theory and policy forward, given the development of the new analytic, mapping and modelling systems described in this chapter, and spurred in part by fears of crime and, even more so, by terrorism. This is because we now have the ability and incentive to capture, display and model vast amounts of information about criminal incidents and settings. Indeed, we have too much data, and coping with this wealth of riches is problematic, with the prospect made somewhat easier by the advent of new data mining and organisational tools. Application of this technology is still in its infancy and much remains to be done. But there exists, for the first time, the possibility of assembling large-scale, longitudinal case study databases about relationships between physical environments, place management, guardianship and crime. This provides the opportunity for long-term comparative empirical research, not unlike the multi-generational population studies conducted by medical researchers. Such work is desperately needed in this field to move theory and public policy forward. It would undoubtedly provide new insights about how crime relates to environ-mental variables and opportunity settings (both physical and managerial) by testing existing theory and practice, and could shed light on an array of current debates, one example being the relationship of street permeability to crime incidence. It could also help us predict how crime niches are likely to change as old crime opportunities become closed and new ones are opened. Such research would be likely to provide the bases for new directions in place-based crime prevention theory, with implications for policy making at national levels and for best-practice advice to local decision makers. The question will always be, of course, whether we can transform the data into knowledge, and that, in turn, into wisdom. Technology can facilitate that transformation, but it must, above all, respect civil liberties and the democratic traditions of open societies.

Fourth, and finally, implicit in the analytic technology described above, and explicit in robotic police and embedded, miniaturised surveillance and warning tools, is the idea that sophisticated gadgets can perform fundamental guardianship functions, a notion at the heart of place-based crime prevention, and especially situational crime prevention. That theory predicates that three essential elements for crime to take place are the convergence of a 'likely offender and a suitable target in the absence of a capable guardian against the offense' (Felson, 2002, p. 21). These ingredients merge within 'favourable' settings, which are often, but not always, physical places. Many of the tools described in this chapter clearly are attempts to produce stand-ins for human guardianship, while others are meant to create settings less favourable to crime by making them riskier or by requiring offenders to expend more efforts to overcome impediments. Walls, confusing street design, bollards, barriers and locking devices certainly fall into the latter category. They augment human intervention by bureaucratising the landscape, providing mechanical solutions that apply equally to users and that economise on decision making.

But newer tools and variants of the older ones above go beyond bureaucracy and have begun to incorporate technologies that promise to do as good a job, or an even *better* job, in protecting us as we can ourselves. Indeed, it is arguable that this may be the future of defensible space and CPTED, especially as physical settings become infused with remote surveillance, sensing and reactive devices such as those made possible by nanotechnology. Given the pace of technological change and the exponential explosion of the fear of terrorism, how far away are truly distal, bionic systems that can sense and react to threats? Beyond bureaucracy, this technology involves actual decision making, albeit programmed in advance. The civil liberty and ethical issues surrounding these developments are yet to be broached, even as comparatively milder interventions, such as the diffusion of CCTV and centralised data mining, have been roundly criticised in the United States and the United Kingdom.

For the present, technology continues to augment, not supplant, human discretion. But computer costs continue to decrease, and our willingness *physically* to police the physical environment against crime and terrorism also decreases. Indeed, a great deal of effort has been expended trying to convince the public and others (including professionals, such as planners and urban designers) that guardianship responsibilities should be spread as broadly as possible since police resources are inadequate to the task, at least in open societies such as the United States and Britain, and that too much *real* policing not only is prohibitively expensive but endangers freedom. The idea that design and technology (separately or bundled together) can do this more cheaply than and as effectively (or more so) as real people and in a politically neutral way is quite attractive. Indeed, one of the guiding notions behind place-based crime prevention is that it is neither a liberal nor a conservative philosophy, but rather one that seeks simply to reduce crime opportunity (Felson, 2002). Nevertheless, theory and policy underpin the funding, deployment, design and programming of technology, especially that used in public spaces. We cannot, therefore, escape ultimate responsibility for it, no matter how attractive the prospect.

Part Three
Conclusions

9

Conclusions

Introduction

What we want to do in this chapter is to pull together some of the threads from the preceding chapters, and to make some suggestions about some ways forward for work in the fields of interest of this book. The first part of this chapter, therefore, revisits Part One (the theory) and Part Two (the practice) to pick out some of what seem to us to be the major points in the material we have presented. We then ask what all of this adds to what we have said previously (Schneider and Kitchen, 2002, chapter 10) about some of the broad propositions we think might guide the future development of the field. We also discuss what we think are some of the important research issues which arise from the material. Finally, we offer some concluding remarks.

The theories revisited

We chose to organise the more theoretical material that we have presented in this book around the idea that there are what we termed some classical theories of place-based crime prevention and also some emerging concepts and trends which in various ways challenge these classical theories. This section therefore revisits what we have said about the current state of the development of theory in this field and seeks to draw it together.

The classical place-based crime prevention theories that we described in Chapter 2 are grounded in the fundamental principles that environment (setting and place) influences behaviour, including criminal behaviour, and that manipulating the environment can mitigate or redirect crime, or prevent it altogether. Each accepts that scientific evidence is necessary to support crime prevention strategies, although there is variable evidence underpinning both defensible space and CPTED across a range of circumstances. Situational criminology and environmental criminology have a larger and more diverse evidence base, including numerous small-scale studies to support their intervention strategies.

All the place-based theories share the notion that the focus on places (or settings, in situational crime prevention) where criminal events occur or can be prevented from occurring is as important (or in some cases more important) in explaining and predicting crime as is concentrating on the disposition of the offender, and all offer a variety of prevention approaches based on this proposition. Despite that, they also consider offenders' rationality, routine activity behaviour and (in Jeffrey's original CPTED formulation) the notion that physical brain processes (such as brain chemistry) affect individual environmental perception in relation to crime. The latter point illustrates an area where science has yet to catch up with theory. In general, however, the place-based theories are much more concerned with spatial, temporal and situational factors than with offender characteristics.

The two oldest place-based theories, defensible space and CPTED, are most often associated with physical design-based explanations for crime, although both have evolved to incorporate and consider management and social factors as well. Situational crime prevention encompasses defensible space and CPTED concepts, and places them within a general opportunity framework, such that crime is predicated to occur in circumstances where likely offenders find targets in the absence of capable guardians and, within this opportunity context, calculate risk, effort and reward, mediated by other factors such as shame and provocation. Offending is therefore seen (in part) as an outgrowth of a combination of environmental, usage and management functions that are crime- and place-specific. Situational crime prevention offers a host of intervention strategies to assist policing and order management efforts in these circumstances, and many of these strategies have been adopted by law enforcement agencies throughout the world.

Environmental criminology incorporates the assumptions of other place-based theories and suggests that crime is not a random event but occurs in patterns across the landscape and is influenced by the physical shape of the environment, including (among other things) pathways, nodes and edges, and by a host of other social, economic and natural factors. Certain types of offending are therefore reasonably predictable given the availability, distribution and accessibility of targets (people or property), the layout of the land, and the normal, everyday activities of offenders across that landscape. Environmental criminology has provided theoretical inspiration for the development of geographic profiling, computer-based crime mapping and other, related technologies that use large data sets to describe, analyse and predict criminal activity, as was discussed in Chapter 8.

It is interesting to note that intense criticism has been directed towards defensible space and CPTED – those theories that generally support community layouts that do not conform to recent planning and design dictates, such as those suggested by new urbanism. On the other side, proponents of these theories emphasise that there is virtually no evidence to support the contrary view, as British research suggests when non-SBD estates are compared with SBD estates (Armitage, 2000). This is reinforced by the experience of police who deal with the on-the-ground reality of permeable street patterns in neighbourhoods, and in Chapter 5 we have discussed the experience and views of two British ALOs in relation to this issue. Situational crime prevention has also been criticised as another 'target hardening' approach that merely displaces crime from one venue to another. However, evidence to refute the idea of automatic crime displacement (or deflection) has come from a variety of sources in the United States, United Kingdom and Australia.

We ended Chapter 2 by suggesting that the evolution of place-based crime prevention theory will most likely be strongly influenced by energy constraints that play out in the development policies and regulations shaping new communities and reshaping existing ones, and by the large amount of resources being devoted to anti-terrorism, including the development of technology at national levels that will filter down to local police agencies. The former point relates very much to debates around how human life in settlements needs to adapt in order to respond appropriately to the challenges of global warming, and while there are still some refuseniks in high places in relation to this agenda, we suggest that its importance can only grow in the coming years. The latter point derives in particular from our assessment in Chapter 7 of the dramatic impact that anti-terrorism planning has had on thinking about planning for crime prevention in the United States, but unless we can find ways of making the world a more stable place such that the threat of terrorism ebbs away, we suggest that this agenda too will inevitably be addressed in many other parts of the globe in subsequent years.

Looking at this body of classical theory as a set, we suggest that the biggest issue it faces is that its worth needs to be demonstrated on the ground much more consistently and continuously than has been the case to date. Too little of the debate that surrounds the application of place-based theories of crime prevention seems to us to be informed by the careful reporting of the results of real-world attempts to apply it. As a consequence, too much of the debate takes the form of 'never mind the facts, here are my opinions'. The primary need, therefore, is to turn this around, so that a much more solid basis of effective evaluation is established. Clearly, this will not happen overnight, but it is an important endeavour for everyone in the field. We suspect that a particular issue in this context is likely to be the extent to which practices and ideas which have largely been established in the developed world (and especially, in terms of the material we have reviewed in this book, in the United States and Britain) will translate effectively to the different cultures and circumstances of the developing world. We know in this latter context that crime is undoubtedly a major issue (United Nations Office on Drugs and Crime, 2005), but in many parts the process of exploring the contribution that the manipulation of the built environment might be capable of making to the amelioration of its impact has scarcely begun, and the tools needed for this task may as yet often be very imperfectly developed. We suspect that this process, when it is attempted, will tell us a great deal about not just how locationally specific but also how culturally specific the successful application of the classical theories of place-based crime prevention might turn out to be; and we suspect that this is an important lesson that the field has still to learn.

Let us turn, then, to some of the contemporary challenges to the classical theories of place-based crime prevention. Chapter 3 reviewed four of these:

work on space syntax, the impact on crime prevention of the application of new urbanism as an urban design concept, the phenomenon of gated communities, and premises liability issues. We revisit each of these in turn below.

In the first section of Chapter 3 we discussed space syntax, a set of complex analytic techniques that aim to describe and decode urban space and movement within space. The results of empirical studies conducted using space syntax approaches reject the theory of territoriality as described by Newman and argue instead that accessibility and permeability of street networks, epitomised in the traditional gridiron layout, provide better solutions to crime prevention than closed or segmented street networks. According to these studies, the movement of strangers and neighbours through places, and especially those where façades open on to the street, makes places safer. Increased opportunity for surveillance is the major predicate for these findings, which suggest that certain crimes tend to cluster in places that are, by structure and placement, less observable. These results stand largely on their own, outside a stream of empirical work that generally contradicts the permeability thesis, but rather than suggesting that this means that space syntax should be rejected outright, we argue that further empirical work, such as that suggested by the *Safer Places* report (Office of the Deputy Prime Minister and the Home Office, 2004), should be done in order to reconcile or reject space syntax as a viable tool in crime prevention planning. We also noted that there are common grounds between space syntax findings and a range of other research and theory on issues related to the dangers of ambiguous space and the value of clearly bounded (though not controlled) urban space, and we think these are matters of considerable significance in their own right.

The second emerging concept reviewed in Chapter 3 in relation to crime prevention was new urbanism, which combines a variety of related ideologies that share an antipathy to the automobile-dominated suburbs that came to symbolise the United States following World War II. Informed by architectural style preferences rather than by empirical research about the experience of crime when living in such layouts, some new urbanists claim that community design that mimics envisioned villages of a bygone American past can promote civic values and, in so doing, deter or prevent crime. Design elements such as connected street layouts and mixed uses are considered important features of new urbanist design that prevent crime inasmuch as they facilitate surveillance and community interaction. Despite this and the fact that many new urbanist communities are undeniably aesthetically appealing, the preponderance of empirical evidence shows that gridiron street layouts and mixed uses are often crime facilitators, not inhibitors. The importance of new urbanist thinking is not limited to the (relatively small) number of whole communities that have been built according to these principles, either, since we have shown in Chapter 4 and elsewhere (Kitchen, 2005) how pervasive new urbanist thinking has become in relation to government advice on urban design in the United Kingdom. The practical consequence of this is that new urbanist ideas influence very many development proposals even when they are not on the scale of the whole neighbourhood, which is the basis of this design philosophy. Given cultural differences and the vast variability of local circumstances, it remains to be seen whether the issues noted above will be reliably replicated in studies elsewhere. However, that may ultimately be less relevant than providing users with context-relevant, empirically based information so that they can make informed and balanced choices.

The third emerging issue reviewed in Chapter 3 was the rapid growth (in the United States in particular) of gated communities both as a form of development from the outset and as a response to problems experienced by existing communities. In this latter context, gated communities tend to privatise formerly public space, where they aggregate people who are generally bound together by formal agreements and the desire for security. Although there is some tangential evidence from studies of alley and street closures that restricting access to neighbourhoods does, in the short term, reduce certain types of crimes, the research is not convincing in relation to long-term applications. Moreover, there is evidence that offenders adapt to changes and that the overall costs of gating may not be balanced by the crime prevention benefits that accrue. The phenomenon of gating as a characteristic of new-build housing seems to be about offering people a sense of greater safety (however real or otherwise that might turn out to be), although it can also be seen as exclusive and in some senses anti-urban. What is undeniable, however, is the rapidity of its spread in some parts of the world, which appears to demonstrate a simple point: security, or at any rate the perception of security, sells.

The final section of Chapter 3 reviewed premises security liability, a subset of premises liability litigation that entails private decisions by property owners, managers and others to protect themselves against damages from negligence, generally attributed to the negligent failure to provide adequate security. It is a variety of tort law that has grown significantly in the United States since the 1960s, and cases have incorporated place-based crime prevention theory and practice, including CPTED and situational crime prevention. We suggest that its use will probably increase in both the United States and Britain as a result of a combination of social and political factors and due to terrorist threats, and that, as a self-help, market-driven force, premises security liability litigation may be in its own way at least as effective a means of implementing place-based crime prevention strategies as efforts made through public (police or planning) authorities.

In sum, Chapter 3 stresses the constant challenge that the classical theories face from emerging concepts and from real-world events, all factors which drive the evolution of these theories and, ultimately, the application of place-based crime prevention interventions in urban communities. Of the four challenges we reviewed, we would conclude that there is still a distance to be travelled before either space syntax or new urbanism (in their different ways) could be said to have established places in the theory of the field supported by empirical studies which convince well beyond the ranks of their true believers. As far as gated communities are concerned, they appear to be here to stay, and thus the field as a whole will have to find a way of accommodating their impact, which as yet it has not done. We suspect that premises liability litigation will grow, and that as a consequence it will be an important element in future actions alongside the efforts of public authorities to promote planning for crime prevention.

The practice revisited

Part Two of this book consists of five chapters where we explore in some depth subject areas that we believe are of importance to the development of the field. Four of these draw on our operational experiences of the processes of planning for crime prevention in the United States and the United Kingdom, and thus in effect represent case studies drawn from those two countries: the impact of the recent emphasis on the development of anti-terrorism measures and applications of new technology to the field from the United States, and the experiences of police ALOs and the development of links between crime prevention and processes of urban regeneration from the United Kingdom. The other chapter in this part of the book presents a partial survey of how planning systems in various parts of the world are beginning to address the crime prevention agenda. As we said in Chapter 1, there are a large number of topics that we could have chosen to handle in this way, but limitations of space (and knowledge) meant that we had to make a limited selection. We believe that the material we have presented in Part Two not only is about issues which are of considerable significance in their own right, but also offers important lessons for other parts of the world facing or considering facing similar issues. We shall return to the conclusions of each of these individual chapters below.

Chapter 4 is about how planning systems engage with crime prevention. This is an important subject because across most of the developed world, and in an increasing number of developing countries, it is planning systems that mediate new development proposals on behalf of the community at large. Thus, if crime prevention is going to be incorporated into development from its outset, as distinct from needing to be tackled at a later date as a retrofitting problem, then it is likely to be via planning systems that any public role in ensuring that this happens will get played out; although, of course, developers and their agents could be encouraged to do this of their own volition. Our survey of this is by no means complete, but as far as we are aware, there has been no attempt to undertake this task anywhere else, and so we offer this review as a contribution to what we regard as a necessary task. The reason why this task seems to us to warrant this description is fairly straightforward. As yet, there appear to be relatively few systematic attempts to get planning systems to see themselves as having a role to play in crime prevention; just as this is a fairly new idea for planning, so it is for planning systems. We suspect, however, that the interest in planning systems' role in crime prevention will undoubtedly grow, and we think it would be inherently desirable if attempts at extending our survey were to be informed by the experience of those systems that are already some way down this road. We have suggested five possible roles for planning systems in this context, and we summarise these below:

- writing appropriate crime prevention policies into plans and associated guidance documents;
- dealing with applications for permissions to undertake development in ways which incorporate crime prevention considerations into the processes of reviewing proposals;
- getting involved in projects which seek to manipulate the physical environment from crime prevention/reduction perspectives;
- encouraging formal monitoring, review and reporting of actions undertaken;
- developing partnership and consultative arrangements.

Planning systems not doing these things at present will not necessarily choose to start all of them together, and the ways in which they are addressed will need to be particular to the extant local circumstances. But we think that this is a useful checklist of potential actions for planning organisations if they wish to begin to develop their capability to contribute to crime prevention.

Chapter 5 looks at the operational experiences of two English ALOs in some depth. As far as we are aware, there are no systematic studies of how police officers who are involved in working with the development industry and with the planning system in order to promote planning for crime prevention actually undertake these tasks, and so these two cases are offered as a start down this road. Clearly, it is quite impossible to say with any authority whether these two cases are even typical of other ALOs working in the British system, much less of police officers doing similar sorts of jobs in other countries around the world. What we do hope, however, is that our process of working with these officers in order to write these case studies will encourage others to attempt this exercise, so that we can build up a better understanding of how processes of this nature actually work. This would be of value not only to the development of the field itself but also to police officers who find themselves in the type of role, who hopefully would be able to learn about what constitutes good practice not just from their own experience but also as part of their training and continuous development from the experiences of others.

Chapter 6 examined how elements of the process of urban regeneration in Britain were addressing crime prevention, given two basic propositions. The first was that urban regeneration was increasingly about improving the quality of people's lives in the more deprived parts of urban areas and was less focused merely on achieving property development in those localities. The second was that it was a common experience that when people were asked about the factors that troubled them about the areas in which they lived, crime, and particularly violent crime, came at or near the top of such lists. Taken together, these two propositions meant that crime prevention over the past decade or so had become a central element in the urban regeneration process, whereas previously it had not figured largely on the regeneration agenda. Of course, the British approach to urban regeneration, with its highly structured sets of partnerships and its strong central government policy drive, would not necessarily be the arrangement adopted elsewhere. But what is likely to be common is the emphasis on using processes of urban regeneration (or similarly described activities) to tackle problems of poor quality of life in established urban areas, and also the recognition of the role that crime prevention initiatives can play in such processes.

Our case studies looked at the part played by the process of thinking strategically about such issues through the medium of the work of the Sheffield First Partnership, and also at a project (the Blackthorn CASPAR project in Northampton) which was addressing a common problem: what to do about a development that was little over 20 years old but that had some design features which could be described as being 'of their time' and which were undoubtedly contributing to a very negative experience of crime on that estate? The former case study showed that there was genuine value in having a process of thinking strategically as part of the adopted approach. The latter (award-winning) case is quite challenging, because what it shows is that it is possible to improve such a situation, in particular through extensive processes of direct engagement with the resident community, but that it still leaves behind the elements of the original design which have contributed to the experience of crime more or less from the outset. The reason why this is particularly challenging, of course, is that the housing stock itself is nowhere near to being at the end of its useful life, and so demolition and starting again is not a practical option (as is often the case). But equally, leaving an existing situation more or less as it was, and not attempting to tackle the negative experience of crime, could also be seen as not being a realistic option, especially for the people likely to be living on that estate for the foreseeable future. So, this is a case which looks at quite a common problem, and which offers some lessons about what might be done to bring about some improvements when tackling the fundamental difficulties at source is not a realistic proposition.

The discussion in Chapter 7 of the impact of the massive increase in attention to anti-terrorist measures in the United States in recent years suggested that one of its consequences had been the growth in interest in CPTED and related place-based crime prevention theory and practice propositions. This was, in part, because these provided a rationale for intervention, given the political imperative to take action following shocking events such as those on 11 September 2001. The likely consequence of this is an acceleration in the development of theory and practice in this field, in all probability more rapidly than would otherwise have been the case, notwithstanding the tiny number of terrorist incidents in the United States as compared with the scale of the crimes that CPTED and related practices seek to ameliorate. It is also likely that this surge of interest will lead to further developments in the application of new technologies to the field, which we discussed in more detail in Chapter 8. Interestingly, Chapter 7 also suggested that the evidence that all of this effort will really lead to more effective protection against terrorist incidents is weak, and that it may well turn out to be the case that investment ostensibly in the name of anti-terrorism will actually generate more tangible crime prevention benefits than anything else – which may not be wholly surprising, given that much of what has been done actually stems from the field of crime prevention.

Of course, in one sense this is the classic example of a field where the last thing that governments actually want to see is their investment in anti-terrorist protection being tested not by simulated means but by a terrorist attack. Essentially, the primary aim here is to deter attacks from taking place in the first place, and only if this does not succeed is the secondary aim to offer the terrorist target as much protection as possible. Sadly, recent experience would suggest that terrorist activities, although in an absolute sense still small in number, must be expected to continue and perhaps even to grow; and just as we have seen in the crime world that one of the propositions that crime prevention activities have to address is the idea of the adaptive criminal, so equally must we expect terrorists to be resourceful in these terms and not to be easily distracted from achieving what they set out to do. One of the other important issues in this context over the next few years will be the extent to which practices developed in the United States are taken up in other parts of the world where the threat of terrorist activities is seen as a growing one; so is the US experience that we report here likely to be unique, or is it the harbinger of developments elsewhere?

We can expect that the process of applying emerging technologies to the field of crime prevention will be more or less continuous, and Chapter 8 has provided a snapshot of this in terms of both direct applications at the point at which a crime might be taking place, and strategic and tactical applications which are designed to improve the process of combating crime. This is probably seamless and endless, and so in detail it is likely that some of the specific examples we use in Chapter 8 will become outdated quickly – because that has always been the fate of some technological applications, and it will continue to be so. But what is constant here is the idea that technologies of all kinds can be applied to the place-based elements of the experience of crime – the *where* of it, which is what particularly distinguishes the subject matter of this book. And what is also constant here is the idea that the process of technological response needs to be ever-changing, faced with a criminal community which includes individuals who constantly adapt to changing circumstances and who often themselves bring technology to bear on this process. We have also suggested that this process is likely to be accelerated as a result of the attention that has been given in recent years in the United States to anti-terrorism measures, especially since much of that activity has itself harnessed a wide range of modern technology. The key point in all of this, though, is whether our technological capability can translate into a human capability to make effective use of the data being generated, and whether the ways in which we choose to use the data can remain consistent with the expectations of the residents of open societies about their civil and personal liberties. To put the problem another way, we can expect the application of technology in this field to become ever more sophisticated; but can we in parallel find ways of using it that are efficient, effective and widely acceptable across our societies?

By virtue of the choices we made about the practice issues where we wished to focus our attention, Part Two of this book represents a collection of material from which it is not easy to draw out linking themes. What we wanted to do here, however, was to identify practice areas where we believed that important developments were taking place, and from which we hoped that valuable lessons would emerge from the process of shining a light on some of the cutting-edge experiences in these fields. So, the process of getting planning systems to address crime prevention does appear to be attracting more interest across the world, and we have offered a model list of tasks for planning systems in this context. Related to this, one of the newly emerging sets of professional relationships is that between police officers and planners, about which very little has been written, and so, to begin the process of improving understanding in this area, we have offered two case studies of British police officers operating in this role. The highly structured British process of urban regeneration, and the processes through which it seeks to engage with crime prevention, may not be found in many other localities, but we have used this arena as a means of examining two more common phenomena: how a strategic approach to this issue can add value, and what a project which seeks through a combination of physical retrofitting and community action to tackle the crime problems of relatively recent housing might be able to achieve. The US experience of terrorism in recent years has led to a flurry of anti-terrorism measures being put in place, and we have highlighted this process, and particularly its links with CPTED and related place-based crime prevention theories and practices, because it has accelerated interest in these fields and seems likely to continue to do so. As concerns about terrorism grow, such applications are likely to spread, intentionally or not, across the globe, with local police at the forefront of implementation. And finally, we have looked at some aspects of the application of new technologies to place-based crime prevention not just because of the intrinsic interest they generate but also because they raise important questions about how we utilise developments of this kind which are fundamentally socio-political in their nature rather than merely technological. In choosing to focus on these areas of practice development (and, therefore, not on others), we hope that Part Two of this book has illustrated how practice and theory are linked in a constant process of evolution.

Some ways forward

We have offered in each of the preceding chapters a series of suggestions about ways forward in relation to the subject matter of those chapters. What we want to do here is to step back from this and look more generally at the development of the field. When we attempted previously to draw some conclusions about the state of play in the field of planning for crime prevention (Schneider and Kitchen, 2002, chapter 10), we did so by offering nine broad propositions which we felt might provide a reliable way forward in a field where there appeared to be more assertion than evidence-based argument. In summary form, these were as follows:

1   Crime and the fear of crime matter greatly to the intended beneficiaries of planning.

2 There are complex relationships between crime, the fear of crime and environmental design.
3 Crime and the fear of crime are different but linked phenomena which both need to be tackled.
4 The careful evaluation and reporting of initiatives are essential.
5 Approaches should be tailored to local circumstances and people.
6 Issues around crime and the design of the built environment do not exist in isolation.
7 Local crime prevention initiatives require partnership working, both between professionals and with local communities.
8 Some of the most extreme problem areas also offer the greatest potential for positive achievement.
9 Context and outcome are of fundamental importance when transplanting ideas from one place to another.

We revisit each of these in turn below, discussing in each case what we would want to add to the proposition as a result of developments in the intervening period and of work on this book.

The first proposition appears to be a self-evident truth. It is indeed the case that crime and the fear of crime are both important elements in people's perceptions of the quality of life in a locality. If planning is about making places better for people (Kitchen, 2007), then it has to address those elements that make places problematic for people, and crime and the fear of crime are high up this list. But as we have shown in our survey in Chapter 4, the extent to which planning systems across the world appear to address planning for crime prevention appears to be very patchy; and even for those planning systems that do accept the need to tackle this agenda, this is likely to be a recent task jostling for attention and resources with more traditional planning tasks. Consequently, there is not yet widespread acceptance that this is a proper task for the planning process, and even in those planning systems where work of this nature has begun, we think it is unlikely that there will be many where all five of the activities we have suggested in the conclusion to Chapter 4 will be fully undertaken.

Of course, the ways in which planning systems will tackle this agenda will vary across the world according to local circumstances, because planning systems are essentially human constructs which work in accordance with the characteristics of the process of governance in the country in question. And the level of development of planning systems across the world is itself very variable. But we believe that the experience of crime in urban areas is a near-universal phenomenon, and that the effective use of planning systems represents one of the ways in which urban societies can respond. It took the British planning system nearly 50 years to begin to address this issue, however, although we think it ought to be possible for much newer planning systems in the developing world to move at a far more rapid rate than this by learning from the experiences of those systems that do see crime prevention as a field to which they need to contribute. Of course, such initiatives require resources, knowledge and political will to work to maximum effect, and any or all of these are often in short supply in many parts of the world.

Part of this process surely needs to be the development of effective relationships between planners and police officers working on place-based crime prevention, both of which groups really ought to see themselves as pulling in the same broad direction. The two British case studies we have presented in Chapter 5 of this book nonetheless suggest that this has not proved to be an easy relationship to develop in the United Kingdom, and while there is a dearth of studies from elsewhere which look at this matter, it would not be too much of a surprise if some of these difficulties were to be repeated. This too must be a field where cross-national learning can contribute to more rapid progress than would otherwise be the case, if only because this offers the opportunity to explore how to intervene in training programmes for both planners and the police in order to facilitate the development of more effective working relationships between them.

The second of our propositions relates closely to the ground we have covered in Part One of this book. There, we tried to show something of the debates that surround both the classical theories of place-based crime prevention and some of the contemporary challenges to those theories. The fact of the matter is that there is no simple linear relationship between an act of environmental design and a predictable consequence in terms of the subsequent experience of crime – although it has to be said that some consequences are more predictable than others. For example, an easily accessible and poorly lit rear of a house that is not overlooked, other things being equal, is likely to experience more burglary than a house without rear access or with a rear access well protected by walls, fencing and landscaping, well lit and overlooked by several neighbours. Barry Poyner (2006, pp. 99–103) has suggested that the way for designers to approach this issue in a residential design context is not to think about applying standardised design solutions but to think strategically in their design process about the kinds of crimes most likely to be committed and therefore how the design can help to deter them. So, he suggests that designers of residential layouts need to think about:

1 A strategy to avoid house burglary, which will usually have three key elements:

   - inhibiting target selection of a house for burglary;
   - protecting the front of a house and the point at which it interfaces with the street;
   - protecting the back of a house.

2 A strategy for providing a safe place to park cars, where the available evidence suggests that risk varies considerably, from communal parking areas (least safe) to secure within-curtilage parking (safest), and where pedestrian access via a segregated footpath system seems to increase the risk as compared with access via footpaths which are part of the street system.

3 A strategy for minimising theft from around the home, including from garages, other outbuildings and gardens, where the essential issues appear to be the need to ensure that spaces and buildings of this nature are secure and overlooked.

4 A strategy for avoiding criminal damage, where the (limited) available evidence suggests that open spaces in front of housing areas should have a degree of separation or some protective landscaping as part of a buffer area (such as an area of sloping ground) between them and the houses.

The importance of this approach is that it does not remove from designers all their creative opportunity by telling them what to do, but rather it invites them to think strategically about finding design solutions to the common kinds of crime problems found in residential areas. This approach might result in a range of possible solutions, but they are likely to be more effective if they are an integral part of the design rather than something tacked on (often reluctantly) as an afterthought or dealt with later as an inevitably constrained retrofit. There are some parallels here with problem-oriented policing (see Chapter 2), where in a similar manner the emphasis is on the analysis of the underlying causes leading to a crime, and not merely on the individual criminal events themselves.

As we said in Chapter 1, this is not a book about fear of crime, and so apart from the introductory remarks we made there, we have not dealt with this issue. That means that we are not in a position to comment any further on the third of our nine propositions, except perhaps to say that nothing that we have seen in the intervening period has changed our view that crime and the fear of crime should be regarded as different but linked phenomena.

One of the main thrusts of our first book was that we wanted to encourage more systematic and more rigorous evaluation and reporting of environmentally based crime prevention initiatives, so that the field would develop in more evidence-based ways rather than by relying on assertion to the extent that we felt it did. In the intervening period we feel that there has been some progress down this road, although the situation is still far from ideal. One of the risks that we think is becoming more visible is the extent to which websites, which are natural vehicles for reporting and reflecting on practice initiatives, are seen by many organisations as being instruments of corporate promotion at least as much as they are seen in this more altruistic role. Thus, instead of reporting and reflecting on initiatives, they tend to become promotional vehicles for their host, which, whatever it may achieve in terms of corporate image, adds little to the understanding and disseminating of the lessons of practice. An example of this problem is the British Secured by Design website, which is less based upon the practice experiences of police ALOs today than it was a few years ago because of a decision following the publication of *Safer Places* in 2004 to make it as consistent as possible with this government guidance. It is not too difficult to see why this was done, but what was sacrificed here was the opportunity for practice experience to influence policy on an ongoing basis.

If readers think this general verdict is unduly harsh, we invite them to think about how many websites they can identify which have reported critically on (their own) initiatives that have not been very successful and that have identified improvement lessons which involve implicit or explicit criticisms of the organisation. We venture to suggest that most readers will find these few and far between; and yet the truth is that not all initiatives are successful. Very often, some of the most instructive lessons can be gleaned from projects which have experienced difficulties, and yet it is just this kind of honest self-evaluation that can be screened out by the process we have described above. We recognise in saying this, of course, that most organisations are properly concerned about their public image, and so we are not asking that this dimension should be ignored in the continuing development of evaluative approaches. Rather, we are suggesting that a sensible balance needs to be struck here in order to ensure that the potential contribution of this particular communication tool to the development of the field and to the development of shared learning is not wasted. A challenge to us all, therefore, is to ensure that reporting and reflecting on initiatives should be as open, honest and accurate as possible, not just in formal reporting situations but also in the less formal practice reporting opportunities that websites often provide.

Of all the nine propositions we advanced in our 2002 book, the fifth one ('*approaches should be tailored to local circumstances and people*') was arguably the most important. Our concern was that we saw too strong a tendency for standardised solutions to be imposed from the outside in too many situations, whereas it was doubtful whether there were proven standardised solutions (other than in the most general of senses), especially when they took no account of the aspirations and knowledge of local people. Two cases we report in this book reinforce this view as far as we are concerned. Stephen Town's work with the local community on the Royds Estate in Bradford (Chapter 5) demonstrates how it is possible to turn around an estate that in so many ways exemplified the label 'problem' through a programme of sensible physical works determined through close cooperation with the local community. The Blackthorn CASPAR project in Northampton (Chapter 6) illustrates that it is possible by getting the local community fully involved in determining what needs to be done to achieve worthwhile gains in a retrofitting project, although the basic design flaws remain, carrying with them the likelihood that certain kinds of crime will not be eliminated over the long term despite the best efforts of the project.

Community involvement is not a panacea, of course, but it is not too difficult to see why projects are more likely to be successful when strong community buy-in has been obtained from the outset. Similarly, the characteristics of places and the ways in which people make use of them are infinitely variable, and so it is inherently much more likely that projects which understand these parameters and seek to start from them will be more successful than projects imposed from the outside without any real thought being given to these features. We have seen many examples of both of these approaches, and we have little doubt that in the field of planning for crime prevention, tailoring to local circumstances and working with local people are characteristics which vastly increase the likelihood of success.

Our sixth proposition, that issues around crime and the design of the built environment cannot be seen in isolation, was simply trying to suggest that place-based crime prevention cannot separate off people's experiences of crime in a particular locality from all the other factors that influence how they use places and what they feel about them. In that sense, as a proposition it strongly reinforces the idea of tailoring approaches to local circumstances and people, discussed above. That said, though, we have certainly come across instances where public projects designed to tackle crime issues are just that – narrowly conceived, with boundaries around what the funding is available for, which severely limit how it can be spent, and often involving people whose perspective is also narrowly focused on the specifics of crime incidents rather than the generalities of the localities within which they occur or on the proximate causes of the incidents themselves. The existence of these sorts of approaches, we suggest, helps to explain why often the process of achieving a meeting of minds between local people and external experts becomes such a struggle. The fact of the matter is that local people are not likely to see their problems as subdivided into neat little administrative packages, and are not likely to be terribly impressed by arguments about what can and cannot be done which bear no relation to what they see as being needed but which are derived from the rules governing organisational budgets and expenditure programmes. Place-based crime prevention should be looked at holistically, because if it is not, the 'place-based' element will be difficult to understand. And effective working with local communities involves trying to understand their perceptions and concerns rather than an extensive explanation of what is and is not possible according to the rules. We think it is vital, therefore, that projects which seek to tackle local crime problems adopt (at any rate at the outset) a broad view of the kind of actions that might be necessary, and structure their budgets and programmes so as to facilitate rather than hinder such an approach.

In the five years or so since we wrote about the importance of partnership working as part of our seventh proposition, we have seen widespread acceptance of this approach in the field of crime prevention. Again, it is not difficult to see why this should be. Essentially, many individuals, many organisations and many different perspectives need to be brought together to tackle something as complex as this, and partnership provides a framework for this kind of activity. This approach has been known and applied for many years in relation to individual projects and short-term bursts of intensive activity. What we have also shown (in our case study of the local strategic partnership in Sheffield in Chapter 6) is its value when thinking strategically – by which we mean thinking about the experiences of crime in large places and their various localities, thinking about tackling crime as a continuous process over long periods of time within each of which specific action programmes take place, and thinking about crime as one of many elements affecting the quality of life in a place rather than as something free-standing. We think the available evidence suggests that, while processes of this nature require a great deal of effort and commitment, often at senior level, they do have the potential to contribute considerably to the fight against crime by providing a framework which helps knit together individual initiatives into a coherent whole. So, we would extend what we previously said about the importance of partnership approaches to incorporate both strategic activity of the kind we have just described and tactical or operational activity at the level of the individual project or initiative.

In one sense, our eighth proposition (that some of the most extreme problem areas offer the greatest potential for positive achievement) was and is a truism: the more that needs to be done, the more room there is for doing. But what we were trying to say was that there was a risk that at times easy options might be chosen in the search for quick wins, and that this might leave some of the more daunting challenges still waiting on the sidelines. If place-based crime prevention is to be effective, it has to offer the opportunity to make progress in a very wide range of circumstances. An approach that only works in middle-class low-density suburbia, for example, may still be of value in other areas of that kind but is clearly very limited when it comes to addressing the problems of high-density, high-rise, multicultural inner-city locations. And other things being equal, the likelihood is that crime rates will be higher in the latter situation than in the former, and so arguably the need for effective action is thereby greater. We have certainly seen clear evidence in the projects we have looked at in this book of a willingness to try to tackle difficult problems, and that is very encouraging, because there can be little doubt that the processes of applying the theories and practices of place-based crime prevention to urban situations across the world will undoubtedly come across many problematic situations where solutions will need to innovate, and it is important that these challenges are both faced and learned from.

Our final proposition (the importance of context and outcome when transplanting ideas from one place to another) also relates to this last point. The process of applying place-based crime prevention measures to an ever-wider range of situations, especially in the developing world, can undoubtedly benefit from learning from experience elsewhere, and this is one of the reasons why we have put such an emphasis on evaluation, reflection and dissemination. This process will undoubtedly be aided by the use of the opportunities offered by new technology in an electronic age, some of which we have discussed in Chapter 8. But the caution here is of fundamental importance: the fact that something appears to have worked in a particular locality (or somebody has said that it has worked, which is not necessarily the same thing) is not a guarantee that it will work elsewhere. Indeed, there is ample evidence that this process of transplanting initiatives, especially when it is done relatively uncritically, achieves very patchy results. What is absolutely critical to drawing the lessons from a project is understanding as broadly as possible the context in which it was originally applied, and then comparing and contrasting that understanding with the context that will apply in the situation under consideration. What is also critical is understanding what the outcomes of the original application were, again in the broadest possible manner – and, in particular, if something appeared to work, understanding why it worked. Often, in practice, several variables contribute to a particular outcome, and if one of them was of special significance to a particular success story, it is important to reflect on whether that element is capable of being replicated in a different set of circumstances. It is sometimes the case also that external circumstances can make a great deal of difference to a particular outcome, in which case success is not necessarily attributable only to the specific variables that were manipulated by the project. What we are really trying to say here is that off-the-shelf approaches which appear to have worked elsewhere need to be looked at very carefully before it is assumed that they are likely to work in the locality being considered, and that the key elements in this process of scrutiny are likely to be context and outcomes.

None of this, of course, is to deny the importance of learning from experience elsewhere. Indeed, we believe that the primary way forward for the field consists of learning from careful research, evaluation and reporting, which includes reflecting on things that may have gone wrong as well as things that have gone well. In a phrase, the field needs to become more evidence based, and to be less swayed by unproven ideas promoted with great zeal by true believers. There is a distance to be travelled before this goal is achieved, but the most important requirement is that all parties are committed to the journey. We have seen some signs of such commitment in recent times, but efforts need to continue to be made to support this approach in the face of pressures that often exist to undermine its longer-term and more incremental characteristics.

Towards a research agenda

We have already made the general point that the field as a whole needs to move in the direction of being more evidence based, with a much stronger commitment to careful evaluation and reporting, and therefore this long-term task needs to be an important part of any research agenda, in particular when it comes to the translation of theory into practice. Over and above this, we want in this section to make a few comments about some of the more specific research implications of the ground we have covered in Part Two.

As far as the experience of planning systems in engaging with the planning for crime prevention agenda is concerned, a first research task is simply around the need to extend the partial survey contained in Chapter 4 so that we have a comprehensive picture of how this task is being tackled across the world. What we suspect that this will show is that in many parts of the world it is not being addressed at all, although we expect that those areas will also contain many urban localities where the experience of crime is a major problem for residents. As a consequence, there is clearly an opportunity in these localities for planning systems to play a role in the process of considering how the physical environment can be manipulated and managed in order to help to address this issue. It is important to understand what the barriers to activities of this nature are and how they can be overcome, and it is important to understand also how less-developed planning systems can learn from those that in this field at least are more developed.

Chapter 5 represents a first attempt as far as we are aware to try to understand in some depth what the experience of police officers working in the field of planning for crime prevention has actually been. As we noted, we have no real idea how representative these two cases are of such experience in the United Kingdom, much less of parallel experiences in other parts of the world, and so there is a need for more case studies of this nature so that we can build up a much better understanding of this role. In many ways, this is a non-traditional and newly emergent role for police services, which means that it inevitably competes for resources and senior management and political attention against more established police functions, but we believe that it is a role that will grow in importance if it is looked at in terms of its potential to reduce future pressures on police resources by eliminating or reducing the opportunity for crime. The process of understanding what officers performing these roles can actually achieve may be of significance in its own right in helping to establish this particular police function alongside many others. It is also likely to be significant in helping to develop training programmes both for officers moving into this work and for those already there. The value of research of this nature, therefore, is not just in terms of the intrinsic gains in understanding that are needed but also in the contribution it is capable of making to the development of this arm of police operations.

The cases looked at in Chapter 6 are probably particular to the structure of urban regeneration as it is practised in Britain. The chapter looked at three common phenomena in this particular context, however: how crime prevention is incorporated into processes of urban regeneration or revitalisation which are taking place in many parts of the world; how processes of partnership can enable crime prevention to be looked at strategically; and how residential areas (in particular) which carry with them the propensity for certain types of crime to be committed by virtue of integral features of their layout can be revisited to try to improve this situation, given that the housing stock itself has still probably a considerable amount of life left in it and is not about to be demolished. In their different ways, all three of these issues are experienced in many parts of the world, albeit often with a very different institutional structure as compard with that of the United Kingdom. The research challenge here is to understand the roles that institutional structures and approaches play in outcomes, and also to try to understand not only what works and what doesn't but why these outcomes occur. These are all likely to be important elements in the portability of solutions, and it is essential that this issue be addressed if we are to get the most out of the opportunity for learning that practice provides.

As we have argued in Chapter 7, there has been relatively little systematic evaluation of anti-terrorism measures as yet, and of course in one sense we would hope that this continues to be the position − because the ultimate evaluation of an anti-terrorism measure may be how it performs in the face of a terrorist attack, and we do not wish to see this particular feature actually happening anywhere. This may be a very optimistic stance to take when looking at a highly unstable world, however, and thus if it turns out that there are more incidents of this nature in future, it will be important to examine carefully what happened. This needs to relate not just to the specific anti-terrorism features that are in place but also to the general philosophy that sits behind them – and, as we have argued in Chapter 7, there are conflicting views about this. But we argued in Chapter 7 that it may well be the case that much of the benefit from anti-terrorism measures will turn out to be in the crossover from this specific intent to more general crime prevention. So, we need to understand how anti-terrorism measures perform in this context as well. This may be different in an important sense from the very occasional terrorist incident which needs to be examined in detail, because it might be about the ongoing performance of a feature or facility in everyday life. We have suggested that a parallel here may be with the US space programme, which has produced all kinds of spin-offs, and if we are to see the full benefit of investment of this nature it is important that we understand all of its consequences.

By its very nature, the material reviewed in Chapter 8 tends to be about the application in practice of the products of processes of research and development. Most fields have as one dimension of their development issues around the application of new technology to them, and the field of place-based crime prevention is no exception. We think it is important here that the research agenda is not just about the development of the technology itself, but about the human problems of adapting and applying it, and about the socio-political issues these processes will inevitably raise. A good illustration of this latter point is the ongoing debate about civil liberties, and about what is acceptable in an open society as technology constantly pushes at the bounds of what is possible. Another important research dimension relates to the concept of the adaptive criminal, where 'adaptive' clearly includes the use of technological innovation in order to make the criminal act easier to accomplish or the undetected escape easier to achieve. The likelihood is that this will continually challenge our notion of what 'secure' actually means, and it is important that we undertake research which explores issues of this nature rather than taking for granted the view that they remain essentially unchanged.

Conclusions

We have tried to pull together in this chapter some threads from the preceding chapters in ways that readers will find helpful. Throughout, we have looked constantly at the interplay between theory and practice in what is at its heart an applied field. The process of manipulating the physical environment in order to reduce the likelihood that certain kinds of crimes will take place is essentially about trying things out, seeing to what extent and in what ways they work, learning from this experience, and then trying to apply it meaningfully elsewhere. We believe that this process has a great deal to offer to the task of combating what appears to be a near-universal experience of crime, not as a panacea but as a valuable contribution alongside many other types of approaches. As such, this activity needs to embrace large numbers of professionals in many of the built environment disciplines as well as police services, and local communities and other political representatives as well as a very wide range of public agencies. Our philosophy is that this task is likely to be done better through an evidence-led process rather than through design or other philosophies which have little or no evaluative basis. We hope that all the parties we have identified as having a contribution to make to this process will feel that this book has been of some help to them in these terms.

Notes

1 Introduction

1 The source for this is the UK government's crime reduction website at www. crimereduction.gov.uk/fearofcrime0216.htm, which we last consulted on 2 June 2006.

2 Classical theories of place-based crime prevention

1 In his foreword to Oscar Newman's monograph for the US Department of Housing and Urban Development, Michael A. Stegman, then Assistant Secretary for Policy Development and Research, notes that 'The appearance of Oscar Newman's *Defensible Space* in 1972 signaled the establishment of a new criminological subdiscipline that has come to be called by many "Crime Prevention Through Environmental Design" or CPTED' (Newman, 1996, p. iii).

2 In a December 2003 email to Stephen Town, Architectural Liaison Officer for Bradford, England, Newman wrote, 'Territorial definition of environments (through the subdivision and assignment of spaces) creates the identification with the space which results in intervention. . . . Jane Jacobs does not understand territorial definition [and] has no theoretical underpinnings and no proof whatever for her ideas.'

3 Von Hoffman (2000) notes that suggestions that Pruitt-Igoe was intended to further segregate St Louis's low-income African-American population by concentrating them in inner-city high-rise structures are not supported by historical evidence.

4 The connection of spatial to social objectives has long been a feature of public housing design in the United States. In this context Vale notes that there is 'a whole history of attempts to use housing as a tool of reform and to see [its] site planning as a means to achieve better citizenship' (2005, p. 71).

5 See http://www.popcenter.org/aboutCPOP.html#cops (last accessed 9 August 2005).

6 The COPS (Community Oriented Policing) programme in the United States is a part of the US Department of Justice and provides millions of dollars worth of grants each year to local agencies to support a wide variety of crime reduction programmes. See http://www.cops.usdoj.gov/Default.asp?Item=34.

7   See   http://www.homeoffice.gov.uk/crime/communitysafety/index.html   (last accessed 10 August, 2005).

8   The British/European COPS project was part-funded by BRE (the Building Research Establishment) and supported by the European Commission. It has involved representatives from Estonia, Germany, Greece, Poland, the Netherlands and the United Kingdom.

9   Horan (1997) gives the example of convenience stores that are revictimised when staff fail to secure large amounts of cash through periodic cash drops at banks. Robbers are rewarded for their efforts, which leads to repeat crimes, even though some perpetrators are arrested. An analysis of the problem suggests that management and training are significant contributing causes of repeat crimes as distinct from other factors.

10   The SARA model includes Scanning, Analysis, Response and Assessment components. See http://www.popcenter.org/about-SARA.htm (last accessed 9 August 2005).

11   In this context, see the extraordinary work of Edward R. Tufte (1997, 2001) on the power of good visual images to convey complex information that help explain phenomena. Hoffman (1998) emphasises this point by noting the enormous importance of vision by virtue of its near-dominance of the cerebral cortex and inasmuch as we use our eyes well before we learn to read, write or even speak. See also Gamman and Pascoe (2004).

12   See, for example, Ned Levine's response to Kim Rossmo's critique of National Institute of Justice geographic profiling methodology at http://www.nedlevine.com/nedlevine5.htm (last accessed 16 August 2005).

13   Some police officers suggest that overt fortressing sends out a message to potential offenders that 'this place has valuable goods'. Gamman and Pascoe (2004) make a cogent argument that the crime prevention literature needs to incorporate more visual imagery, as well as standards and measurement scales with which to describe types and levels of 'fortressing' clearly, among other descriptive but essentially vague terms in the crime prevention literature that are difficult to compare across communities, much less cultures.

3 Emerging concepts and trends affecting place-based crime prevention theory and practice

1   The spatial types include three primary types – convex, axial and isovist spaces – which, in turn, are associated with convex, axial and isovist maps (Klarqvist, 1993).

2   As we noted in Chapter 2, Jeffrey suggests (1971, 1977) that the *physical* brain mediates the environment–behaviour connection and that such linkages provide unique individual experiences that cannot be easily generalised.

3   That said, there is evidence that territoriality per se is indeed less powerful than Newman suggested. For example, in their study of Atlanta neighbourhoods Greenberg *et al.* (1982) concluded that design changes were more important than territorial feelings in accounting for differences between low- and high-crime urban neighbourhoods. But their findings (and others noted below) also cast doubt on the space syntax contention that permeable places tend to be safer ones. They report that 'The flow of outsiders into and out of low crime neighborhoods was inhibited because land use was more homogeneously residential, there were fewer major arteries, and boundary streets were less traveled than was the case in high crime neighborhoods' (p. 163).

4 Personal conversations in 2006 with Officer Art Hushen, who, until recently, directed the CPTED unit in Tampa, Florida, and who served as longtime President of the Florida CPTED Network. Personal conversation in 2005 with Constable Stephen Town, ALO for the West Yorkshire Police in Bradford.

5 It could be argued that recent new urbanist thinking has come to incorporate broader connections with landscape architecture and planning. For example, Duany advocates 'transect' planning, which he defines as 'geographical cross sections of a region used to reveal a sequence of environments' (2005, p. 1). Transects are employed to organise the built and natural environments, and they form the basis for some new urbanist zoning and related land development and building codes.

6 For example, relative to crime and street surveillance, the Kitty Genovese murder in Queens, New York, makes the point that neighbours do not always look after neighbours, no matter how compelling the circumstances. So, while on the whole it is better to be seen (or at least heard) than not, surveillance is a variable and fragile tool in crime prevention, perhaps especially when it is looked at as a free-standing element. There may be more to be said for natural surveillance working in partnership with other crime prevention tools.

7 The US Census Bureau defines gated communities as 'secured communities' and says that they are 'typically residential communities in which public access by nonresidents is restricted, usually by physical boundaries, such as gates, walls, and fences, or through private security. These communities exist in a myriad of locations and development types, including high-rise apartment complexes, retirement developments, and resort and country club communities'. Source: Appendix A, Definitions US Census, American Housing Survey 2001, http://www.census.gov/hhes/www/housing/ahs/ahs01/appendixa.pdf.

8 The website is 'Expert Pages.Com' at http://expertpages.com/all/394.

9 The *Premises Liability Report* can be accessed at http://www.straffordpub.com/products/plr/.

10 The September 11th Victim Compensation Fund of 2001 is one of three key features of the Air Transportation Safety and System Stabilization Act of 2001 ['ATSA'], Title IV of Pub. L. 107–42, 115 Stat. 230, 49 U.S.C. Section 40101.

4 A global perspective on integrating crime prevention into planning systems

1 Formal processes through structures of governance at various levels are assisted in the European case by the existence of the European Designing Out Crime Association (E-DOCA), which is in turn the European chapter of the International CPTED Association. E-DOCA's membership includes a wide range of profes-sionals, academics and people involved in governance agencies interested in urban safety planning and CPTED, and as well as keeping members up to date via its website, it organises formal and informal events of various kinds where information and experience can be exchanged. More information can be found on the E-DOCA website at http://www.e-doca.net//frameset-00.htm.

2 The information about both the Durban and the Nairobi projects has been taken from the UN-HABITAT Safer Cities website, consulted on 8 March 2006. Its address is www.unhabitat.org/programmes/safercities/projects.asp. The devel-opment of thinking about planning for crime prevention at city scale in Durban is being complemented by strategic activity at provincial scale, where in KwaZulu-Natal it is now a requirement that integrated development plans covering the

major urban areas must include both crime prevention policies and women's safety audits.

3   The two Nairobi City Residents Conventions took place in November 2004 and November 2005. This was done as a two-stage process because of the perceived need in the first instance for a familiarisation stage, and so the formal agreement by residents of the Urban Pact on Safety and the two-year Action Plan took place at the second of these two events.

4   The reference here is to the English planning system rather than to the British planning system because the effects of devolution throughout the United Kingdom include the fact that planning in Scotland, Wales and Northern Ireland is now overseen by their own Parliaments or Assemblies rather than by the UK national government (Tewdwr-Jones, 2002). So, this section of text is explicitly about how the planning system in England has taken increasing account of crime prevention issues, and the situation in the other constituent parts of the United Kingdom is a little different.

6   Crime prevention and urban regeneration: developing practice in the United Kingdom

1   The Blackthorn CASPAR project has some characteristics in common with 'weed and seed', a community-based strategy sponsored by the US Department of Justice with over 300 sites in the United States, with populations ranging from 3,000 to 50,000. It involves a two-pronged approach. The 'weed' element involves law enforcement agencies collaborating to weed out violent criminals and drug abusers, and the 'seed' element involves public agencies and community organisations collaborating to improve the locality in various ways. For more details, see the Office of Justice Programs website at http://www.ojp.usdoj.gov/cedo/ws/welcome.html.

2   The data on theft from inside cars are affected by changes in definition of what constitutes this category of crime between 1987 and 2000. Poyner therefore uses the word 'probably' to describe his conclusion that this category of crime had fallen between the two dates (2006, p. 80). He also argues that car theft (i.e. both of cars and from cars) has been reduced over this period by the much greater attention being paid by car designers to building security aspects into the initial design of vehicles.

7   The development of place-based anti-terrorism strategies in the United States

1   Michalak (2002) argues that terrorists' major goals are usually unrealised unless they are part of a broader military or political strategy. He uses examples of the Viet Cong during the Vietnamese War and the Palestinian struggle against the Israelis to prove his points. In the latter case he suggests that 'the success of Yasir Arafat had much more to do with western dependence on Arab oil than upon the terrorist tactics of the PLO, Hamas, or Hezbollah' (p. 5) This is an interesting argument which assumes that Arafat's performance was indeed successful.

2   In the United States the term 'critical infrastructure' is defined as 'systems whose incapacity or destruction would have a debilitating impact on the defence or economic security of the nation'. See section 1016(e) of the US Patriot Act of 2001 (42 U.S.C. 5195c(e)).

3 See Mark Burgess (2003) *A Brief History of Terrorism* at http://www.cdi.org/ program/relateditems.cfm?typeID=(7)&programID=39 (last accessed 15 March 2006).

4 The 'Mad Bomber' was George Metesky, a deranged and disgruntled former utility company employee. See http://www.crimelibrary.com/terrorists_spies/ terrorists/metesky/2.html (last accessed 16 March 2006) for further details about the case.

5 The 'Unabomber' was Theodore John Kaczynski, a brilliant mathematician turned radical environmental activist. See http://www.crimelibrary.com/terrorists_spies /terrorists/kaczynski/1.html for further details about the case (last accessed 16 March 2006).

6 For starters, we suggest a review of Kean *et al.* (undated), *The 9/11 Commission Report: Final Report of the National Commission on Terrorist Attacks upon the United States*, W. W. Norton, New York and London.

7 See the National Housing Act of 1954, Public Law no. 560, section 910, 68 Stat. 590 (1954).

8 These are the first eight offences listed in the Federal Bureau of Investigation's Uniform Crime Reports (UCR), also called 'index crimes'. They identify the most serious violent and property crimes in order of their presumed seriousness. They consist of murder and non-negligent manslaughter, forcible rape, robbery, aggravated assault, burglary, larceny-theft, motor-vehicle theft and arson. The UCR consists of crimes reported to the police, which in turn are reported to the Program Support Section of the FBI. It is a voluntary process on the part of local jurisdictions, although more than 90 per cent participate in the United States. Index crimes are used to compare crime rates nationally and across jurisdictions. Part II crimes are less serious and consist of arrest reports for such crimes as curfew and loitering violations, disorderly conduct, drug abuse, and a host of other, non-traffic violations.

9 The five basic questions were:

- how the threat of terrorism affects the transportation security decisions of agencies;
- how such decisions have changed after the events of 11 September 2001;
- how agencies effectively identify and assess vulnerabilities in their transport systems;
- what measures they are taking to increase transit security; and
- the relative importance they place on different security strategies such as CPTED, public education and user outreach, policing, and security hardware and technology (p. 4).

10 See, for example, *Indicators of School Crime and Safety, Indicator 18*, where students report that restrooms are the most feared and avoided places at schools. Institute of Education Science, US Department of Education. See http://nces.ed. gov/programs/crimeindicators/Indicators.asp?PubPageNumber=18&ShowTable Page=TablesHTML/table_18.1.asp (last accessed 27 March 2006).

11 'Force protection' is a military term defined as 'Any measure or combination of measures used to reduce the risk of injury to our [Britain's] security forces, or damage to their assets'. See http://www.defence-structures.com/glossary.htm (last accessed 31 March 2006).

12 According to the US Department of Defense, 'BRAC' is an acronym which stands for base realignment and closure and it is 'the process DoD has previously used to reorganize its installation infrastructure to more efficiently and effectively

support its forces, increase operational readiness and facilitate new ways of doing business'. See http://www.dod.mil/brac/definitions_brac2005.html. The BRAC process derives from the provisions of Title II of the Defense Authorization Amendments and Base Closure and Realignment Act (Pub. L.100-526, 102 Stat. 2623, 10 U.S.C. S 2687 note), or the Defense Base Closure and Realignment Act 1990 (Pub. L. 100-526, Part A of Title XXIX of 104 Stat. 1808, 10 U.S.C. S 2687 note).

13   A lone wolf narcotics dealer is an individual operator as distinguished from someone who is part of one of the major drug cartels. At the time, most drug busts were considered a cost of doing business for the major cartels, given the vast amounts of illegal narcotics they moved into the United States each day. For a lone wolf operator, the loss of one shipment might mean life and death, in both a business and a literal sense.

8   The application of new technologies to place-based crime prevention

1   This conclusion is based on conversations with numerous police officers, including Art Hushen, Director of the City of Tampa, Florida's CPTED unit; Sgt Tim Merrill, criminal investigator with the Alachua County, Florida Sheriff's Office; Justin Hill, Division Chief of Jacksonville, Florida's Sheriff's Office; Stephen Town, West Yorkshire Police Architectural Liaison Officer for Bradford; and Peter Knowles, Bedfordshire Police Architectural Liaison Officer. The work of the last two of these officers makes up the case studies used in Chapter 5.

2   See, for example, http://www.probarrier.com/faq/certify.asp (last accessed 17 April 2006) for one vendor's discussion of the certification process.

3   See, for example, http://www.engadget.com/2004/09/14/kryptonite-evolution-2000-u-lock-hacked-by-a-bic-pen/ (last accessed 25 April 2006) and http://www.wired.com/news/culture/0,1284,64987,00.html (last accessed 25 April 2005).

4   We came across another example of the symbiotic relationship between adaptive criminals and ever-developing technology in the experience of burglary in Sheffield as a result of talking to police as part of the process of researching this book. Apparently, a common *modus operandi* for burglary used to be the use of a brick or similar implement to smash a rear window, with the remaining pieces of glass then being brushed away by the burglar before gaining entry. One of the risks with this action, however, is that the burglar sustains cuts from the shards of glass dealt with in this process, and therefore leaves traces of DNA at the site. As the technology of collecting, disseminating and comparing evidence like this has improved, more burglars have found themselves confronted with evidence of old crimes from this source. News of this has travelled through the burgling community, and the consequence is that today the old *modus operandi* of using a brick to break a rear window has become relatively rare. Instead, the burglar is more likely to attack the window frame in an attempt to remove the whole structure, which of course can be a more difficult task, given a robust form of window frame construction.

5   See, for example, http://www.smartersecurity.com/outdoor/smarterfence/index.html (last accessed 22 April 2006) for an example of one of many electronic perimeter fence systems offered by commercial vendors.

6   Some earlier, sound-based systems were modelled after earthquake sensing technology. See, for example, http://quake.wr.usgs.gov/prepare/factsheets/Gunshots/.

7   See especially the Annual Crime Mapping Conference series sponsored by the US National Institute of Justice. The eighth conference was held in Savannah, Georgia, in 2005 and hosted participants from across the world.

8   See http://www.ojp.usdoj.gov/nij/maps/links.html (last accessed 2 May 2006) for a listing of crime mapping websites in the United States.

9   For example, spatial analysis tools allow crime analysts to depict crime densities, so that crime hot spots are immediately identifiable. See references at the International Association of Crime Analysts website, http://www.iaca.net/Software.asp (last accessed 1 May 2006).

10 As of December 2005, virtually all new cell phones in the United States were required by federal law (Federal Communications Commission E911 Mandate) to be able to identify callers' locations, but only a relatively small percentage of existing phones actually incorporate GPS chips, which can locate callers much more accurately than other means available.

11 For example, police learn about 'hot products' – desirable items for theft – through field interrogations and arrests. An acronym for these goods is 'CRAVED', which stands for those that are 'Concealable, Removable, Available, Valuable, Enjoyable, and Disposable' (Clarke, 1999).

12 Matrix aggregated public records (including such issues as property ownership, bankruptcy filings, professional licences, business liens) with law enforcement records (including criminal histories, driver licences, motor vehicle registration) and made that information available to police. The system was de-funded by the US Justice Department because of privacy concerns arising, in part, out of the fact that the data were stored in private companies. See 'Matrix Unplugged' at http://www.privacyinternational.org/article.shtml?cmd%5B347%5D=x-347-205261 (last accessed 8 May 2006).

13 See http://www.karrysafe.com/home.html (last accessed 2 May 2006) for examples of these products.

14 In this regard, see 'Talking Trash Cans Keep Berlin Clean', CNN.Com International at http://edition.cnn.com/2005/TECH/09/27/spark.rubbish/index.html. 28 September 2005 (last accessed 1 May 2006).

References

Addison & Associates with Arup, 2004, *Evaluation of Planning Delivery Grant, 2003/04*, Office of the Deputy Prime Minister, London.

Akins K., 2003, 'Fighting Fire with Fire: Quantification of the Public Realm Walk 21', *IV Proceedings*, http://www.americawalks.org/ACCESSIB/ACC_PAPE/AAkins.doc, p 4.

Alexander C., 1977, *A Pattern Language: Town's – Buildings – Construction*, Oxford University Press, New York.

Altman I., 1975, *Environment and Social Behavior: A Social Learning Approach*, Wadsworth, Belmont, CA.

Ambrose S., 2002, 'Beware the Fury of an Aroused Democracy', *Wall Street Journal*, 1 October, p. A24.

American Academy of Actuaries, 2004, *P/C Terrorism Insurance Coverage: Where Do We Go Post-Terrorism Risk Insurance Act?*, American Academy of Actuaries, Washington, DC. See at http://www.actuary.org/pdf/casualty/tria_may04.pdf.

American Housing Survey, 2002, HUD User Policy Development and Research Information Service, Washington, DC. Located at http://www.huduser.org/datasets/ahs/ahsdata01.html.

American Society of Landscape Architects, 2005, *Designing with CPTED and Emerging National Security Standards*, Conference tape. See at https://www.nrstaping.com/asla/asla1005.php.

Ames Research Center (2003) 'Nanotechnology's Homeland Security Potential to Be Explored at NASA Ames Research Center Forum'. See at http://www.comspace watch.com/news/viewpr.html?pid=13199 (last accessed 7 November 2006).

Appleton J., 1975, *The Experience of Place*, Wiley, London.

Appleyard D., 1980, *Livable Streets, Protected Neighborhoods*, University of California Press, Berkeley, CA.

Archibald R., Medby J., Rosen B. and Schachter J., 2002, *Security and Safety in Los Angeles: High-Rise Buildings after 9/11*, Rand Corporation, Santa Monica, CA.

Armitage R., 2000, 'An Evaluation of Secured by Design Housing within West Yorkshire', Home Office Briefing Note 7/00, Home Office, London.

Armitage R., 2001, 'Secured by Design in West Yorkshire', Presentation at the Architectural Liaison Officers' Conference (ACPO), Blackpool, UK, 2–4 May.

Associated Press, 2005, 'Cameras Have Ear on Crime', *Gainesville Sun*, 5 July, p. 1.

Atlas R., 1999, 'Is There a Difference in Designing for Crime or Terrorism?', CPTED

Training Convention. See http://www.cpted-security.com/cpted2.htm. See also http://www.cpted-security.com/presentations/NEOCON%206-18-03.pps#267, 1, Designing for Security with CPTED.

Atlas R. and LeBlanc W., 1994, 'Environmental Barriers to Crime', *Ergonomics in Design*, 9–16 October.

Augur T., 1948, 'The Dispersal of Cities as a Defense Measure', *Journal of the American Institute of Planners*, Summer, pp. 29–35.

Baker K. and Merriam D., 2004, *Update on Homeland Security and Land Use: Homeland Security and Premises Liability ALI-ABA Course of Study*, Land Use Institute: Planning, Regulation, Litigation, Eminent Domain and Compensation, Center for Urban and Environmental Solutions and Government Law Center, Boston, MA, pp. 1–17.

Barr R. and Pease K., 1990, 'Crime Placement, Displacement, and Deflection', in M. Tonry and N. Morris (eds) *Crime and Justice*, vol. 12, University of Chicago Press, Chicago.

Bates N., 2005, *Major Developments in Premises Security Liability III*, Liability Consultants, Inc., Boston, MA.

Baum A., Davis A. G. and Aiello J. R., 1978, 'Crowding and Neighbourhood Mediation of Urban Density', *Journal of Population*, 1, pp. 266–279.

Beavon D. J. K., Brantingham P. L. and Brantingham P. J., 1994, 'The Influence of Street Networks on the Patterning of Property Offences', in R. V. Clarke (ed.) *Crime Prevention Studies*, vol. 2, Monsey, NY, Criminal Justice Press, pp. 115–148. Also see the paper at http://www.popcentre.org/Library/Crime Prevention/Volume%2002/2002/06beavon.pdf.

Beck M., 1983, 'Inquest on a Massacre', *Newsweek* 102, 7 November, pp. 85–89.

Ben-Joseph E., 1995, 'Livability and Safety of Suburban Street Patterns: A Comparative Study', Working Paper 641, Berkeley, CA, Institute of Urban and Regional Development, University of California.

Bennett T. and Wright R., 1984, *Burglars on Burglary: Prevention and the Offender*, Gower, Aldershot, UK.

Bentham J., 1907, *An Introduction to the Principles of Morals and Legislation*, Clarendon Press, Oxford (original work published 1789).

Bevis C. and Nutter J., 1977, *Changing Street Layouts to Reduce Residential Burglary*, American Society of Criminology, Atlanta, GA.

Bjor J., Knutsson J. and Kuhlhorn E., 1992 'The Celebration of Midsummer Eve in Sweden: A Study in the Art of Preventing Collective Disorder', *Security Journal*, 3(3), pp. 169–174.

Black H. (ed.), 1968, '*Black's Law Dictionary*', revised 4th ed., West Publishing, St Paul.

Blakely E. J. and Snyder M. G., 1997, *Fortress America: Gated Communities in the United States*, Brookings Institution Press, Washington DC.

Blandy S., Lister D. F., Atkinson R. and Flint J., 2003, 'Gated Communities: A Systematic Review of the Research Evidence', CNR Paper 12, April, pp. 1–65 at http://www.bris.ac.uk/sps/cnrpaperspdf/cnr12pap.pdf.

Blandy S, 2005, 'Housing Responses to a Less than Perfect World: Where Do Gated Communities Fit In?' , Public presentation at Sheffield Hallam University, 12 October.

Block R. L. and Block C. R., 1995, 'Space, Place, and Crime: Hot Spot Areas and Hot Places of Liquor-Related Crime', in J. E. Eck and D. Weisburd (eds) *Crime Prevention Studies*, vol. 4: *Crime and Place*, Criminal Justice Press, Monsey, NY.

Boba R., 2005, *Crime Analysis and Crime Mapping*, Sage Publications, Thousand Oaks, CA.

Booth A., 1981, 'The Built Environment as a Crime Deterrent', *Criminology*, 18(4), pp. 557–570.

Bothwell S., Gindroz R. and Lang R., 1998, 'Restoring Community through Traditional Neighbourhood Design: A Case Study of Diggs Town Public Housing', *Housing Policy Debate*, 9(1), pp. 89–114 at http://www.fanniemaefoundation.com/programs/hpd/pdf/hpd_0901_bothwell.pdf.

Boulay B., Bremond F. and Thonnant M., 2006, 'Applying 3D Human Model in a Posture Recognition System', *Elsevier Science*, 18 January. 2006. See at http://www-sop.inria.fr/orion/Publications/Articles/patternrecognitionBoulay05-1.pdf.

Brantingham P. J. and Brantingham P. L., 1975, 'The Spatial Patterning of Burglary', *Howard Journal of Criminal Justice*, 14, pp. 11–23.

Brantingham P. J. and Brantingham P. L., 1981, *Environmental Criminology*, Sage, Beverly Hills, CA.

Brantingham P. J. and Brantingham P. L., 1991, *Environmental Criminology*, Waveland Press, Prospect Heights, IL.

Brantingham P. J. and Brantingham P. L., 1998, 'Environmental Criminology: From Theory to Urban Planning Practice', *Studies on Crime and Crime Prevention*, 7(1), pp. 31–60.

Brantingham P. L. and Brantingham P. J., 1981, 'Mobility, Notoriety, and Crime: A Study in the Crime Patterns of Urban Nodal Points', *Journal of Environmental Systems*, 11(1), pp. 89–99.

Brantingham P. L. and Brantingham P. J., 1993a, 'Paths, Nodes, Edges: Considerations on the Complexity of Crime and the Physical Environment', *Journal of Environmental Psychology*, 13, pp. 3–28.

Brantingham P. L. and Brantingham P. J., 1993b, 'Environment, Routine, and Situation: Toward a Pattern Theory of Crime', in R. V. Clarke and M. Felson (eds), *Routine Activity and Rational Choice*, New Brunswick, NJ, and London, Transaction Publishers.

Brantingham P. L., and Brantingham P. J., 2004, 'Computer Simulation as a Tool for Environmental Criminologists', *Security Journal*, 17(1), pp. 21–30.

Brantingham P. L., Rondeau M. B. and Brantingham P. J., 1997, 'The Value of Environmental Criminology for the Design Professions of Architecture, Landscape Architecture and Planning', draft paper, Second Annual CPTED Conference, ICA, Orlando, FL.

Briggs A., 1982, *Victorian Cities*, Pelican Books, London.

British Urban Regeneration Association (BURA), 2002, *The Office of the Deputy Prime Minister's Award for Urban Renaissance 2002*, BURA, London.

Brooks M. P., 2002, *Planning Theory for Practitioners*, American Planning Association, Chicago.

Brown B. and Altman I., 1991, 'Territoriality and Residential Crime: A Conceptual Framework', in P. J. Brantingham and P. L. Brantingham (eds) *Environmental Criminology*, Waveland Press, Prospect Heights, IL, pp. 55–76.

Brown B. B. and Bentley D. L., 1993, 'Residential Burglars Judge Risk: The Role of Territoriality', *Journal of Environmental Psychology*, 13, pp. 51–61.

Brown J., 1999, 'An Evaluation of the Secured by Design Initiative in Gwent, South Wales', MSc, Scarman Centre for the Study of Public Order, University of Leicester.

Brunn S. D., Raposo R., Stoyanov P., Coy M. and Webster C., 2004, *The Privatization of Urban Space: Gated Communities – A New Trend in Global Urban*

Development?, Annual Symposium by the Universities of New Orleans and Innsbruck, New Orleans, 28 February, at http://www.gated-communities.de/Abstracts%20New%20Orleans.htm.

Buck A. J., Hakim S. and Rengert G. F., 1993, 'Burglar Alarms and the Choice Behavior of Burglars: A Suburban Phenomenon', *Journal of Criminal Justice*, 21, pp. 497–507.

Bureau of Justice Assistance, 2005, *National Criminal Intelligence Sharing Plan*, United States Department of Justice, Office of Justice Program. Washington, DC. See at http://it.ojp.gov/documents/National_Criminal_Intelligence_Sharing_Plan. pdf.

Burgess M., 2003, *A Brief History of Terrorism*, Center for Defense Information, Washington, DC. See at http://www.cdi.org:80/program/document.cfm? DocumentID=1381&StartRow=11&ListRows=10&&Orderby=D.DateLastUpdate d&ProgramID=39&typeID=(7)&from_page=relateditems.cfm.

Burson S., 2006, 'Sonic Device Allows Shopkeepers to Repel Youngsters Only', *Western Mail*, 17 February. See at http://www.officer.com/article/article.jsp?site Section=20&id=28732.

Cambridge (Massachusetts) Police Department, 1997, *Annual Crime Report: Crime Factors*. See at http://www.ci.cambridge.ma.us/cpd/reports/1997/factors.html (last accessed 7 November 2006).

Canter D., 2003, *Mapping Murder: The Secrets of Geographic Profiling*, Virgin Books, London.

Casella S., 2003, 'Let Cities Be Cities', Viewpoint, APA website, www.planning. org/viewpoints/letcities.htm.

CEN (European Committee for Standardization), 2003, *Prevention of Crime: Urban Planning and Design*, Part 2: *Urban Planning*, ENV 14383-2, CEN Management Centre, Brussels.

Chainey S. and Smith C., 2006, 'Review of GIS-Based Information Sharing Systems', Home Office, Home Office Online Report 02/06. See at http://www.home office.gov.uk/rds/pdfs06/rdsolr0206.pdf.

Chapin F. S., 1974, '*Human Activity Patterns in the City: Things People Do in Time and Space*', John Wiley, New York.

Chesney K., 1970, *The Victorian Underworld*, Temple Smith, London.

Cisneros H. G., 1995, *Defensible Space: Deterring Crime and Building Community*, Department of Housing and Urban Development, Washington, DC.

Clarke R. V., 1997, *Situational Crime Prevention: Successful Case Studies*, 2nd edn, Harrow & Heston, Albany, NY.

Clarke R. V., 1999, 'Hot Products: Understanding, Anticipating and Reducing Demand for Stolen Goods', Police Research Series Paper 112, Policing and Reducing Crime Unit, Home Office, London.

Clarke R. V., 2003, *Closing Streets and Alleys to Reduce Crime: Should You Go Down This Road?*, Problem-Oriented Guides for Police Response, Response Guides Series, no. 2. Office of Community Oriented Policing Services, US Department of Justice, Washington, DC. See at http://www.popcentre.org/Responses/PDFs/Closing_alleys_and_streets.pdf.

Clarke R. V. and Felson M., 1993, *Routine Activity and Rational Choice: Advances in Criminology Theory*, Transaction Publishers, New Brunswick, NJ.

Clarke R. V. and Weisburd D., 1994, 'Diffusion of Crime Control Benefits: Observations on the Reverse of Displacement', in R. V. Clarke (ed.) *Crime Prevention Studies*, vol. 2, Criminal Justice Press, Monsey, NY.

Clarke R. V., Kemper R. and Wyckoff L., 2001, 'Controlling Cell Phone Fraud in the US: Lessons for the UK', *Security Journal*, 14(1), pp. 7–22.

Code of Federal Regulations (United States) (Title 28, Judicial Administration, Subpart P, Federal Bureau of Investigations, Section 0.85, Subsection L).

Coleman A., 1990, *Utopia on Trial: Vision and Reality in Planned Housing*, Hilary Shipman, London.

Colquhoun I., 2004, *Design Out Crime: Creating Safe and Sustainable Communities*, Architectural Press, Oxford.

Committee on Transportation and Infrastructure, 1996, Hearing on Federal Building Security before the Subcommittee on Public Buildings and Economic Development, US House of Representatives, April 24 1996. See at http://www.fas.org/irp/congress/1996_hr/hpw104-70_0.htm.

Cornish D. and Clarke R. V., 1986, *The Reasoning Criminal: Rational Choice Perspectives on Offending*, Springer-Verlag, The Hague.

Cornish D. B. and Clarke R. V., 2003, 'Opportunities, Precipitators and Criminal Decisions: A Reply to Wortley's Critique of Situational Crime Prevention', in M. Smith and D. B. Cornish (eds) *Theory for Practice in Situational Crime Prevention*, Crime Prevention Studies vol. 16, Criminal Justice Press, Monsey, NY, pp. 41–96. Also available at http://www.popcenter.org/Library/CrimePrevention/Volume%2016/OpportunitesPrecipitators.pdf.

Cozens P., Hillier D. and Prescott G., 2001, 'Crime and the Design of Residential Property: Exploring the Theoretical Background, Part 1', *Property Management*, 19(2), pp. 136–164. See at http://www.e-doca.net/Resources/Articles/PROPERTYMNGMNT2.PDF.

Cozens P. M., Pascoe T. and Hillier D., 2004, 'Critically Reviewing the Theory and Practice of Secured By Design (SBD) for Residential New-Build Housing in Britain', *Crime Prevention and Community Safety: An International Journal*, 6(1), pp. 13–29.

Crouch S., Shaftoe H. and Fleming R., 1999, *Design for Secure Residential Environments*, Longman, Harlow, UK.

Crowe T., 1991, *Crime Prevention through Environmental Design*, 1st edn, Butterworth-Heinemann, Boston.

Crowe T., 1997, 'Crime Prevention through Environmental Design Strategies and Applications', in L. J. Fennelly (ed.) *Effective Physical Security*, 2nd edn, Butterworth-Heinemann, Boston.

Crowe T., 2000, *Crime Prevention through Environmental Design*, 2nd edn, Butterworth-Heinemann, Boston.

Dain D. P. and Brennan R. L. Jr, 2003, 'Negligent Security Law in the Commonwealth of Massachusetts in the Post-September 11 Era', *New England Law Review*, 38(1), pp. 73–96.

Demkin J. (ed.), 2003, *Security Planning and Design: A Guide for Architects and Building Design Professionals*, American Institute of Architects, John Wiley, Hoboken, NJ.

Department of Homeland Security, 2003, *The Office for Domestic Preparedness Guidelines for Homeland Security*, US Department of Homeland Security, Washington, DC. See at http://www.ojp.usdoj.gov/odp/docs/ODPPrev1.pdf.

Department of the Environment, 1977, *Inner Area Studies: Liverpool, Birmingham and Lambeth: Summaries of Consultants' Final Reports*, HMSO, London.

Department of the Environment, 1994, *Planning Out Crime*, Circular 5/94, HMSO, London.

Department of the Environment, Transport and the Regions, 2000, *Our Towns and Cities: The Future: Delivering an Urban Renaissance*, Cm 4911, HMSO, London.

Dershowitz A., 2002, *Why Terrorism Works*, R. R. Donnelly, Chicago.

Dietrick B., 1977, 'The Environment and Burglary Victimization in a Metropolitan

Suburb', Paper given at the Annual Meeting of the American Society of Criminology, Atlanta, GA.

Ditton J. and Duffy J., 1983, 'Bias in the Newspaper Reporting of Crime News', *British Journal of Criminology*, 23, pp. 159–165.

Ditton J. and Innes M., 2005, 'The Role of Perceptual Intervention in the Management of Crime Fear', in N. Tilley (ed.) *Handbook of Crime Prevention and Community Safety*, Willan, Cullompton, Devon, UK, pp. 595–627.

Donald I. and Wilson A., 2000, 'Ram Raiding: Criminals Working in Groups', in D. Canter and L. Alison (eds) *The Social Psychology of Crime: Groups, Teams and Networks*, Offender Profiling Series, Ashgate, Brookfield, VT.

Donnelly P. and Kimble C. E., 1997, 'Community Organizing, Environmental Change, and Neighborhood Crime', *Crime and Delinquency*, 43(4), pp. 493–522.

DTLR and CABE, 2001, *By Design: Better Places to Live: A Companion Guide to PPG3*, Thomas Telford, Tonbridge, UK.

Duany A., 2003, 'Neighbourhood Design in Practice', in P. Neal (ed.) *Urban Villages and the Making of Communities*, Spon, London, pp. 85–101.

Duany A., 2005, *SmartCode: A Comprehensive Form-Based Planning Ordinance*, vol. 6.5 at http://tndtownpaper.com/images/SmartCode6.5.pdf.

Dudley Metropolitan Borough Council, 2002, *Design for Community Safety: Supplementary Planning Guidance*, Dudley MBC, Dudley, UK.

Dudley M. Q., 2001, 'Sprawl as Strategy: City Planners Face the Bomb', *Journal of Planning Education and Research*, 21 (1), pp. 52–63.

Duffy C., 1979, *Siege Warfare: The Fortress in the Early Modern World, 1494–1660*, Routledge & Kegan Paul, London.

Edgar, B. and Taylor, J., 2000, 'Housing', in P. Roberts and H. Sykes (eds), *Urban Regeneration: A Handbook*, Sage, London.

Edwards K., 1999, 'Bing Crosby, Acne, Police and Youth', *On Line Opinion*, 15 August at http://www.onlineopinion.com.au/view.asp?article=1308.

Egilmez S., 2004, 'How to Battle Incidents of Graffiti: CRrAS Citywide Graffiti Abatement Program', *Crime Mapping News*, Police Foundation, 6(2), Spring, pp. 2–3.

Eisinger P., 2004, 'The American City in the Age of Terror: A Preliminary Assessment of the Effects of 9/11', Address before the Urban Affairs Association 11–14, 30 March – 3 April. See at http://www.culma.wayne.edu/pubs/eisinger/Terrorism%20manuscript.pdf.

Ekblom, P., 1997a, 'Can We Make Crime Prevention Adaptive by Learning from Other Evolutionary Struggles?', Home Office Research, Development and Statistics Directorate, London. Home Office Research, Development. See also at http://www.e-doca.net/Resources/Articles/Can%20we%20make%20crime%20prevention%20adaptive.pdf.

Ekblom P., 1997b, 'Gearing Up against Crime: A Dynamic Framework to Help Designers Keep Up with the Adaptive Criminal in a Changing World', *International Journal of Risk, Security and Crime Prevention*, 214, pp. 249–265. See at www.homeoffice.gov.uk/rds/pdfs/risk.pdf.

Ekblom P., 1999, 'Can We Make Crime Prevention Adaptive by Learning from Other Evolutionary Struggles?', *Studies on Crime and Crime Prevention*, 8(1), pp. 27–51. See at www.bra.se/web/english.

Ekblom P., 2002, 'Future Imperfect: Preparing for the Crime to Come', *Criminal Justice Matters*, 46, Winter 2001/02, pp. 30–40.

Ekblom P., Law H. and Sutton M., 1996, *Safer Cities and Domestic Burglary*, Home Office Research Study 164, Home Office, London.

European Crime Prevention Network, 2005, *A Review of Scientifically Evaluated*

Good Practices for Reducing Feelings of Insecurity or Fear of Crime in the EU Member States, Building Research Establishment, Garstang, London.

Farrall S., Bannister J., Ditton J. and Gilchrist E., 1997, 'Questioning the Measurement of Fear of Crime: Findings from a Major Methodological Study', *British Journal of Criminology*, 37(4), pp. 657–678.

Farrell G. and Pease K., 2006, 'Criminology and Security', in M. Gill (ed.) *Handbook of Security*, Palgrave Macmillan, Basingstoke, UK.

Farrington D. and Welsh B., 2002, *Effects of Improved Street Lighting on Crime: A Systematic Review*, Home Office Research Study 251, Home Office, London.

Federal Bureau of Investigation, 2004, 'Crime in the United States 2004', US Department of Justice. See at http://www.fbi.gov/ucr/cius_04/offenses_reported/index.html.

Federal Emergency Management Agency, 2003a, *Integrating Human-Caused Hazards Into Mitigation Planning*, FEMA Publication no. 386-7, Version 2.0, Government Printing Office, Washington, DC. See at http://www.fema.gov/pdf/plan/mitplanning/howto7.pdf.

Federal Emergency Management Agency, 2003b, *Reference Manual to Mitigate Potential Terrorist Attacks against Buildings*, (FEMA) Risk Management Series Publication no. 426, Government Printing Office, Washington, DC. See at http://www.wbdg.org/pdfs/fema426.pdf.

Federal Emergency Management Agency, 2003c, *Primer for Design of Commercial Buildings to Mitigate Terrorist Attacks*, (FEMA) Risk Management Series, Publication no. 427, Government Printing Office, Washington, DC. See at http://www.wbdg.org/pdfs/fema427.pdf.

Federal Emergency Management Agency, 2003d, *Primer to Design Safe School Projects in Case of Terrorist Attacks*, Publication no. 428, Government Printing Office, Washington, DC. See at http://www.wbdg.org/pdfs/fema428.pdf.

Federal Emergency Management Agency, 2005, *Risk Assessment: A How-To Guide to Mitigate Potential Terrorist Attacks against Buildings*, (FEMA) Risk Management Series, Publication no. 452, Government Printing Office, Washington, DC. See at http://www.wbdg.org/pdfs/fema452.pdf.

Federal Transit Administration, 2006, *Crime and Anti-terrorism*, 17 March 2006. See at http://www.fta.dot.gov/11227_11229_ENG_HTML.htm.

Feinberg J., 2002, 'Viewpoint', APA website, March, at www.planning.org/planning/member/2002mar/viewpoint.htm.

Felson M., 2002, '*Crime in Everyday Life*', 3rd edn, Sage, Thousand Oaks, CA.

Felson M. and Clarke R. V., 1998, 'Opportunity Makes the Thief: Practical Theory for Crime Prevention', Police Research Series Paper 98, Home Office Research, Development and Statistics Directorate, London.

Feynman R, 1960, 'There's Plenty of Room at the Bottom, An Invitation to Enter a New Field of Physics', *Engineering and Science*, February. See http://www.zyvex.com/nanotech/feynman.html.

Fisher B. and Nasar J., 1992, 'Fear of Crime in Relation to Three Exterior Site Features, *Environment and Behavior*, 24, pp. 35–65.

Flint A., 2002, Oscar Newman quoted in 'Safeguards in Cities Could Get New Look', *Boston Globe*. See http://www.boston.com/globe/nation/packages/after_sept11/07702.htm.

Florida Department of Education, 2003, *Florida Safe School Design Guidelines: Strategies to Enhance Security and Reduce Vandalism*, Florida Department of Education, Tallahassee, FL, available at http://www.firn.edu/doe/edfacil/safe schools.htm.

Fountain H., 2006, 'The Camera Never Blinks, but It Multiplies', *New York Times*, 23 April, p. 14.

Fowler F. Jr and Mangione T. W., 1986, 'A Three-Pronged Effort to Reduce Crime and Fear of Crime: The Hartford Experiment', in D. P. Rosenbaum (ed.) *Community Crime Prevention: Does It Work?*, Sage, Beverly Hills, CA.

Franck K. A. and Mostoller M., 1995, 'From Courts to Open Spaces to Streets: Changes in the Site Design of US Public Housing', *Journal of Architectural and Planning Research*, 12(3), pp. 186–220.

Freedonia Group, 2003, 'US Electronic Access Control Products and Systems Demand to Reach $7.3 Billion in 2007', at http://www.findarticles.com/p/articles/mi_go2519/is_200310/ai_n6431749.

Friedmann J., 2002, 'City of Fear or Open City', *Journal of the American Planning Association*, 68(3), Summer, pp. 237–243.

Gamman L. and Pascoe T., 2004, 'Seeing Is Believing: Notes towards a Visual Methodology and Manifesto for Crime Prevention through Environmental Design', *Crime Prevention and Community Safety: An International Journal*, 6(4), pp. 9–18.

Gamman L., Thorpe A. and Willcocks M., 2004, 'Bike Off! Tracking the Design Terrains of Cycle Parking: Reviewing Use, Misuse and Abuse', *Crime Prevention and Community Safety: An International Journal*, 6(4), pp. 19–36.

Gans H. J., 1982, *The Urban Villagers*, Free Press, New York.

General Services Administration, 2002, *Facilities Standards for Public Building Service*, PBS-P100, November.

Gilchrist E., Bannister J., Ditton J. and Farrall S., 1998, 'Women and the Fear of Crime', *British Journal of Criminology*, 38, pp. 283–298.

Gilling D., 2005, 'Partnership and Crime Prevention', in N. Tilley (ed.) *Handbook of Crime Prevention and Community Safety*, Willan, Cullompton, Devon, UK, pp. 734–756.

Giordano S, 1997, 'Hotel Room Keys and Endangered Species', *American City Business Journal*, 29 August, at http://www.bizjournals.com/seattle/stories/1997/09/01/focus5.html.

Glasgow Housing Association Ltd (GHA), 2004, 'Summary Evaluation: Secured by Design Installations in GHA Communities', at http://www.securedbydesign.com/pdfs/glasgow.pdf.

Goodchild B., 1997, *Housing and the Urban Environment*, Blackwell, Oxford.

Gordon L. and Brill W., 1996, 'The Expanding Role of Crime Prevention Through Environmental Design in Premises Liability', *National Institute of Justice Research in Brief*, April, pp. 1-7.

Graham S., 2005, 'In a Moment: On Global Mobilities and the Terrorised City', at http://www.acturban.org/biennial/DOC_planners/inamoment.doc, pp. 1–9.

Gratz R. B., 2003, 'Authentic Urbanism and the Jane Jacobs Legacy', in P. Neal (ed.) *Urban Villages and the Making of Communities*, Spon, London, pp. 17–29.

Greenberg S. W. and Rohe M. W., 1984, 'Neighborhood Design and Crime: A Test of Two Perspectives', *Journal of the American Planning Association*, 50(1), pp. 48–61.

Greenberg S. W., Rohe W. M. and Williams J. R., 1982, 'Safety in Urban Neighborhoods: A Comparison of Physical Characteristics and Informal Territorial Control in High and Low Crime Neighborhoods', *Population and Environment (Historical Archive)*, 5(3), September, pp. 141–165. See the abstract at http://www.springerlink.com/(n5aft5jlijr3ek55ee0z5i55)/app/home/contribution.asp?referrer=parent&backto=issue,2,4;journal,60,77;linkingpublicationresults,1:405738,1.

Hajer M., 2005, 'Rebuilding Ground Zero: The Politics of Performance', *Planning Theory and Practice*, 6(4), pp. 445–464.

Hakim S., Rengert G. F. and Shachamurove Y. (2001) 'Target Search of Burglars: A Revised Economic Model', *Papers in Regional Science*, 80, pp. 121–137.

Hall P., 1990, *Cities of Tomorrow: An Intellectual History of Urban Planning and Design in the Twentieth Century*, Blackwell, Oxford.

Halsall P., 1997, Internet Modern History Sourcebook: M. Robespierre, *On the Moral and Political Principles of Domestic Policy*, speech of 5 February 1794. Quoted in http://www.marx.org/history/france/revolution/robespierre/1794/terror.htm   (last accessed 15 March 2006).

Hanson R. K., 1998, 'Liability on Franchise Premises: Footing the Bill for Crime', *Business Horizons*, July/August. See also at http://www.findarticles.com/cf_0/m1038/n4_v41/21015195/print.html.

Harries K., 1999, *Mapping Crime: Principle and Practice*. Research Report, US Department of Justice, Office of Justice Programs, National Institute of Justice, Washington, DC. See at http://www.ncjrs.gov/pdffiles1/nij/178919.pdf (last accessed 7 November 2006).

Hawley A., 1950, *Human Ecology*, Ronald, New York.

Helsley R. W. and Strange W. C., 1999, 'Gated Communities and the Economic Geography of Crime', *Journal of Urban Economics*, 46(1), pp. 80–105.

Hesseling R. B. P., 1994 'Displacement: A Review of the Empirical Literature', in R. V. Clarke (ed.) *Crime Prevention Studies*, vol. 3, Monsey, NY, Criminal Justice Press.

Heyman D., 2002, *Anthrax Attacks: Implications for US Bioterrorism Preparedness, A Report on a National Forum for Biodefense*, Center for Strategic and International Studies and the Defense Threat Reduction Agency, Washington, DC.

Hillier B, 1996, *Space Is the Machine*, Cambridge University Press, Cambridge.

Hillier B., 1998, 'The Common Language of Space: A Way of Looking at the Social, Economic and Environmental Functioning of Cities on a Common Basis', http://www.bartlett.ucl.ac.uk/spacesyntax/publications/commonlang.html.

Hillier B., 2004, 'Can Streets Be Made Safe?', *Urban Design International*, 9(1), pp. 31–45.

Hillier B. and Hanson J., 1984, *The Social Logic of Space*, Cambridge University Press, Cambridge.

Hillier B. and Shu S., 1999, 'Designing for Secure Spaces', *Planning in London*, 29, April, pp. 36–38.

Hinman E. E., 1995, 'Designing Blast Resistant Buildings: Lessons Learned from Oklahoma City – Ground Zero', *Security Management*, October, pp. 26–31.

Hoffman D. D., 1998, *Visual Intelligence: How We Create What We See*, W. W. Norton, New York.

Horan D. J., 1997, *The Retailer's Guide to Loss Prevention and Security*, CRC Press, Boca Raton, FL.

Hughes R. and Stanard M., 2004, 'North Carolina's Experimental Use of GPS to Provide an "Integrated" GIS Analysis for Truck Involved Crashes and Commercial Vehicle Enforcement Activities', *Crime Mapping News*, Police Foundation, 6(2), Spring, pp. 1–7.

Hulme Regeneration, 1994, *Rebuilding the City: A Guide to Redevelopment in Hulme*, Hulme Regeneration Ltd, Manchester.

Illuminating Engineering Society of North America (IESNA), 2003, *Guideline for Security Lighting for People, Property and Public Space*, G-1-103, New York.

Imrie R. and Thomas H., 1999, *British Urban Policy: An Evaluation of the Urban Development Corporations*, Sage, London.

Institute of Nanotechnology, 2003, 'Nanotechnology in Crime Prevention and Detection', Conference Agenda, 28 and 29 October. See at http://www.nano.org.uk/crime6.doc.

International Association of Chiefs of Police (IACP), 2005, *From Hometown Security to Homeland Security*, White Paper, IACP, Alexandria, VA. See at http://www.theiacp.org/leg_policy/HomelandSecurityWP.PDF.

Jacobs J, 1961, *The Death and Life of Great American Cities*, Vintage Books, New York. Also published in 1964 by Pelican in Britain (Harmondsworth, Middlesex).

Jacques C., 1998, *Ram Raiding: The History, Incidence and Scope for Prevention in Crime at Work*, Studies in Security and Prevention. See at http://www.popcenter.org/Problems/Supplemental_Material/Burglary/Jacques.pdf.

Jandura K. J. and Campbell D. R., 2004, 'Courthouse Security', in B. A. Nadel (ed.) *Building Security: Handbook for Architectural Planning and Design*, McGraw-Hill, New York, pp. 6.1–6.24.

Jardin X., 2005, 'Focused Sound Laser for Crowd Control', National Public Radio. See at http://www.npr.org/templates/story/story.php?storyId=4857417.

Jeffrey C. R., 1971, *Crime Prevention through Environmental Design*, Sage, Beverly Hills, CA.

Jeffrey C. R., 1977, *Crime Prevention through Environmental Design*, revised edn, Sage, Beverly Hills, CA.

Jeffrey C. R., 1990, *Criminology: An Interdisciplinary Approach*, Prentice-Hall, Englewood Cliffs, NJ.

Jeffery C. R. and Zahm D. L., 1993, 'Crime Prevention through Environmental Design, Opportunity Theory, and Rational Choice Models', in R. Clarke and M. Felson (eds) *Routine Activity and Rational Choice, Advances in Criminological Theory*, vol. 5, Transaction Publishers, New Brunswick, NJ.

Jenkins R., 2005, 'CCTV Used to Spy on Woman in Bathroom', *The Times*, 7 December, p. 11.

Jenkins B. M. and Gerston L. 2001, *Protecting Public Surface Transportation against Terrorism and Serious Crime: Continuing Research on Best Security Practices*, Mineta Transportation Institute 277, Norman Y., Mineta International Institute for Surface Transportation Policy Studies, San Jose, CA.

Kaminsky A., 1995, *A Complete Guide to Premises Security Litigation*, American Bar Association, Chicago.

Kaplan D., 2006, 'Spies among Us', *US News and World Report*, 8 May, pp. 41–49.

Katzman M., 1981, 'The Supply of Criminals: A Geo-economic Examination', in S. Hakim and G. F. Rengert (eds) *Crime Spillover*, Sage, Beverly Hills, pp. 119–134.

Kay J. H., 2001, quoted in 'Planning after September 11', in Dateline, APA website, www.planning.ord/dateline/2001/date100101.htm.

Keefe P., 2006, 'Can Network Theory Thwart Terrorists?', *New York Times Magazine*, 12 March. See at http://www.nytimes.com/2006/03/12/magazine/312wwln_essay.html?ei=5070&en=47b5f8d275fe747a&ex=1146196800&adxnnl=1&adxnnlx=1146024866-MftLpHtl7MeFYwLh8kMeNg.

Kennedy D. B., 1993, 'Architectural Concerns Regarding Security and Premises Liability', *Journal of Architectural Planning and Research*, 10, pp. 105–129.

Kennedy D. B. and Hupp, T. R., 1998, 'Apartment Security and Litigation: Key Issues', *Security Journal*, 11, pp. 21–28.

Killen ., 2005, 'The First Hijackers', *New York Times Magazine*, 16 January, pp. 22–25.

Kitchen T., 2001, 'Planning in Response to Terrorism: The Case of Manchester, England', *Journal of Architectural and Planning Research*, 18(4), Winter, pp. 325–340.

Kitchen T., 2002, 'Crime Prevention and the British Planning System: New Responsibilities and Older Challenges', *Planning Theory and Practice*, 3(2), pp. 155–172.

Kitchen T., 2005, 'New Urbanism and CPTED in the British Planning System: Some Critical Reflections', *Journal of Architectural and Planning Research*, 22(4), Winter, pp. 342–357.

Kitchen T., 2007, *Skills for Planning Practice*, Palgrave Macmillan, Basingstoke, UK.

Kitchen T. and Schneider R. H., 2005, 'Crime and the Design of the Built Environment: Anglo-American Comparisons of Policy and Practice', in J. Hillier and E. Rooksby (eds) *Habitus: A Sense of Place*, Ashgate, Aldershot, UK, pp. 258–282.

Klarqvist B., 'A Space Syntax Glossary', *Nordisk Arkitekturforskring*, 2, 11–12.

Knowles P., 2003a, 'Designs on Crime', *Police Review*, 18 July, pp. 22 and 23.

Knowles P., 2003b, 'The Cost of Policing New Urbanism', *Community Safety Journal*, 2(4), pp. 33–37.

Kostof S., 1991, *The City Shaped*, Little, Brown, Boston. Also published in 1991 by Thames & Hudson, London.

Kostof S., 1992, *The City Assembled*, Little, Brown, Boston.

Kunstler J. H., 1993, *The Geography of Nowhere: The Rise and Decline of America's Man-Made Landscape*, Touchstone, New York.

Kunstler J. H., 1996, *Home from Nowhere: Remaking Our Everyday World for the Twenty-First Century*, Touchstone, New York.

LaGrange R. and Ferraro K. F., 1989, 'Assessing Age and Gender Differences in Perceived Risk and Fear of Crime', *Criminology*, 27(4), pp. 697–719.

Landman K., 2003, *A Survey of Gated Communities in South Africa*, CSIR Publication BOU/1 347, Pretoria.

Langdon P., 2004, 'Three Years after 9/11 Security Mindset Threatens Civic Design', *New Urban News*, 9(6). pp. 1–5.

Lasley J., 1998, *'Designing Out' Gang Homicides and Street Assaults*, Research in Brief, National Institute of Justice, Washington, DC.

League of Nations, 1937, Convention for the Prevention and Repression of Terrorism, Resolution of 10 October 1936, reproduced in League of Nations, International Conference, *Proceedings on the Repression of Terrorism*, Geneva, 16 November 1937, League of Nations Doc. C.94.M.47.1938.V (League of Nations Archives, Geneva: Council Members Docs Vol. 1103), Annex I, at 183.

Leavitt P., Ellis Z. L. and Vaughan J. F. (eds), 1997, *Avoiding Liability in Premises Security*, 3rd edn, Strafford, Atlanta, GA.

Lipton E., 2005, 'To Fight Terror, New York Tries London's "Ring of Steel"', *New York Times*, 24 July.

Llewellyn Davies, 2005, *The Draft Bedfordshire Community Safety Design Guide*, Bedfordshire Community Safety Working Group, Bedford.

Lo Scalzo J., 2006, 'A Line in the Sand', *US News and World Report*, 20 March, pp. 40–45.

Lodha S. K. and Verma A., 1999, 'Animations of Crime Maps Using Virtual Reality Modeling Language', *Western Criminology Review* 1(2). See at http://wcr. sonoma.edu/v1n2/lodha.html.

Lombroso C., 1876, *L'uomo delinquente*, Hoepli, Milan. Partially translated in 1911 as *Criminal Man*, Putman, New York; reprinted in 1972 by Patterson Smith, Montclair, NJ.

Luedtke G. D. & Associates, 1970, *Crime and the Physical City: Neighbourhood Design Techniques for Crime Reduction*, US Department of Justice. Washington, DC.

Lum C., Kennedy L. and Sherley A., 2006, *The Effectiveness of Counter-terrorism Strategies: A Campbell Systematic Review*, pp. 1–49. See at http://www. campbellcollaboration.org/CCJG/reviews/CampbellSystematicReviewOnTerroris m02062006FINAL_REVISED.pdf.

Lynch K., 1960, *The Image of the City*, MIT Press, Cambridge, MA.

McCahill M. and Norris C., 2003, 'Estimating the Extent, Sophistication and Legality of CCTV in London', in M. Gill (ed.) *CCTV*, Perpetuity Press, Leicester.

McCrie R. D., 2006, 'A History of Security', in M. Gill (ed.) *Handbook of Security*, Palgrave Macmillan, New York, pp. 21–44.

MacDonald J. E. and Gifford R., 1989, 'Territorial Cues and Defensible Space Theory: The Burglar's Point of View', *Journal of Environmental Psychology*, 1989(9), pp. 193–205.

Macintyre S. and Homel R., 1997, 'Danger on the Dance Floor: A Study of Interior Design, Crowding and Aggression in Nightclubs', in R. Homel (ed.) *Crime Prevention Studies: Policing for Prevention: Reducing Crime, Public Intoxication and Injury*, vol. 7, pp. 91–113, Criminal Justice Press, Monsey, NY.

Maguire M., 1982, *Burglary in a Dwelling*, Heinemann, London.

Manchester City Council, 1995, *Manchester: 50 Years of Change*, HMSO, London.

Marcuse P., 2000, 'The New Urbanism: The Dangers So Far', *DISP*, 140, pp. 4–6.

Margolis M., 2006, 'Mapping Crime: Police around the World Are Using Technology to Anticipate Where the Bad Guys Will Strike Next', *Newsweek International Edition*. See at http://www.msnbc.msn.com/id/12334548/site/newsweek/.

Mather A., 2005, personal communications with Alan T. Mather, former Chief of Physical Security for the Joint InterAgency Task Force East (JIATFE).

Matthews R., 1997, 'Developing More Effective Strategies for Curbing Prostitution', in R. Clarke (ed.) *Situational Crime Prevention: Successful Case Studies*, 2nd edn, Criminal Justice Press, Monsey, NY, pp. 74–82.

Mawby R. I., 1977, 'Kiosk Vandalism: A Sheffield Study', *British Journal of Criminology*, 17, pp. 30–46.

Mayhew P. and van Dijk J. J. M., 1997, *Criminal Victimisation in Eleven Industrialised Countries*, Key findings from the 1996 International Crime Victims Survey, Ministry of Justice, Wetenschappelijk Onderzoek- en Documentatiecentrum (WODC), The Hague.

Mayhew P., Clarke R. V., Burrows J. N., Hough J. M. and Winchester S. W., 1979, *Crime in Public View*, no. 2049, Home Office Research Study, British Home Office Research Publications, London.

Mayhew P., Clarke R. V. and Elliot D., 1989, 'Motorcycle Theft, Helmet Legislation, and Displacement', *Howard Journal of Criminal Justice*, 28(1), pp. 1–8.

Michalak S., 2002, 'What College Students Learn about Terrorism: A Case Study of IR Textbooks', *Newsletter of FPRI's Marvin Wachman Fund for International Education*, 7(6), November, p. 2. See also http://www.fpri.org/footnotes/0706. 200211.michalak.whatcollegestudentslearnaboutterrorism.html.

Mollenkamp C. and Haughney C., 2006, '"Ring of Steel" for New York?', *Wall Street Journal*, 25 January.

Morton C. and Kitchen T., 2005, 'Crime Prevention and the British Planning System: Operational Relationships between Planners and the Police', *Planning Practice and Research*, 20(4), pp. 419–431.

Moussatche H., Hayes R., Schneider R., McLeod R., Abbott P. and Kohen M., 2004, 'Retailing Best Practices: Through Store Design and Layout', unpublished Report for the Gillette Corporation, Loss Prevention Research Team, Gainesville, FL.

Mumford L., 1961, *The City in History: Its Origins, Its Transformations, and Its Prospects*, Harcourt, New York.

Murray C., 1994, 'The Physical Environment', in J. Q. Wilson and J. Petersilia (eds), *Crime*, Institute for Contemporary Studies, San Francisco.

Nadel B. A., 2004 'Industrial Facilities and Office Buildings: Safety, Security, Site Selection, and Workplace Violence', in B. A. Nadel (ed.) *Building Security: A Handbook for Architectural Planning Design*, McGraw-Hill, New York, pp. 13.1–13.10.

Nasar J. L., 1981, 'Environmental Factors and Commercial Burglary', *Environmental Systems*, 11(1), pp. 49–56.

National Academy of Sciences, 2003, *The Global Positioning System: The Role of Atomic Clocks*. See at http://www.beyonddiscovery.org/content/view.article.asp ?a=458.

National Capital Authority (NCA) (2003) See at http://downloads.nationalcapital.gov. au/corporate/publications/misc/Urban_Design_Guidelines_LR.pdf.

National Capital Planning Commission (NCPC), 2002a, Draft Plan, July 2002: National Capital Urban Design and Security Plan, NCPC, Washington, DC.

National Capital Planning Commission (NCPC), 2002b, *National Capital Urban Design and Security Plan*, NCPC, Washington, DC, October. Also available at http://www.ncpc.gov/publications_press/udsp/Final%20UDSP.pdf.

National Capital Planning Commission (NCPC), 2004, *National Capital Urban Design and Security Plan, November 2004, Addendum*, at http://www.ncpc.gov/ publications_press/udsp/NCUDSP2004Addendum.pdf.

National Capital Planning Commission (NCPC), 2005, *National Capital Urban Design and Security Plan Objectives and Policy*, at http://www.ncpc.gov/planning_init/ security/NCUDSP%20Addendum050505.pdf.

National Counterterrorism Center, 2006, *A Chronology of Significant International Terrorism for 2004*, at http://www.tkb.org/documents/Downloads/NCTC_Report. pdf.

New Urbanism website at http://www.newurbanism.org/index.html; http://www.new urbanism.org/pages/416429/index.htm.

Newman O., 1973, *Defensible Space: Crime Prevention through Urban Design*, Macmillan, New York.

Newman O., 1976, *Design Guidelines for Creating Defensible Space*, National Institute of Law Enforcement and Criminal Justice, Washington, DC.

Newman O., 1981, *Community of Interest*, Anchor Press/Doubleday, Garden City, NY.

Newman O., 1996, *Creating Defensible Space*, US Department of Housing and Urban Development, Washington, DC.

Newman O., 2001, quoted in *Planning Practice – Expert Advice*, APA website at www.planning.ord/planningpractice/2001/dec01.htm.

Nicholas S., Povey D., Walker A. and Kershaw S., 2005, *Crime in England and Wales 2004/05*, Home Office, London.

Norman T., 2004, 'Understanding Threats', in J. Demkin (ed.) *Security Planning and Design: A Guide for Architects and Building Design Professionals*, American Institute of Architects, John Wiley, Hoboken, NJ, pp. 21–35.

Northamptonshire Planning Authorities and Northamptonshire Police, 2004, *Planning Out Crime in Northamptonshire*, Northamptonshire Planning Authorities and Northamptonshire Police, Northampton.

Oc T. and Tiesdell S. (eds), 1997, *Safer City Centres: Revising the Public Realm*, Paul Chapman, London.

Office of the Deputy Prime Minister (ODPM), 2005a, *Planning Policy Statement 1: Delivering Sustainable Development*, ODPM, London.

ODPM, 2005b, *Sustainable Communities: People, Places and Prosperity*, ODPM, London.

ODPM, 2005c, *Consultation Paper on a New Planning Policy Statement 3 (PPS3): Housing*, ODPM, London.

ODPM, 2006, *State of the English Cities*, Urban Research Summary 21, ODPM.

ODPM and the Home Office, 2004, *Safer Places: The Planning System and Crime Prevention*, HMSO, London.

Onishi N., 2006, 'South Korea Wants a Robot in Every Home', *New York Times*, 2 April.

Osborn D. R., Ellingworth D., Hope T. and Truckett A. 1996, 'Are Repeatedly Victimized Households Different?', *Journal of Quantitative Criminology*, 12(2), pp. 223–245.

O'Toole R., 2001, 'The Folly of Smart Growth', *Regulation*, Fall, pp. 20–25.

Oxley J., Reijnhoudt P., van Soomeren P., Beckford C., Jorgejan A. and Jager J., 2005, *Crime Opportunity Profiling of Streets (COPS)*, Building Research Establishment, Garstang, UK.

Pain R., 2000, 'Place, Social Relations and the Fear of Crime: A Review', *Progress in Human Geography*, 24(3), pp. 365–387.

Painter K. and Farrington D. P., 1997, 'The Crime Reducing Effect of Improved Street Lighting: The Dudley Project', in R. V. Clarke (ed.) *Situational Crime Prevention: Successful Case Studies*, 2nd edn, Harrow & Heston, Albany, NY, pp. 209–226.

Parkinson M., Hutchins M., Simmie J., Clark G. and Verdonk H., 2004, *Competitive European Cities: Where Do the Core Cities Stand?*, Office of the Deputy Prime Minister, London.

Pascoe T., 1999, *Evaluation of Secured by Design in Public Sector Housing*, Final Report, BRE, Watford, UK.

Pascoe T. and Lawrence G., 1998, 'Are Intruder Alarm Systems Effective as Crime Prevention Measures?', *Aerospace and Electronic Systems Magazine, IEEE*, 13(2), pp. 8–15.

Pascoe T. and Topping P., 2000, 'Countering Household Burglary through the Secured by Design Scheme: Does It Work? An Assessment of the Evidence, 1989–1999', *Security Journal*, 13(4), October, pp. 71–78.

Pease K., 1998, *Repeat Victimisation: Taking Stock*, Home Office. London.

Peiser R. B. and Chang A., 1998, 'Situational Crime Prevention in Cerritos and Paramount Industrial Parks', in M. Felson and R. B. Peiser (eds) *Reducing Crime through Real Estate Development and Management*, Urban Land Institute, Washington DC, pp. 91–101.

Phelan G. F., 1977, 'Testing Academic Notions of Architectural Design for Burglary Prevention. How Burglars Perceive Cues in Suburban Apartment Complexes', Paper given at Annual Meeting of the American Society of Criminology, Atlanta, GA.

Phillips P. D., 1972, 'A Prologue to the Geography of Crime', *Proceedings, Association of American Geographers*, 4, pp. 86–91.

Pictometry, 2005, *Pictometry Used by Gwinnet County Police in the Capture of the Atlanta Courthouse Shootings Suspect*, at http://www.pictometry.com/press release/gwinnettgapressrelease.asp.

Pitts J., Porteous D. and Wolfson M., 2002, *An Evaluation of the CASPAR Project in Bellinge, Blackthorn, Briar Hill and Spring Boroughs, Semilong, Northampton*, University of Luton, Luton, UK.

Plater-Zyberk E., 1993, 'Five Qualities of Good Design', *ANY*, no. 1, July/August, p. 12.

Polgreen L., 2004, 'The Pen Is Mightier than the Lock', *New York Times*, 17 September.

Poyner B., 1983, '*Design against Crime: Beyond Defensible Space*', Butterworths, London.

Poyner B., 2006, *Crime-Free Housing in the 21st Century*, UCL Jill Dando Institute of Crime Science, London.

Poyner B. and Webb B., 1991, *Crime Free Housing*, Butterworth Architecture, Oxford.

Prescott J., 2003, Speech to the Prince's Foundation Traditional Urbanism Conference on 20 November.

Public Technology Net, 2006, 'High-Resolution Aerial Imaging and GPS Pilot to Improve Police Road Investigations', 4 March. See at http://www.public technology.net/modules.php?op=modload&name=News&file=article&sid=4743.

Pyle D., 2003, *Business Modelling and Data Mining*, Morgan Kaufman, San Francisco.

Ratcliffe J., 2002, 'Burglary Reduction and the Myth of Displacement', *Trends and Issues in Crime and Criminal Justice*, no. 232, pp. 1–6. See at http://www. jratcliffe.net/papers/Ratcliffe%20(2002)%20Burglary%20reduction%20and%20t he%20displacement%20myth.pdf.

Ratcliffe J. and Makkai, T., 2004, 'Diffusion of Benefits: Evaluating a Police Operation', *Trends and Issues in Crime and Criminal Justice*, no. 278, pp. 1–6. See at http://www.aic.gov.au/publications/tandi2/tandi278.pdf.

Ratte F., 1999, 'Architectural Invitations: Images of City Gates in Medieval Italian Painting', *Gesta*, 38(2), pp. 142–153. See at http://www.jstor.org/view/0016920 x/ap030066/03a00030/0?frame=noframe&userID=80e33936@ufl.edu/01cc99 33970050ba18c&dpi=3&config=jstor&charset=t.

Rengert G. and Hakim S., 1998, 'Burglary in Affluent Communities: A Planning Perspective', in M. Felson and R. B. Peiser (eds) *Reducing Crime through Real Estate Development and Management*, Urban Land Institute, Washington, DC, pp. 39–52.

Rengert G. F. and Wasilchick J., 1985, *Suburban Burglary*, Charles C. Thomas, Springfield, IL.

Reps J., 1965, *The Making of Urban America*, Princeton University Press, Princeton, NI.

Rhodes W. M. and Conly C., 1981, 'Crime and Mobility: An Empirical Study', in P. J. Brantingham and P. L. Brantingham (eds) *Environmental Criminology*, Sage, Beverly Hills, CA, pp. 167–188.

Richtel M., 2004, 'A Student ID That Can Also Take Roll', *New York Times*, 17 November. See at http://select.nytimes.com/search/restricted/article?res=F50 814F9395B0C748DDDA80994DC404482.

Roberts P. and Sykes H., 2000, *Urban Regeneration: A Handbook*, Sage, London.

Robespierre, M., 1794, *On the Moral and Political Principles of Domestic Policy*, in P. Halsall, 1997, *Internet Modern History Sourcebook*, http://www.marx.org/ history/france/revolution/robespierre/1794/terror.htm.

Robinson R. B., 1996, 'The Theoretical Development of "CPTED": 25 Years of Response to C. Ray Jeffrey', Paper presented at the American Society of Criminology, Chicago, Illinois, November 1996.

Robson B., Bradford M., Deas I., Hall E., Harrison E., Parkinson M., Evans R., Garside P., Harding A. and Robinson F., 1994, *Assessing the Impact of Urban Policy*, HMSO, London.

Rondeau M. B., Brantingham P. L. and Brantingham P. J., 2005, 'The Value of Environmental Criminology for the Design Professions of Architecture, Urban Design, Landscape Architecture, and Planning', *Journal of Architectural and Planning Research*, 22(4), Winter, pp. 294–304.

Rosen J., 2001, 'A Watchful State', *New York Times Magazine*, 7 October, pp. 38–43.

Rossmo K., 1999, *Geographic Profiling*, CRC Press, Boca Raton, Florida.

Royse C. and Johnson B., 2002, 'Security Considerations for Microbiological and Biomedical Facilities', *Anthology of Biosafety V*, BSL4 Laboratories, chapter 6 at http://www.absa.org/0200royse.html.

Rubenstein H., Murray C., Motoyama T., Rouse W. V. and Titus R., 1980, *The Link between Crime and the Built Environment*, National Institute of Justice, US Department of Justice, Washington, DC.

Rudlin D. and Falk N., 1999, *Building the 21st Century Home: The Sustainable Urban Neighbourhood*, Architectural Press, Oxford.

Sahoo S., 2006, 'Exploring "Transparent Security": A Case Study of the Alachua County Entrance Lobby in Gainesville, Florida', Master's thesis, University of Florida, Gainesville, Florida.

Sampson R., 2003, 'The Problem of False Burglar Alarms', Center for Problem Oriented Policing. See at http://www.popcenter.org/Problems/problem-false-alarms.htm.

Samuels R., 2005, 'After-Dark Design, Night Animation, and Interpersonal Interaction: Toward a Community-Security Paradigm', *Journal of Architectural and Planning Research*, 22(4), Winter, pp. 305–319.

Sandercock L., 2005, 'The Democratization of Planning: Elusive or Illusory?', *Planning Theory and Practice*, 6(4), pp. 437–441.

Saul B., 2006, 'The Legal Response of the League of Nations to Terrorism', *Journal of International Criminal Justice*, 4(1), pp. 78–102, doi:10.1093/jicj/mqi096, Oxford University Press.

Saville G. and Cleveland G., 1998, '2nd Generation CPTED: An Antidote to the Social Y2K Virus of Urban Design', Paper presented at the Third Annual International CPTED Conference, Washington, DC, December.

Saville G. and Cleveland G., 2003, 'An Introduction to 2nd Generation CPTED: Parts 1 and 2', *CPTED Perspectives*, 6(1), 7–9; 6(2), 4–8.

Schneider R. H., 2003, 'American Anti-terrorism Planning and Design Strategies: Applications for Florida Growth Management, Comprehensive Planning and Urban Design', *University of Florida Journal of Law and Public Policy*, 15(1), Fall, pp. 129–154.

Schneider R. and Kitchen T., 2002, *Planning for Crime Prevention: A Transatlantic Perspective*, Routledge, London.

Sheffield First for Safety, 2002, *Sheffield's Crime Reduction Strategy, 2002–2005*, Sheffield First for Safety Partnership, Sheffield.

Sheffield First Partnership, 2005, *Sheffield's Future: Be Part of It*, Sheffield First Partnership, Sheffield.

Sheffield First Safer Communities Partnership, 2005, *The Safer Communities Strategy: Sheffield's Crime Reduction Strategy and Drugs Strategy, 2005–2008*, Sheffield First Safer Communities Partnership, Sheffield.

Sherman L. W., Gottfredson D. C., Mackenzie D. C., Eck J., Reuter P. and Bushway S. D., 1997, *Preventing Crime: What Works, What Doesn't, What's Promising*, National Institute of Justice Research in Brief, US Department of Justice, Washington, DC.

Shu S., 2000, 'Housing Layout and Crime Vulnerability', *Urban Design International*, 5(3–4), pp. 177–188.

Sidener J., 2006, 'Implant ID Chips Called Big Advance, Big Brother', SignOnSan Diego.Com. See at http://www.signonsandiego.com/news/computing/20060312 -9999-1n12chip.html (last accessed 8 June 2006).

Skinner B. F., 1938, *The Behavior of Organisms: An Experimental Analysis*, Appleton-Century, New York.

Smith E. and Gadher D., 2005, 'Spy Cameras to Spot Drivers' Every Move', *Sunday Times*, 13 November, p. 5.

Smith M., 1996 '*Crime Prevention through Environmental Design in Parking Facilities*', Series: NIJ Research in Brief, National Institute of Justice, April, 24 pages available at http://www.ncjrs.gov/txtfiles/cptedpkg.txt.

Social Exclusion Unit, 1998, *Bringing Britain Together: A National Strategy for Neighbourhood Renewal*, Cm 4045, HMSO, London.

Social Exclusion Unit, 2001, *A New Commitment to Neighbourhood Renewal: National Strategy Action Plan*, HMSO, London.

Southworth M., 2003, 'New Urbanism and the American Metropolis', *Built Environment*, 29(3), pp. 210–226.

Southworth M. and Owens P. M., 1993, 'The Evolving Metropolis: Studies of Community, Neighborhood, and Street Form at the Urban Edge', *Journal of the American Planning Association*, 59(3), pp. 271–287.

Spraggs D., 2004, 'Detectives and Crime Scene Investigators Are Using 3D Technology to Bring Crime Scenes to Life', *Police*. See at http://www.policemag. com/t_cipick.cfm?rank=90463.

Taraska J., 2005, 'MoMA's Safety Check', MetropolisMag.Com. See at http://www. metropolismag.com/cda/story.php?artid=1572, 20 September.

Taylor B., Loukaitou-Sideris A., Liggett R., Fink C., Wachs M., Cavanagh E., Cherry C. and Haas P., 2005, *Designing and Operating Safe and Secure Transit Systems: Assessing Current Practices in the U.S. and Abroad*, Mineta Transportation Institute, San Jose, CA.

Taylor R. B., 1999, *Crime, Grime, Fear and Decline: A Longitudinal Look*, US Department of Justice, Office of Justice Programs, National Institute of Justice, Washington, DC.

Taylor R. B., 2002, 'Crime Prevention through Environmental Design (CPTED): Yes, No, Maybe, Unknowable, and All of the Above', in R. B. Bechtel and A. Curchman (eds) *Handbook of Environmental Psychology*, John Wiley, New York, pp. 413–426.

Taylor R. B. and Harrell A. V., 1996, *Physical Environment and Crime*, a final summary report presented to the National Institute of Justice, US Department of Justice, Office of Justice Programs, NCJ 157311, Washington, DC.

Tewdwr-Jones M., 2002, *The Planning Polity: Planning, Government and the Policy Process*, Routledge, London.

Tijerina R., 2001, Appendix B: 'Lighting Design for Exterior Areas', in A. Zelinka and D. Brennan (eds), *SafeScape: Creating Safer, More Liveable Communities through Planning and Design*, Planners Press, Chicago, pp. 254–259.

Tilley N., 2005, *Handbook of Crime Prevention and Community Safety*, Willan, Cullompton, Devon, UK.

Timberg S., 2005, 'Classical Music as Crime Stopper', *Los Angeles Times*, 18 February. See at http://www.freenewmexican.com/artsfeatures/10701.html.

Topping P. and Pascoe T., 2000, 'Countering Household Burglary through the SBD Scheme: Does It Work? An Assessment of the Evidence, 1989–1999', *Security Journal*, 13(4), pp. 71–78.

Town S. and O'Toole R., 2005, 'Crime-Friendly Neighbourhoods: How "New Urbanist" Planners Sacrifice Safety in the Name of "Openness" and "Accessibility"', *Reason*, 36(9), February, pp. 30–36.

Town S., Davey C. and Wootton A., 2003, *Design against Crime: Secure Urban Environments by Design: Guidance for the Design of Residential Areas*, University of Salford, Salford, UK.

Tufte E. R., 1997, *Visual Explanations: Images and Quantities, Evidence and Narrative*, Graphics Press, Cheshire, CT.

Tufte E. R., 2001, *The Visual Display of Quantitative Information*, 2nd edn, Graphics Press, Cheshire, CT.

UN-HABITAT, 2005, *Responding to the Challenges of an Urbanizing World*, UN-HABITAT, Nairobi.

UN-HABITAT, undated, *The Safer Cities Programme: Making Cities Safer from Crime*, UN-HABITAT, Nairobi.

United Nations Office on Drugs and Crime, 2005, *Crime and Development in Africa*, UNODC, Vienna.

Urban Task Force, 1999, *Towards an Urban Renaissance*, Spon, London.

Urban Task Force, 2005, *Towards a Strong Urban Renaissance*, Urban Task Force, London.

US Department of State, 2003, *Architectural Engineering Design Guidelines*, 5 vols (For Official Use Only), Government Printing Office, Washington, DC.

Vale L., 2005, 'Standardising Public Housing', in E. Ben-Joseph and T. Szold (eds) *Regulating Place*, Routledge, New York, pp. 67–101.

van Nes A., 2005, 'Burglaries in the Burglar's Vicinity', at http://www.bk.tudelft.nl/users/internet/spacecrime.pdf.

Vernon R. L. and Lasley J. R., 1992, 'Police/Citizen Partnerships in the Inner City', *FBI Law Enforcement Bulletin*, 61(5), pp. 18–22.

von Hoffman A., 2000, 'Why They Built Pruitt-Igoe', in J. F. Bauman, R. Biles and K. M. Szylvian (eds) *From Tenements to the Taylor Homes: In Search of an Urban Housing Policy in Twentieth Century America*, Pennsylvania State University Press, University Park, PA.

Wallace H., 1998, *Victimology: Legal, Psychological, and Social Perspectives*, Allyn & Bacon, Boston.

Walt V., 2001, 'Unfriendly Skies Are No Match for El Al', *USA Today*, 1 October.

Warner J., 2004, *John the Painter: Terrorist of the American Revolution*, Thunder's Mouth Press, New York.

Weisburd D. and McEwen J. T. 1997, (eds), *Crime Mapping and Crime Prevention*, Crime Prevention Studies vol. 8, Willow Tree Press, Monsey, NY.

Weisburd D. and Mazerolle L. G., 2000, 'Crime and Disorder in Drug Hot Spots: Implications for Theory and Practice in Policing', *Police Quarterly*, 3(3), September, pp. 331–349.

Weisel D., 2005, *Burglary of Single-Family Houses. Problem Oriented Guides for Police*, Problem Specific Guide Series no. 18, Community Oriented Policing Services, US Department of Justice, Washington, DC.

Welsh B. and Farrington D., 2003, 'Effects of Closed-Circuit TV on Crime', *Annals of the American Society of Political and Social Sciences*, 587(1), pp. 110–135.

White G. F., 1990, 'Neighbourhood Permeability and Burglary Rates', *Justice Quarterly*, 7(1), pp. 57–67.

White House, 2003, *The National Strategy for the Physical Protection of Critical Infrastructures and Key Assets (2003)*, at http://www.whitehouse.gov/pcipb/physical_strategy.pdf.

Wilcox P., Quisenberry N., Cabrera D. T. and Jones S., 2004, 'Busy Places and Broken Windows? Toward Defining the Role of Physical Structure and Process in Community Crime Models', *Sociological Quarterly*, 45(2), pp. 185–207.

Williams G. and Wood R., 2001, *Planning and Crime Prevention: Final Report*, University of Manchester School of Planning and Landscape, Manchester.

Wilson-Doenges G., 2000, 'An Exploration of Sense of Community and Fear of Crime in Gated Communities', *Environment and Behavior*, 32(5), pp. 597–611.

Wood E., 1961, *Housing Design: A Social Theory*, Citizens' Housing and Planning Counsel, New York.

Wood E., 1967, *Social Aspects of Housing and Urban Development*, United Nations, no. 67.IV.12, New York.

Wright G., 2001, 'Searching for a Moral in Disorder Legislation', *Planning Newspaper*, no. 1426, 27 April, p. 32.

Wright R. T. and Decker S. H., 1997, *Armed Robbers in Action: Stickups and Street Culture*, Northeastern University Press, Boston.

Yaar E. and Hermann T., 2004, 'Peace Index/Most Israelis Support the Fence, Despite Palestinian Suffering', Haaretz.Com, 11 November, at http://www.haaretz.com/hasen/pages/ShArt.jhtml?itemNo=402996&contrassID=1.

Yang Xiaowen, 2006, 'Exploring the Influence of Environmental Features on Residential Burglary Using Spatial-Temporal Pattern Analysis', Ph.D. dissertation, University of Florida, Gainesville, FL. Available at http://etd.fcla.edu/UF/UFE 0013390/yang_x.pdf.

Yin P. P., 1980, 'Fear of Crime among Elderly: Some Issues and Suggestions', *Social Problems*, 27(4), pp. 492–504.

Zahm D., 2005, 'Learning, Translating and Implementing CPTED', *Journal of Architectural and Planning Research*, 22(4), pp. 284–293.

Zelinka A. and Brennan D., 2001, *SafeScape: Creating Safer, More Liveable Communities through Planning and Design*, Planners Press, Chicago.

Ziegler E., 2005, 'American Cities and Sustainable Development in the Age of Global Terrorism: Some Thoughts on Fortress America and the Potential for Defensive Dispersal II', *Environmental Law and Policy Review*, 30(1), Fall, pp. 95–151.

Index